Strategic Sports Event Management

The Hospitality, Leisure and Tourism Series

Butterworth-Heinemann's Hospitality, Leisure and Tourism series of books is aimed at both academic courses and management development programmes. The series represents a planned and targeted approach to the subject and the portfolio of titles provide texts that match management development needs through various stages from introductory to advanced. The series gives priority to the publication of practical and stimulating books that are recognised as being of consistent high quality.

The Series Editor

Professor Conrad Lashley is Professor of Leisure Retailing, Centre for Leisure Retailing at Nottingham Business School, UK. His research interests have largely been concerned with service quality management, and specifically employee empowerment in service delivery. He works closely with several major industry organisations including the British Institute of Innkeeping, Scottish and Newcastle Retail and McDonald's Restaurants Limited.

Strategic Sports Event Management

An International Approach

Guy Masterman

ELSEVIER
BUTTERWORTH
HEINEMANN

AMSTERDAM • BOSTON • HEIDELBERG • LONDON • NEW YORK • OXFORD
PARIS • SAN DIEGO • SAN FRANCISCO • SINGAPORE • SYDNEY • TOKYO

Elsevier Butterworth-Heinemann
Linacre House, Jordan hill, Oxford OX2 8DP
200 Wheelers Road, Burlington, MA 01803

First published 2004

Permissions may be sought directly from Elsevier's Science &
Technology Rights Department in Oxford, UK: phone: (+44) (0) 1865
843830; fax: (+44) (0) 1865 853333; e-mail: permissions@elsevier.co.uk.
You may also complete your request on-line via the Elsevier homepage
(http://www.elsevier.com), by selecting 'Customer Support' and then
'Obtaining Permissions'

British Library Cataloguing in Publication Data
A catalogue record for this book is available from the British Library

Library of Congress Cataloguing in Publication Data
A catalogue record for this book is available from the Library of
Congress

ISBN 0 7506 5983 1

For information on all Elsevier Butterworth-Heinemann
publications visit our web site at http://books.elsevier.com

Typeset by Charon Tec Pvt. Ltd, Chennai, India
Printed and bounded in Great Britain

Contents

Contents

List of figures and tables

Figures

Tables

List of Event management boxes

List of Case studies

Glossary of terms

AELTC	All England Lawn Tennis Club, owners of the Wimbledon Tennis Championships
AFC	African Football Confederation
AFL	American Football League
After-use	The continued use of legacies after the event has ended
After-users	The organizations that manage after use
ANOCA	Association of National Olympic Committees of Africa
ATP	Association of Tennis Professionals, organizers of the men's tennis professional tour
AUS $	Australian dollar
BERL	Business and Economic Research Ltd
BOC	British Olympic Committee
BOCOG	Beijing Organizing Committee for the Olympic Games
BRA	British Racketball Association, NGB of British racketball
BSA	British Surfing Association, NGB for British surfing
BUSF	British Universities Sports Federation
BWSF	British Wheelchair Sports Federation, the NGB for British wheelchair sport
CAF	Confederation Africaine de Football
CAN $	Canadian dollar
CONCACAF	Confederation of North, Central Americas and Caribbean Association Football
CONMEBOL	Confederation Sudamericana de Football
CRM	Customer Relationship Management, marketing technique
DM	German Deutschmark
EAC	Equivalent advertising costs, advertising evaluation technique

ECT	Estimated completion time (project management)
EOC	European Olympic Committees
E-tail	Retail operations via web sites
FA	Football Association, NGB for football in England
FIA	Federation Internationale de L'Automobile, IGB for motor sport
FIBA	International Basketball Federation, the IGB for basketball
FIFA	Federation Internationale de Football Association, the IGB for football
FINA	Federation Internationale de Natation, the IGB for swimming
FISU	International University Sports Federation
FITA	International Archery Federation, the IGB for archery
49ers	San Francisco 49ers, American Football Team/Franchise
GAISF	General Association of International Sports Federations
Gantt Chart	Project management technique
GBRF	Great Britain Racquetball Federation, the NGB for British racquetball
GDP	Gross domestic product
GLA	Greater London Authority
Grand Slam	Australian Open Championships, French Open Tennis Championships, Wimbledon Championships and US Open Championships
HKSDB	Hong Kong Sports Development Board
IAAF	International Association of Athletic Federations, the IGB for athletics
IABA	International Amateur Boxing Association, the IGB for amateur boxing
IASF	International Amateur Swimming Federation, the IGB for swimming
ICC	International Cricket Council, the IGB for cricket
IF	An international sports federation (same as an IGB)
IGB	An international governing body of sport (same as an ISF)
IMC	Integrated Marketing Communications, marketing technique
IMG	International Management Group
IOC	International Olympic Committee
IRB	International Rugby Board, the IGB for rugby union
ISMWSF	International Stoke Mandeville Wheelchair Sports Federation, the IGB for wheelchair sport
ITF	International Tennis Federation, the IGB for tennis

IWGA	International World Games Association
KRONOS	UK based research services company
LASEC	Los Angeles Sports and Entertainment Commission
London 2012	London 2012 Olympic Bid Organization
MASC	Minnesota Amateur Sports Commission
MkIS	Marketing Information System, marketing support system
MUFC	Manchester United Football Club
NBA	National Basketball Association, the professional major league for basketball in the US
NCAA	National Collegiate Athletic Association, US Colleges Sports Organization
NF	National Federation of sport (same as an NGB)
NFL	National Football League, the professional major league for football in the US
NHL	National Hockey League, the professional major league for ice-hockey in North America
NGB	A national governing body of sport (same as an NF)
NOC	National Olympic Committee
NSW	New South Wales, Australia
NYC2012	New York 2012 Olympic Bid Organization
OCA	Olympic Council of Asia
OCF	Oceania Football Confederation
OCOG	Organizing Committee of the Olympic Games
OGKS	Olympic Games Knowledge Service
PASO	Pan-American Sports Organization
PEST	Political, economical, sociological and technological analyses, management evaluation technique
PGA	Professional Golf Association (US and European PGAs), organizers of professional golf tours
PIs	Performance indicators, used in evaluation of management performance
POS	Point of sale, marketing technique
PR	Public relations
PSL	Personal seat licences
SKY	BSkyB Television Company, UK
SMART	Specific, Measurable, Achievable, Relevant and Timely objectives
SOBL	Sydney Olympics 2000 Bid Ltd
SOCOG	Sydney Organizing Committee of the Olympic Games
SWOT	Strengths, weaknesses, external opportunities and threats or situational analysis, management evaluation technique
TOK	Transfer of Olympic Knowledge, IOC support information system

TOP	The Olympic Partners, IOC and Olympic sponsorship programme
TWI	Trans-World International, IMG Owned television production organization
UEFA	Union European Football Association
UK	United Kingdom
UK Sport	UK Government agency controlling elite sport development
UMass	University of Massachusetts, USA
Universiade	World Student Games
USA	United States of America
USA Basketball	NGB for US basketball
USATF	USA Track and Field, the NGB of US athletics
USOC	US Olympic Committee
USRA	US Racquetball Association, the NGB for US racquetball
VAT	Value-added tax, UK Government taxing system
VIPs	Very important persons
WBS	Work breakdown structures (project management)
WCT	World Championship Tennis Inc
WOM	Word of mouth
WRC	World Rally Championships
$	US dollar
£	Great Britain pound

Acknowledgements

The family support which I have received throughout my career has made this book a possibility and so its publication is dedicated to them.

My love and thanks also go to Emma for her support and encouragement throughout this very enjoyable project.

An introduction

The Olympic oaths

In the name of all competitors, I promise that we shall take part in these Olympic Games, respecting and abiding by the rules that govern them, in the true spirit of sportsmanship, for the glory of sport and the honour of our teams, committing ourselves to a sport without doping and without drugs.

In the name of all the judges and officials, I promise that we shall officiate in these Olympic Games with complete impartiality, respecting and abiding by the rules which govern them in the true spirit of sportsmanship.

IOC (2003)

Setting the scene

The importance of the role of sports event management is reflected in these short declarations, taken by an athlete and judge from the home nation at the opening ceremony of an Olympic Games. The oaths themselves have developed over time and are indicative of the importance of flexible management. At the ancient Olympics athletes swore that they had trained properly and that they would abide by the rules of the Games. The importance of the oath is reflected in the fact that the trainers, brothers and fathers of athletes would also make such declarations. In more recent times the oaths have been changed to accommodate social trends and in order to protect the integrity of an event that is seen by many to be at the pinnacle of the sports events industry. In 1920, when the first modern Olympic oath was taken, a spirit of chivalry rather than sportsmanship was required, and in 2000, for the Sydney Olympics, the commitment to participation without doping and drugs was deemed a necessary addition and a reflection of the times.

Abiding by the rules are important criteria for the success of the event but it may take more than a declaration to ensure such compliance. The development of the control of sport by governing bodies in their creation and application of rules is therefore important. Events also provide the best vehicle by which to exercise this control as they can be implemented and controlled as they happen.

The glory of sport may represent two perspectives. The first being the individual success of sporting achievement and the second, the encouragement that this achievement gives to others to then participate themselves. This is the essence of sports development and the role events play is clearly significant in putting both the participants and the event as a whole in the shop window.

The linking of the glory of sport and the honour of teams (formerly country) is an important social and cultural aspect of the athlete oath. The honour at this level has been seen to have bearing on national pride and identity, manifested in large television viewing figures of key moments and providing dominant conversation topics, if only in the short term. Many host cities show even greater faith in the ability of major events to assist in the development of socio-cultural legacies by declaring them long-term event objectives.

These oaths, said in ceremony, may also indicate a longer-term perspective that implicates a wider view of the role of event management. A role that is responsible for the implementation of an event that has wide reaching and long-term impact. That is not to say that the International Olympic Committee (IOC) has any greater aim than the provision of a successful event and athlete experience. Indeed, Jacques Rogge the current President of the IOC, declared that a successful event for spectator and athlete are their priority (Rogge, 2002). There are no IOC objectives that are concerned with the development of long-term commercial and physical legacies for Olympic host cities and yet these have developed, in recent years, as key municipal objectives with the event being seen as a catalyst for their achievement. The IOC has recognized this requirement in the recent development of its Transfer of Olympic Knowledge (TOK) programme and in staging its own Symposium on the Legacy of the Olympic Games, (Lausanne, November 2002). It is beginning to acknowledge the need for its own strategic understanding of host cities and their requirements for a return on investment. An investment that may entail wider and longer-term benefits than from just the staging of an Olympic event itself.

The promise of wider benefits in the form of socio-cultural and economic impact is not just an objective that is set by Olympic event organizers. Organizers of events of all scales can seek to maximize such impact by using sports events more strategically. The implementation of one event can be planned so that it has a positive effect on the next. A private event organization for example, in developing relationships with its customers at an event can increase revenue at the next. A charity can raise more funds.

A municipal authority, in researching local needs, can stage an annual programme of sports events that will provide positive economic impact across its area as well as provide wider associated community activities. Sports governing bodies at all levels can utilize their events to develop future participation and audience if they facilitate opportunities at the time and incorporate appropriate follow-up mechanisms. A strategic approach to event management is therefore of benefit across the whole industry.

Unfortunately this is not a widespread approach. There are notable and high profile examples where strategic planning has been lacking, including Sheffield, UK and Sydney, Australia. Sheffield City Council is still paying for its staging of the 1991 World Student Games and recently required long-term mortgage facilities to enable it to do so (Mackay, 2001). Sydney meanwhile, nearly 4 years after staging the 2000 Olympics, struggles to make a success of its Olympic showpiece, Stadium Australia (Holloway, 2001; The Sydney Morning Herald, 2002). The President of the IOC is reported to have referred to it as a white elephant in 2001 (Hansard, 2001). The sports event management industry would appear to be still in its infancy in this respect.

This infancy is also reflected in a lack of research, writing and theory on the strategic management of sports events. Few books have been published in this specific area and whilst there are more that are concerned with event management as a whole, they are ostensibly focused on the implementation of events as opposed to their strategic development and any long-term perspective. This book is an attempt to start bridging that gap by providing a strategic approach for sports event management that may also usefully serve across the whole event industry.

It is useful to explain one important element of the book title. Most people will have a perception of the nature, types and scales of sports events and these are discussed in Chapter 1. The meaning and use of the word strategy in this text requires explanation here. Consult a dictionary and the entry for strategy reveals military implications. A stratagem is a plan for deceiving an enemy or gaining an advantage, and strategy is the art of conducting and manoeuvring armies. A strategic position would be a position that gives its holder a decisive advantage (Chambers, 1992). Small wonder then that the word became synonymous with business.

Management theory maintains that business strategies are a means to an end (Johnson and Scholes, 2002; Mintzberg et al., 1998; Thompson, 2001) but beyond this there are various views and definitions, for example, on whether both goals and objectives are implemented strategically. Mintzberg (Mintzberg et al., 1998) offers five views of strategy, as a plan, as a ploy, as a pattern, as a position and as a perspective and maintains that an eclectic view that considers all these is less confusing than trying to arrive at one single definition. Johnson and Scholes (2002), however, are clear that strategy for business is concerned with the direction and scope of an organization over the long term and for the achievement of advantage.

Further exploration of corporate strategy theory is not essential here. It is more important to identify the approach that has been adopted in this book. Strategy means different things to different people and so in order to offer an approach an appropriate context is required. This book is essentially concerned with the implementation of events and the process required to achieve a successful outcome. The key theme that runs throughout is that this success may be measured against short, medium and/or long-term objectives that may or may not be achieved solely upon the execution of the event. The aim of the book is to inspire lateral, innovative and thorough planning in the management of sports events, whatever their scale, in order to achieve objectives. These objectives may involve the implementation of an event with short or long planning periods and may or may not involve aspects that the event is only a catalyst for. This may require planning that goes beyond those realms that have so far been traditionally considered a part of the business of event management.

The focus is also on the management of events and not the management of organizations. This is an important distinction. Events are ephemeral by nature and even though they may be staged again and again, each staging is a separate and different project. The book therefore considers the management of events on two levels, the management of single events and the management of events that have a role in event programmes and series. The latter perhaps requiring a wider and longer-term strategic view.

The strategic approach in this text is therefore concerned with the direction and scope of an event in order to achieve its objectives.

Book structure

Chapters 1 and 2 serve as an introduction to the sports event industry. The former provides some historical background on the emergence of sports events by initially focusing on ancient Greece and a path through to the modern Olympics. It also considers the importance of events in society by analysing the types of events and the scale of the industry. Further consideration is given to the structures of events, an identification of the roles of all participants, the emergence of event management as a discipline and what the future holds for event managers. Chapter 2 considers the nature and structure of international sport by focusing on the roles of both international and national sports governing bodies. It then reviews the importance of the IOC and the Olympic Movement and the role of other events on the world stage. Lastly it considers the various types of other event owners, operators and organizers.

The key to the overall approach of the book is a proposed new event planning process, discussed in Chapter 3. The process, intended as being appropriate whatever the scale of event, is iterative in nature and consists of nine stages plus a bidding stage if appropriate. The process forms a backbone for the book and whilst the subsequent chapters do not follow the prescribed stages in order, the process is consistently used to identify how various planning requirements relate to each other.

Chapter 4 evaluates the successes and failures of events by generally considering what the potential impacts and legacies from sports events are. An evaluation of the strategies used and considerations for management are also discussed.

The next chapters are more directly related to the stages of the event planning process. Chapters 5 and 6 go hand in hand and are concerned firstly with the financial control and planning that is required prior to the decision to go ahead with an event. Secondly, in order to maximize revenue potential and even to simply get an event underwritten, the various revenue streams that are available to an event manager are evaluated.

Chapter 7 considers the management of a bid and the process undergone in strategizing to win the right to host a sports event. There is a particular focus on the bids for the 2012 Olympics. Chapter 8, whilst concerned with the implementation of the event itself, does focus on what is strategically required for the longer term, including the requirements for handover and post-event evaluation.

The next three chapters are marketing orientated. The marketing planning process and how the marketing plan is implemented is covered in Chapter 9, an innovative approach to the event communications mix is in Chapter 10, and developing successful sponsorship programmes is considered in Chapter 11.

The final chapter is focused on research and from two perspectives. The first is the importance of conducting research throughout the event planning process and how that contributes to the strategic development of events. The second is concerned with the use of research post the event and in particular on the importance of evaluating events against their objectives. A strategic approach to event evaluation is concerned with research and then evaluation immediately after the event, but if there are longer-term objectives that involve legacies, then they too require evaluation and it is critical that event managers plan for this too.

At appropriate places there are Case studies. There are 21 in all and they cover a whole range of different scales and types of sports and events in order to exemplify key points in the text. In addition there are examples of all types of sports event from all around the world that are used throughout the text to show both similarities and differences in the business of event management. In particular there are a number of references used from three Case studies where research has been conducted, Manchester and Sheffield in the UK, and Sydney in Australia. To further support key points, there is also the use of Event management boxes, where specific practices are further explained.

To aid both student and professor there are questions and references at the end of each chapter.

Finally, one humorous introductory note that is worthy of consideration and perhaps not as far-fetched as it first sounds. Whilst the sports calendar is undoubtedly crowded, new sports events continue to emerge and grow. In order to be competitive therefore, an event manager has to be aware of an ever-increasing market and deliver an innovative and wonderful product. For this, the event manager has to know what the future will bring.

> In February 1971, Captain Alan Shepard of Apollo 14, drove two golf balls on the moon with his Spalding 6-iron (Fotheringham, 2003).

References

Chambers English Dictionary (1992). 7th edition. Edinburgh, W & R Chambers.

Fotheringham, W. (2003). *Fotheringham's Sporting Trivia*. London, Sanctuary.

Hansard (2001). House of Commons Hansard Debates. 11 December 2001. United Kingdom Parliament. www.parliament.the-stationery-office.co.uk/pa/cm200102/cmhansrd/vo011211 (accessed 6 January 2004).

Holloway, G. (2001). After the party, Sydney's Olympic blues. www.europe.cnn.com.2001 (accessed 13 March 2002).

IOC (2003). www.olympic.org/uk/games/past/index_uk (accessed 7 January 2003).

Johnson, G. and Scholes, K. (2002). *Exploring Corporate Strategy*. 6th edition. Harlow, FT Prentice Hall.

Mackay, D. (2001). Sheffield calls off bid. *The Guardian*, 28 November, Manchester, The Guardian Media Group.

Mintzberg, H., Quinn, J. and Ghoshal, S. (1998). *The Strategy Process*, Revised European Edition. Hemel Hempstead, Prentice Hall.

Rogge, J. (2002). Opening address at the *IOC Annual Symposium: Legacy*, Olympic Museum, November 2002. Lausanne, IOC.

The Sydney Morning Herald (2002). ANZ kills off stadium's debt deal, 30 November, 2002. www.smh.com.au/articles/2002/11/29/1038386316792 (accessed 6 January 2004).

Thompson, J. (2001). *Understanding Corporate Strategy*. London, Thomson Learning.

CHAPTER 1

The sports event industry

After studying this chapter, you should be able to:

- understand the origins of sports events and the sports event industry.

- determine the international importance of sports events.

- identify the importance of scale in planning and managing sports events.

- identify the different structures and formats of sports events.

- identify the range of roles of the personnel at sports events.

Introduction

Putting today's sophisticated sports events industry into historical perspective is important if an understanding of how modern day sports events are governed and structured is to be achieved. The importance of organized sport in early Greek, Chinese and Egyptian cultures has ultimately led to what exists today, an industry that consists of a multi-levelled range of events, varying in scale from the locally to the globally significant. This chapter briefly considers an historical perspective and moves on to dissect the industry into various components by considering the importance of the industry at large, not simply from an economic viewpoint, but also its social, political and technological impact. Then the different scales of event, event ownership and governance and event formats, including competition structures, are discussed. It is people that are at the heart of all industries, and so finally the role of the event manager is considered.

Historical perspective

The study of the history of sport is a considerable academic area and the question of a chronological order for the development of sport is a fascinating focus for these studies. When and how sports events were first and then subsequently organized throughout history is important for an understanding of how current events emerged. However, this is not sports history text. What is required here is an awareness, of what are considered to be the origins of organized sport.

It perhaps comes as no surprise that there is some debate regarding these origins. The credit lies somewhere between Greek, Chinese and Egyptian historical accounts and indeed it is only in the last 20 years or so that research from beyond the Mediterranean has come to light. Chinese scholars have added to the wealth of western knowledge with the publication of numbers of studies, in English, that at least raise questions about the chronology of the origins of sports (Peiser, 1996).

There are archaeological finds that have led to the dating of sports. The 1994 Winter Olympics in Lillehammer, Norway commercially utilized the images of 4000-year-old rock carvings of sports people in action. There are the somewhat younger 2000-year-old drawings on pharaonic monuments in Egypt that depict competitive action such as the tug-of-war, swimming, boxing and others that have led to the claims that the Egyptians laid down rules for games, had player uniforms and that there were awards for winners. In literature, Homer's Iliad reports on an athletic competition as being part of a funeral event (Graham et al., 2001). The more widely acknowledged history refers to the origins of what are now the Olympic Games. The ancient games of Olympia in Greece were also a part of a wider festival. From humble beginnings the games at Olympia may have existed as early as the 10th or 9th century BC where they were a part of a religious festival in honour of Zeus, the father of mythological Greek Gods. Olympia, in the Peloponnesos region of Greece, was a rural sanctuary, and the original festival was attended by those who only spoke the same language and shared the same religious beliefs (University of Pennsylvania, 2003). As the games became more widely known they attracted athletes from farther afield until in 776 BC what is accepted as the ancient Olympic Games first started. From that time on the games were held in Olympia every 4 years for possibly 10 centuries. Sports were added each year and in the 5th century BC and at its height the festival consisted of a 5-day programme (Toohey and Veal, 2000), that consisted of athletic events including three races on foot (the stadion, the diaulos and the dolichos) and the pentathlon which consisted of the five sports of discus, javelin, long jump, wrestling and a foot race.

The games at Olympia were not the only sporting festival of the time. They were one of four that are now referred to as the Panhallenic Games. The others were the Pythian Games in Delphi (every 4 years and 3 years after the games at Olympia in celebration of the God Apollo), the Isthmian Games in Corinth (every 2 years in celebration of the God Poseiden) and the Nemean Games in Nemea (every 2 years and in the same year as the Isthmian Games in celebration of the God Zeus) (Toohey and Veal, 2000). The games at Olympia are believed to have drawn crowds of up to 40 000 at their peak.

The ancient Olympic Games faded and finally came to a halt in 393 AD when the Christian Roman Emperor, Theodosius I, abolished them because of their links to Zeus. They were rejuvenated as the modern games in 1896. The Frenchman Baron Pierre de Coubertin was responsible, having first proposed the idea in 1894 with the intention of reviving the games in 1900 in Paris. Instead it was decided that the first modern Olympics should be returned to Greece and were staged in Athens in 1896. The 4-year cycle was re-adopted but significantly for a different location each time and later in 1924 a Winter games was introduced. More recently in 1994, the Winter Olympics cycle was altered so that every other year would be an Olympic year. See Table 1.1.

We now have a number of multi-sport events in addition to the Summer and Winter Olympics and whilst they are not of the same scale, they are nevertheless of importance to societies. These would include, amongst others, the Commonwealth Games that purports to develop trade links between countries of the Commonwealth, the World Wheelchair Games that helps to develop sport for the disable bodied, and the Islands Games that create links between many small island communities around the world.

A key point in recent history has been the gradual change in definition of amateur status and the emergence of professionalism across sports that not too long ago were sacrosanct and

Year	Summer	Winter
1896	Athens	
1900	Paris	
1904	St Louis	
1908	London	
1912	Stockholm	
1916	No games were organized during the World War I	
1920	Antwerp	
1924	Paris	Chamonix
1928	Amsterdam	St Moritz
1932	Los Angeles	Lake Placid
1936	Berlin	Garmisch-Partenkirchen
1940	No games were organized	
1944	during the World War II	
1948	London	St Moritz
1952	Helsinki	Oslo
1956	Melbourne	Cortina d'Ampezzo
1960	Rome	Squaw Valley
1964	Tokyo	Innsbruck
1968	Mexico City	Grenoble
1972	Munich	Sapporo
1976	Montreal	Innsbruck
1980	Moscow	Lake Placid
1984	Los Angeles	Sarajevo
1988	Seoul	Calgary
1992	Barcelona	Albertville
1994		Lillehammer
1996	Atlanta	
1998		Nagano
2000	Sydney	
2002		Salt Lake City
2004	Athens	
2006		Torino
2008	Beijing	
2009	Vancouver	

Source: IOC (2003).

Table 1.1

The modern Olympic Games

commercially untouchable. The emergence of professional tennis in the 1960s and the eventual acceptance of the grand slam 'Opens' for professional players for example. Earlier in the century there were illegal payments to UK footballers and as a result clubs like Leeds City Football Club were disbanded. In the US in the1880s the major controversy in college sports was the use of professional coaches and the use of 'tramp' players (those who would regularly switch teams sometimes for inducements).

Importance of sports events

How important are sports events? History reveals that they have played a significant role in the development of society and that key individuals have managed, sometimes against all odds, to start from small beginnings a wide reaching sports events industry. The eventual transformation of illegal bareknuckle prize fights into the Marquis of Queensberry 1867 rules for boxing is an example of the development of a sport over a very long period. Other and varied examples include the development of a sport intended as a recreational indoor game at a New England School for Christian Workers by James Naismith in 1891. He developed the original 13 rules of basketball, a game that is now played in events all over the world by over 300 million people (Basketball Hall of Fame, 2003). On Christmas Day in 1914 it is reported that World War I enemies contested an inter-trench football match, and although reports are varied, the idea at least has affected many and is legend now, (Bancroft-Hinchley, 2000). Shortly after World War II in 1948, Ludwig Guttmann organized a competition for war veterans with spinal cord injuries in Stoke Mandeville in the UK. Four years later the Paralympics was founded, the first games taking place in Rome in 1960 (Paralympic Games, 2003). Tom Waddell is credited with having conceived the idea of the Gay Games, originally intended as the Gay Olympic Games but as an event that would have no minimum ability as criteria for participation, and the first event was held in 1982 in San Francisco. Gay Games VIII will be staged in Montreal in 2006. More recently in 2003 football became the number one sport for women in the UK, a game that has traditionally been developed and played by men, and England will host the 2005 Union European Football Association (UEFA) European Women's Championship (FA, 2003). In 1999 the US team won the Federation International de Football Association (FIFA) Women's World Cup in front of a crowd of 90 125 in the Rose Bowl, Pasadena (Blum, 2003). These varied examples over time go some way to explain and explore the importance of sports events.

The contribution to society made by these and other events is an individual perception and whilst there is no research to show that there is undivided acceptance of say Gay sports events, their existence is a reflection of the flexibility of society. The creation of these events clearly helped trailblaze for issues that were of wider significance to society than just the staging of a sport event.

The breadth of the industry is so great that to establish market data is a far-reaching task. It is made difficult in having to decide which sectors should be included. Consider two different perspectives. Economically there is venue revenue, the monies spent on the leveraging of sports sponsorship as well as event revenues themselves, and from a sports development perspective, there is the vast range of participation numbers, from school sports days to major international events. Sports participation figures are available for certain sports and they can also be supplemented by percentage year on year growth. Unfortunately, the availability of data is sparse on anything more than a national scale and beyond only a selected number of countries. However, the data is useful when available. Using US soccer as an example again, it is reported that in that country 5.5 million women (7 years old and above) played the game at least once in 2002. This represented an increase of 37.8 per cent on the previous year whereas the corresponding figures for the men's game are 14.5 million participants and a 4.7 per cent increase (National Sporting Goods Association, 2003).

Keeping politics out of sport is a recurring issue. On the one hand there is the argument that sport should be considered above all politics and governmental and party politics. This is a debate-able area of course and when it comes to certain events it may simply not be possible. All scales of events are influenced polit-ically in many ways as there is no getting away from the require-ment to conform to numerous sets of regulation such as the likes of those for health and safety, employment, fiscal reporting, and licensing. On the other hand, political intervention is quite differ-ent and there are all levels of politician that see fit to play a role in the management of sports events and/or use such for political ends. Prime ministers have been seen to increase their opinion poll results and political messages have been made all the more vehemently by individuals and minority groups as a result of associating themselves with major events (see Chapter 4).

The role of technology in sport has been intrinsically involved in the development of events. Customer expectations and the demands of the media again have led to all kinds of innovation and its use in the advancement of the presentation and control of sports events. Examples include tennis where wooden to metal to carbon fibre racket development has led to the enhancement of player performance. Footballs for the FIFA 2002 World Cup were lighter in an attempt to make the game more entertaining although the expected shooting and goals from long range did not appear to materialize. The development of a reflective ball in the 1980s was intended to lead to an increased, and much needed, television coverage of the sport of squash as was the use of one-way see-through glass. Call centre services have made ticket sell-ing a less frustrating customer activity and giant plasma screens have made the action replay possible at an event. Digital timing has clearly enhanced athletes' performance indicators and the introduction of Cyclops (equipment for judging line calls) has made a contentious name for itself in tennis line calls. Technological development of broadcast equipment has improved the televised viewing of events and also works hard to improve viewing fig-ures technology such as Hawkeye (simulation software) for wicket taking analysis in cricket thus helping to educate viewers.

One can see how much of this technology has also added to the communication potential of events by increasing the opportunities for an event to increase spectator and viewer numbers and at the same time increase revenue with various types of sponsorship and advertising vehicles. The FIFA 2002 World Cup 'fevernova' footballs were provided by Adidas and digital timing and scoring services, supplied by various organizations such as Siemens, receive on-air television exposure. Plasma screens not only attract the eye towards replays, they also show advertisements. Lastly, though probably not finally, the Internet has clearly had an effect by becoming a major vehicle for marketing communications, not just for tickets, but for event webcasting and merchandise sales.

The development of sport itself relies on the unique showcase that events supply. The more people that watch a sports event the more likely it is that sports participation figures will increase and participation led events are vehicles for newcomers as well as more experienced performers. However, this is not necessarily sustained development. In the UK the public tennis courts appear to fill up during Wimbledon fortnight. The task of governing bodies is clearly not just to make use of events as showcases and as opportunities to see and try, but also to ensure there are mechanisms that convert these experiences into long-term participation.

Scale of the industry

The industry can be dissected into various conceptual dimensions in order to ascertain the scale involved. Sports events are organized throughout the world for able and disable bodied men and/or women of all ages. There are single and multi-sport formats, some of which are universally available and others that are specific to only one region of one country. In a time dimension there are various competition formats from one-day tournaments to year round championships. In a socio-economic dimension there are amateur and professional events and those that are spectator or participant led. There is also the dimension of ability and attainment, at the heart of competition, with grassroots sports events for those who are new to the sport and elite events that are organized for skilled performers.

Some events can be classed as being either spectator or participant led. This is essentially a commercial classification in that the main revenue is earned via one or the other. For example, a 32-player draw badminton tournament may be watched by thousands of spectators if it is a national competition such as the British Open. However, if it is a club competition it is unlikely that many more than friends, family and other players will watch. Revenue for the former would probably be predominantly made up of spectator ticket sales whereas the latter may involve only player entry fees. For multi-sports events such as the Commonwealth Games, Olympic Games and Pan-American Games however, there is a case for classifying them as both spectator and participant led, such is the extent of the revenue and numbers of both spectators and participants.

Event organizers and owners determine who participates in their event and a diverse range of sectors are involved. Educational institutions are possibly the first to introduce most sports at the earliest ages, and schools, colleges, universities are all involved with events at intra- and inter-competition levels. Television, as an informer, also plays an ever-increasing role. Events are staged at schools, colleges and universities and at district, county, state, regional, national and international levels. Similarly, there are sports clubs for all ages, some of which have their beginnings entrenched in religiously based institutions such as church groups. Some older clubs were founded for amateur sport but evolved into professional organizations. For example, the founding member teams of the English Football League started out from such beginnings.

Many sports events are a part of a wider entertainment delivery. Larger events that cover a range of leisure and recreational activities may have sports as one element but with arts, music and other socially integrating elements alongside. Multi-sported events such as the Olympics and Commonwealth Games have sports competitions as their central focus but incorporate programmes of events that often extend well before and after these take place. The Spirit of Friendship Festival began in Manchester in early 2002 and several months before the Commonwealth Games. It incorporated arts, music and educationally based activities for all age ranges of local residents as well as tourists. Their torch relay, modelled on Sydney's 2000 Olympic event, took 3 months to tour Commonwealth countries and the UK and was the catalyst for municipal events in many towns and cities.

Not all sports related events have sports activity and competition at their heart. There are also sports related exhibitions and conferences, sports product launches, sports personality appearances at corporate events, and whilst there is no sports activity at the BBC's Sports Personality of the Year Award ceremony there is certainly competition for the coveted prize.

Whilst this text is predominantly concerned with those events that consist of sports competition it is important to place this industry into the more generic sports industry. The sports industry consists of three elements: consumers of sport, sports products, and suppliers of sports related products (Shank, 2002).

Consumers

Amongst other sports products, there is the consumption of sports events themselves. In this sense consumers can be spectators and of two basic kinds, corporate and individual. Corporate consumers at sports events can be sponsors, corporate hospitality purchasers and guests. Individual spectators may be ticket buying, complimentary guests or free entrants. Sports event consumers can also be participants in the form of teams or individual competitors as well as their entourage of trainers, medical staff and even agents. Officials such as referees, umpires and judges are also included here because they too take part and consume the event. An event is a consumer too as it is supplied with necessary resources. There are also consumers of other sports products.

Products

These products consist of sports goods and equipment. There is also sports information and data including results, and media fed broadcast, live or by delay. There are also training services and facilities that are provided to those that require them. Funding, grants and commercial input can also be described as products from an events perspective. An event itself is also a product or an offering.

Suppliers

The suppliers of such products are therefore not just limited to the manufacturers of sporting goods and equipment. They also include sponsors and other organizations with the supply of equipment and services as well as funds. The media are the suppliers of information and broadcasts to both individual consumers and are of course brought in as event partners. Agents can also be suppliers of elite performers as well as the facilitators of broadcast deals for events.

One concept prevails across all sports events. They are all entertainment. This is true whether the event has spectators or not because participants take part for their own entertainment, even if they sometimes make it look like hard work. Of course there are poor experiences for both spectators and those taking part, and the aftermath may well be one of negative reflection, however, sports events are a significant part of the entertainment industry. Whatever the scale there is a show to be put on.

Establishing the three elements of the wider sports industry above provides an understanding of the relationships that are important for the event. What should be clear is that the sports events industry, in its concern for the provision of entertainment, is no different from any other industry and that the focus for those that provide events has to be on the needs of the consumer.

There has been mention of large- and small-scale events, and in identifying so many different kinds of events it becomes clear that terminology may be an issue. For example, what is a mega event and how much lesser is a minor event than a major event, and in what ways?

These differences in the definitions and terms occur in event planning literature. An event, according to Getz (1997) is temporary, can be planned or not, has a fixed length and most importantly is unique. The field of event management is concerned with those events that are planned and to mark the differences some refer to these events as special events (Allen et al., 2002; Getz, 1997). At this point the terminology differs. There are hallmark, mega, major and minor events referred to by various authors. Goldblatt (1997) and Hall (1992) refer to any Olympic Games as a hallmark event whereas Getz (1997) and Allen et al. (2002) bill them as mega events and describe hallmark events as those that recur in a particular place where the city and the event become inseparable, take for instance Wimbledon, the tennis championships. Getz (1997) identifies mega-events by way of size and significance that have a high yield of tourism, media coverage, prestige and economic impact for the host.

Jago and Shaw (1998) offer a model that appears to encapsulate all these terms in a ranked structure that indicates scale and size, and offers an explanation of the relationship between the various types of event. They describe a relationship between major, hallmark and mega events. Their model begins with events that are either ordinary (unplanned) or special (planned). Secondly, special events are minor, festivals or major. Thirdly, major events are either hallmark events that are either infrequent and belong to a particular place, or mega events that are one-off and on an international scale (see Figure 1.1). They define a major event as a special event that is high in status or prestige, one that attracts

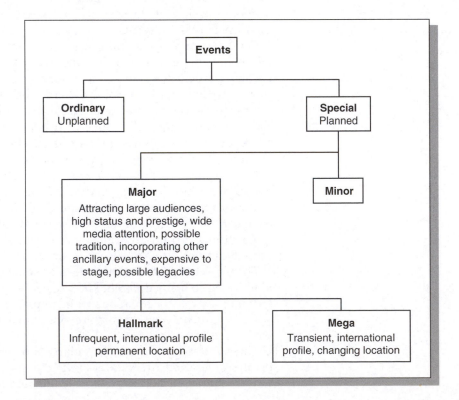

Figure 1.1
A definition for events
Adapted from Jago and
Shaw (1998).

a large crowd and wide media attention, has a tradition and incorporates festivals and other types of events, are expensive to stage, attract funds to the host region, lead to demand for associated services, and leave behind legacies.

In accordance with this definition, major events can be one-time or recurring events, one or several days in nature, and size and scale can differ enormously. Thus the sorts of major international sports events referred to in this text vary greatly in scale and profile. On the one hand there are the Winter and Summer Olympics, FIFA World Cup, UEFA European Championship, Super Bowl, Rugby Union World Cup, and many sports international championships such as those for athletics, swimming, judo, cycling and so on, which are all one-time staged as far as the hosts are concerned and are often bid for. On the other hand there are recurring events such as the four Grand Slams in tennis, the Football Association (FA) Cup Final, and Formula One motor racing Grand Prix.

There would be no advantage gained here in reviewing the literature further. The purpose in doing so at all is to show that there are no standards in the use of terminology. It might be argued that a standard use of definition and terminology across the events industry might be beneficial for those writing about it, and it could serve that purpose here. However, most event attendees, whatever type of consumer they might be, will not need to know if the event is mega or hallmark, or major or minor, they will be able to determine the scale themselves. The same may be said of event managers.

Structures

Each and every year there are many sports events staged all around the world and the structures and formats of these events are determined by a number of different kinds of owners. These owners fall into one or more of several categories, local government and authorities, sports governing bodies and competition organizations, corporate organizations, volunteer and charitable organizations and educational institutions and organizations. These are discussed in greater detail in Chapter 2. In many instances, particularly when the impact of the event is wider spread, there are collaborations between two or more of these owners and organizers in the control, development and implementation of their event. These event-managing bodies determine the kinds of competition and entertainment that goes on show.

Whether it is the local church, scout group, regional sports body or a host city, the same basic competition formats are available. These formats have been developed over time and as a result of the influence of key drivers, such as increasing consumer expectations and more recently, for some events, televised expectations. For example, straightforward knockout draws have been made more sophisticated with seeding in order to keep the better players in the event longer and the better matches until later in the event. These have been further developed with the introduction of earlier staged mini-leagues or round-robin formats where more matches can be seen by partisan fans. The spectacle of knock-out can then still be enjoyed but between those competitors that were able to sustain their efforts, in other words protecting the interests of the supposed better performers. This can mean more ticket revenue as well as improved media rights take up for larger events. There is nothing wrong with this. It is good commercial sense and remains consumer focused.

Competition formats are universal. They are applicable in any scale of event. Knockout tournaments, long- or short-term league championships, round robins, challenge tables, pre-qualification and group stages are formats that can be used by all event managers although some are more common at certain sizes of event. The basic principles behind each format are explained, using examples, in Case study 1.1.

Case study 1.1

Event competition formats

Knockout tournament

Entries are received from interested participants (teams or individuals) by a certain time (entry deadline). The number of entrants may be limited to a certain number too (limited draw) and the eventual number of entrants determines the shape of the draw. The draw consists of the random selection of each entrant against an opponent whereby the match can be played by or at a certain time or date that can be prescribed or self-arranged. The aim of the draw is to end up with an even number of matches/fixtures (rounds) so that quarter finals, semi-finals and a final can result. This provides a winner. For example an entry level of 128 participants will result in there being four quarter finals, two semi-finals and one final (127 matches in all). It is of course possible to have any number of entrants and still devise a draw that results in the same way.

An example of the results of the final rounds of the 2002 US Tennis Open Men's Singles event that began as a 128-man draw is given in the following table.

The numbers in brackets behind the names in the first column (quarter-final round) are the seedings that were given to those players. Seedings are a ranking starting with the favourite at number one. They are decided by tournament directors or committees and are used to keep the better players apart until their respective seedings bring them together. A seeding process that has been 100% successful would have the top eight seeds winning through to the quarter finals, with the top four seeds going through to the semi-finals and the top two seeds playing each other in the final. In this particular example it can be seen that the seedings were not that successful with the number six seed playing the number 17 in the final and the latter, the irrepressible Pete Sampras winning.

Completed tournaments of this sort produce a regular update of results and make it available to competitors and spectators as well as the media. After the event the result sheet would feature every match score.

US Men's Open (2002)

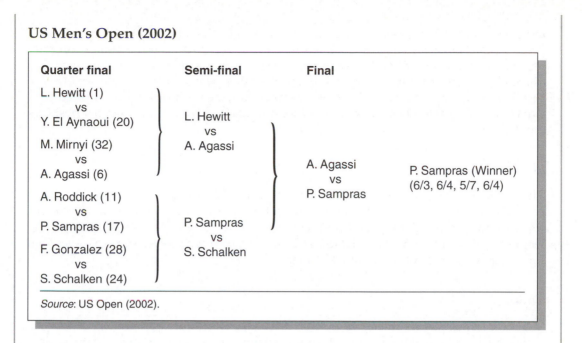

Quarter final	Semi-final	Final

L. Hewitt (1)
vs
Y. El Aynaoui (20)

L. Hewitt
vs
A. Agassi

M. Mirnyi (32)
vs
A. Agassi (6)

A. Agassi
vs
P. Sampras

P. Sampras (Winner)
(6/3, 6/4, 5/7, 6/4)

A. Roddick (11)
vs
P. Sampras (17)

P. Sampras
vs
S. Schalken

F. Gonzalez (28)
vs
S. Schalken (24)

Source: US Open (2002).

Knockout stalemate solutions

A number of elements have been introduced to knockout competition formats in order to make them more attractive and efficient. Those matches that end in draws or stalemates have previously required a replay, sometimes on neutral territory at a later date. Extra time at the end of normal time has long been used to find a winner but of more recent use have been shoot-outs or penalty competitions, silver goals and golden goals systems (first goal wins scenarios). Tie-breaks in racket related sports have also been introduced in order to keep the duration of matches manageable, not just for participants and spectators but also for event managers.

Leagues

Leagues are generally used over longer competition periods and involve everyone or every team playing each other at least once. Each participant is then automatically placed in rank in the league according to points won for winning or drawing matches. Most leagues also accumulate the points, goals, tries, runs, etc. for each participant, to also determine ranking.

Round Robin

Round-robin competitions are where every one plays each other. They are appropriate for limited entry day-long events. They are used productively in combinations, see below.

Challenge tables

These are more appropriately used when the competition is long term or flexible and for individually played sports such as tennis, racquetball, squash and badminton. Entrants are placed on a ladder or league whereby they are ranked in order, probably by a seeding process. Challenge rules are then agreed whereby a participant on the ladder can challenge someone above them (possibly up to two places). A match is self-arranged and played. If a challenger wins they move into the other persons place and everyone else below moves down one place. If the other person wins, the positions remain unaltered. At a declared time/date all challenges are ceased and a ladder winner and all other positions are determined.

Group stages

These consist of mini leagues usually with small numbers of participants whereby round-robin matches are played over a given time and then the group winners and or runners-up go through to further competition. This can involve the use of further mini-leagues such as for the UEFA Champions League where there are two group stages then followed by a knockout competition format.

Tours

Tours consist of a series of events and can result in end of tour champions, possibly via a play-off event. Usually the same players, probably with some kind of tour registration, play each event. The idea may well have originated out of the same athletes visiting ancient games and now we have the likes of the Professional Golf Association (PGA) Tour and the Association of Tennis Professionals (ATP) Tour. The latter takes its top eight players over the year round tour and stages an end of tour championship play-off that uses a combination of competition formats; two groups of four players in a round robin with the top two in each group going through to knockout semi-finals and then a final.

Pre-qualification stages

These consist of competitions of any format and they are staged prior to the main competition in order to provide participants for the main event. Some pre-qualifying events only provide limited numbers of places in the main competition where others can be the sole providers of entrants for the main event albeit with a prescribed number of places available. An example of the latter would be the qualifying rounds of the FIFA World Cup where there are international group zones and the fixtures take over a year to complete. Group winners, and some runners-up, qualify for the finals.

Stroke play

Used widely in golf where unlike in most other sports the players are hitting their own ball and trying to keep as low a score as possible by getting around the course in as few strokes as possible. The lowest stroke count overall wins. Competitions can be organized whereby participants play in groups, usually of two or four, and each group starts their round (usually an 18 hole course) at a certain time (tee-off). Any number of participants can take part and because it is your own number of strokes at stake there is no real handicap in who you partner in your group. When all rounds have concluded the participants are ranked according to their stokes played and prizes can be awarded. Golf is unique in this way but there are other games where you play your own ball. For example, croquet, ten-pin bowling and crown green bowling where there is the added interest of the opportunity to hit and affect your opponent's shots.

Combination formats

As can be seen in some of the above examples there are a number of events that combine competition formats in order to be more efficient, conclude within certain time limitations and as a result provide more exciting and entertaining spectacles for those who watch and play.

Participants

The participants of a sports event are often perceived as being only the sportsmen and women who take part in the competition. Of equal importance however are a number of other 'players' as intimated above in the list of sports industry consumers. These stakeholders can be considered to be participants as the event may well be worse off without them.

Competitors

The men and women who compete against each other either as individuals or in teams of two or more and either for their own gratification and achievement or for some representative body such as a school, club, district, county, state, region, league, conference or nation. Competitors can take part in an event by paying an entry fee and may also buy tickets for themselves and their families. They can also spend money at the event in a variety of ways. At larger events of course there are those participants that are needed by the event to help it sell itself and so prize money structures and appearance fees play a part. To go out of the competition in the first round at Wimbledon earned 64 male tennis players £8630.00 each and 64 female tennis players £6900.00 each in 2003 (Wimbledon, 2003).

Officials

Sometimes professional but often volunteers, the officials at sports events include scorers and recorders as well as the referees, umpires and judges that are required for arbitrary decisions and keeping score. The call for volunteer parental assistance here is often the difference between being able to stage the event or not. Whilst officials are an intrinsic part of the management of the event, they are also stakeholders in that they watch the event when they are not officiating and often spend their own money at the event on event services and products.

The entourage

This is a collective description for the men and women who accompany the competitors, sometimes through necessity and sometimes as a result of indulgence. Whatever, the reason the event manager has to be aware that the trainer or coach, the wife and children, the doctor or physiotherapist may need tickets, car parking, accommodation and somewhere to provide whatever service they provide. There are also official governing body executives and council members, team managers and agents to consider too. At larger events they require event expenditure but they may also spend their own money.

Suppliers

Suppliers include all the providers of equipment and services that are required by the event. They may be front line services where there is direct contact with other stakeholders and they of course may be stakeholders themselves. Security services, sponsors, sports equipment manufacturers and caterers all come into this category.

Event management

Event managers, whether they be owner/operators or not, make the event the show it needs to be. As owners they are shareholders and whether they are employed or contracted they are stakeholders.

Staffing

In addition to management there are also paid casual employees or volunteers who staff the event in all kinds of roles. These include stewarding, table waiting, kiosk manning, ticket selling and being a part of the ball-boy/girl team. They are both spectators and money spenders at the event in many cases.

Spectators

Spectators are all those who watch the event whether they buy a ticket or not and as such they are very much a part of the event. The interactions between a peanut seller and a seat holder at a major league baseball game can provide much needed entertainment between innings. The interaction between fans and the response of audience to action are also a fundamental part of the event. Empty stadiums do not attract strong media interest nor do they impress those who attend. Event managers have just as much a job to do with the empty seats as they do the full ones in this respect. If people on seats are important, then contingency plans to fill them at the last minute are a key management responsibility and contingency.

Media

The provision for the representatives of the media at events is becoming increasingly sophisticated. Elaborate media centres with state of the art technology and dedicated communications and liaison executives are now common at many events. In this sense they are stakeholders. The media are also an important vehicle for the delivery of information to others before, during and after the event.

Very important people

The very important people (VIPs) who attend an event do not often have to pay anything for anything but they are nevertheless key consumers. They can be sponsors, government officials or other stakeholders whose opinion and/or influence are important for the future of the event. They can also be important additions to the event programme in that they can present trophies at awards ceremonies or simply adds presence to the spectacle of the event. Why else would we want to classify our celebrity lists from A to C?

The discipline of event management

Clearly event managers and the skill of event management have been around for a long time but it is only in the last decade that both literature and qualifications in the field have emerged to any great extent.

Much of the literature that has been written on the practice of event management is first of all related to the industry as a whole. It is a practical approach that has been adopted by most, with an emphasis on planning and operation. Authors such as Allen, O'Toole, McDonnell and Harris in Australia; Catherwood, Van Kirk, Getz and Goldblatt in the US; and Hall from New Zealand, have contributed much to the development of the discipline and the emergence of event management courses in higher education in the US, Australia and the UK in particular.

There are few dedicated sports event management English texts though the subject does receive coverage to some extent in sport management and sport marketing related literature.

In the early 1990s event management certification emerged in the US, principally at George Washington University. Not too much later, in 1996, Leeds Metropolitan University in the UK launched the first BA Honours degree in event management with a Higher National Diploma in 2000 followed by a Masters degree in 2002. By September 2003 there were over 70 institutions offering higher education qualifications in event management in the UK, thus demonstrating significant development in just 10 years. The emergence of sports event management as an integral part of this provision has been a natural development and the likelihood of a first sports event management degree in the UK is not too far away. In the US, sports events management has for some time been a part of the delivery of wider sports management programmes.

There are numbers of event industry related associations. This provides a point of contention. There is a distinct lack of cooperation between these bodies and the formation of more universal representation. There are those that advocate that this is a necessity and yet the simple consideration of the extent of the industry, its broad inclusion of arts, music, conference, exhibition, festivals, and sports sectors is perhaps evidence enough that single body representation is barely a practical opportunity. Those that organize sports events are inextricably linked if not articled with national and international governing, organizing and owning bodies and are therefore, well served with information and support by such. The International Olympic Committee (IOC) itself is also involved in the endorsement of educational programmes. Along with the European Olympic Committees it supports the delivery of a postgraduate degree in sports administration that is based at different sites across Europe. In the sports sector of event management at least the bodies that exist serve well.

Event managers

There have clearly been sports event managers long before any formal qualifications were available. This begs the question, is there a need for formal qualification in an area that has been well served by expertise from all kinds of other disciplines? Great event managers have emerged from backgrounds in law, marketing, human resources and accounting, and indeed out of non-certificated routes into management. The reason for their success is that event management encompasses all of these disciplines and an event requires a multitude of management and business skills. Event management qualifications from higher education institutions are not able to offer these disciplines in as much singular depth but they do allow for a multi-skilled and equipped graduate that can only be of benefit to the industry. The recent development of so many new programmes is a result of industry asking for more qualification in this area.

The future

What of the future? There are perhaps several areas of concern for the future of sports events. One is the development of some sports at the expense of others. In 1999 in the UK the top 10 sports received 90% of all the money spent on sponsorship and of those, the top two sports, motor sport and football, received the majority of the increase in spend (Mintel, 2000). The concern is the increasing influence borne by television revenue, the related attraction of sponsorship to events and as a result a polarization effect. Whilst the successful get more so, is this at the expense of minor sports that may well be regressing? Significantly, events may disappear as a result of lesser demand from television and thus much needed sponsorship funding. The irony of this is that there will then be fewer events to help develop those sports.

The increasing influence of the media on sport goes still further. It is now a common occurrence for televised games across many sports to be scheduled according to the timings of commercial breaks and for peak audiences. This has meant that the traditional Saturday fixtures for many sports have now become Sundays and Mondays and at all kinds of kick-off times. A Sunday 4.05 p.m. kick-off time for a Sky televised football match in the UK allows for two pre-game advertising slots within 5 minutes. In addition, those sports with natural time-outs can get more coverage because they allow for more commercial breaks.

There are other examples of where the drive for success and commercial gain is having an effect on the integrity of sport. The opportunity for drug abuse and performance enhancement has increased and sport has had to move with that to control it. Sports marketing techniques are so well advanced that there are now sophisticated controls developed to protect against ambush marketing. All these developments are indicative of the external commercial forces that are at play and of the extent of the skills that are now required in order to put on the event successfully.

These concerns for the future are indicative of the importance that is placed on sport. The popularity of sports events in society have led to increased commercial interest and greater competition on and off the field that have in turn led to the need for increased controls to keep sport within the limits of social standards and values.

Summary

The origins of modern sports events can be clearly seen in the models that were created in ancient cultures. From the likes of the ancient Greek Games have emerged sports events that have played significant roles in the development of society. The industry now is important on a global scale, economically, socially, politically and technologically.

In determining the scale of the sports events industry this chapter has considered various conceptual dimensions, the structures of competition and the stakeholders involved. These stakeholders include the organizers, competitors, suppliers and spectators of events that can range from local to international in profile. The identification of the various roles that stakeholders play is important in understanding the relationships that event managers have with each stakeholder group. The management of events is clearly historically important, however, the academic discipline of event management, both in terms of certificated education and writing, is more recent. As it develops, these relationships, and the issues that arise out of them, will become the focus for further understanding and thus, better performance within the industry.

Questions

1 Sports events are an important social phenomenon. Critically discuss this statement.

2 Analyse how scale is important in the planning of sports events by using examples of events from your own research.

3 Explain how the basic sports competition formats have developed into the sophisticated events that exist today and identify the driving forces that have led to them.

4 Identify the relationships between, and the roles played by, the various participants of a sports event of your choice.

References

Allen, J., O'Toole, W., McDonnell, I. and Harris, R. (2002). *Festival and Special Event Management*, 2nd edition. Queensland, Australia, John Wiley & Sons, Chapter 1.

Bancroft-Hinchley, T. (2000). *Football Match between First World War Enemies on Christmas Day 1914 really took place*. www.english. pravda.ru/sport/2001/01/01/1795 (accessed 22 May 2003).

Basketball Hall of Fame (2003). www.hoophall.com/halloffamers/ Naismith (accessed 22 May 2003).

Blum, R. (2003). *US: Sweden Place Women's World Cup Bids. Miami Herald*. www.miami.com/mld/miamiherald/sports/5896707 (accessed 22 May 2003).

FA (2003). *The F.A. Women's Challenge Cup*. www.thefa.com (accessed 22 May 2003).

Getz, D. (1997). *Event Management and Tourism*. New York, Cognizant, Chapter 1.

Goldblatt, J. (1997). *Special Events: Best Practices in Modern Event Management*. New York, John Wiley & Sons, Chapter 2.

Graham, S., Neirotti, L. and Goldblatt, J. (2001). *The Ultimate Guide to Sports Marketing*. New York, McGraw-Hill, Chapter 1.

Hall, C.M. (1992). *Hallmark Tourist Events – Impacts, Management and Planning*. London, Bellhaven Press, Chapter 1.

IOC (2003). www.olympic.org/uk/games/index_uk (accessed 27 January 2004).

Jago, L. and Shaw, R. (1998). Special events: a conceptual and differential framework. *Festival Management and Event Tourism.* **5**(1/2), 21–32.

Mintel (2000). *Sponsorship 2000.* Sports Sponsorship: Market Overview. 5 July.

National Sporting Goods Association (2003). *2002 Participation – Ranked by Total Participation.* www.nsga.org/public/pages/index (accessed 22 May 2003).

Paralympic Games (2003). *Paralympic Games.* www.paralympic.org/games/01 (accessed 22 May 2003).

Peiser, B. (1996). *Western Theories about the Origins of Sport in Ancient China.* www.umist.ac.uk/sport/peiser2 (accessed 7 May 2003).

Shank, M. (2002). *Sports Marketing: A Strategic Perspective*, 2nd edition. Upper Saddle River, NJ, Prentice Hall, Chapter 1.

Toohey, K. and Veal, A. (2000). *The Olympic Games: A Social Science Perspective.* Oxon, CABI, Chapters 2 and 3.

University of Pennsylvania (2003). www.upenn.edu/museum/Olympics/olympicorigins (accessed 7 May 2003).

US Open (2002). *2002 US Open Draw.* www.usopen.org (accessed 25 May 2003).

Wimbledon (2003). *Prize Money for the 2003 Championships.* www.wimbeldon.org/pressreleases/prizemoney 29 April (accessed 28 May 2003).

Event organizations

After studying this chapter, you should be able to:

- understand the structure of international sport.
- identify the role played by sports governing bodies in the governance of sport on a local to a worldwide level.
- identify the various types of sports event owners and organizers and the roles they play.

Introduction

Who do event managers work for if they want to organize sports events and for those that have the ambition, who are the best and the most deserved of emulation in the industry? This chapter considers the bodies and organizations that play key roles in the sports events industry. Firstly, it is important to describe the structure of international sport and the mechanisms that are used to govern and control sport. This governance is ostensibly universal and thus applies to all owners and organizers of sports events whether they are national governments or local authorities, professional sports franchises or amateur sports clubs. Secondly, the various types of event owners and organizers and the key relationships that exist between them will be discussed.

International sport

International and national governing bodies

Whilst there are a plethora of bodies that represent the interests of sports, the basic structure of international sport and its governance is not difficult to understand. The accepted and guiding principle, though not universal across all sports, is that there is one recognized international governing body (IGB). Even where this is not the case it is generally accepted that it is the optimum aspiration. This one body is responsible for the development and control of that sport including its rules of competition. This control is exercised and maintained via membership whereby all those who wish to play a sport, particularly at events, are governed by the rules and conditions of that body. For example, the rules for archery, basketball and cricket are governed by three organizations: the International Archery Federation (FITA), the International Basketball Federation (FIBA) and the International Cricket Council (ICC), respectively. These bodies govern their sports at all levels, and therefore control the rules whether played by children or adults, by amateurs or professionals, or at school or the Olympics.

When new sports develop sometimes a number of organizing bodies may emerge but generally and ultimately one body becomes the recognized power. The most widely developed sports on a global basis are those with long established IGBs. For example, those of athletics, boxing, football and swimming are the International Association of Athletic Federations (IAAF), International Amateur Boxing Association (IABA), Federation Internationale de Football Association (FIFA) and International Amateur Swimming Federation (IASF). Collectively these governing bodies are referred to as IGBs in the US and UK or International Federations (IFs) by the Olympic Movement and most are members themselves of the General Association of International Sports Federations (GAISF), a forum that allows for discussion on common issues and policy. They can also be a part of the Olympic Movement either as an Olympic participating or Olympic recognized sport.

The more widespread the sport the more levels there are in the organizational structure that is then developed by the IGB in order to maintain governance. Control is maintained essentially in two ways. Firstly, only one national governing body or national federation (NGB or NF) can be recognized in each country and secondly, that national body governs its territory according to the international rules and regulations set by the respective IGB. In between the international and national forums there may also be international regional bodies, generally called confederations. For example, the Football Association of England (The FA) is a member of Union European Football Association (UEFA) that ultimately sits under the governance of FIFA. UEFA operates within a territory (Europe) and alongside similar confederations that operate within Africa, Asia, North and Central America and the Caribbean, Oceania and South America. The international structure of football and how it relates to local member clubs and players in England is illustrated in Case study 2.1. Similar structures and relationships between bodies apply for each NGB of football.

There are other relationships that are peculiar to each IGB/NGB and are concerned with the organization of competitions and events and this is where the structure is more sophisticated. In some cases the organizations that emerge as event and competition organizers are perceived as being just as powerful as the governing bodies. For example the Football League and the Premier League in England are responsible for various professional football competitions and events but play to the rules of the game as prescribed by FIFA and as controlled at national level by the FA. The Association of Tennis Professionals (ATP) runs the worldwide tour (ATP Tour) of men's tennis tournaments but to the rules of tennis as laid down by the International Tennis Federation (ITF). As powerful as the National Basketball Association (NBA) is in the US, the matches are played to rules that derive out of FIBA and its nationally affiliated body, USA Basketball.

In addition IGBs and NGBs own and/or organize their own events and competitions. To illustrate the point and use the same sports, UEFA has its Champions League (for club teams) and European Championships (for national teams), the ITF has the Davis Cup and FIBA has World Championships for national men's and women's teams at senior, youth and junior levels as well as for wheelchair teams.

For some sports the international body appears to be less powerful than say a prominent national body. This tends to represent a relatively early stage in the life-cycle of that body and its influence on an international basis. The game of racquetball has been a significant sport within the US since the 1960s and has had a strong NGB in the US Racquetball Association (USRA) since 1968. In the

Case study 2.1

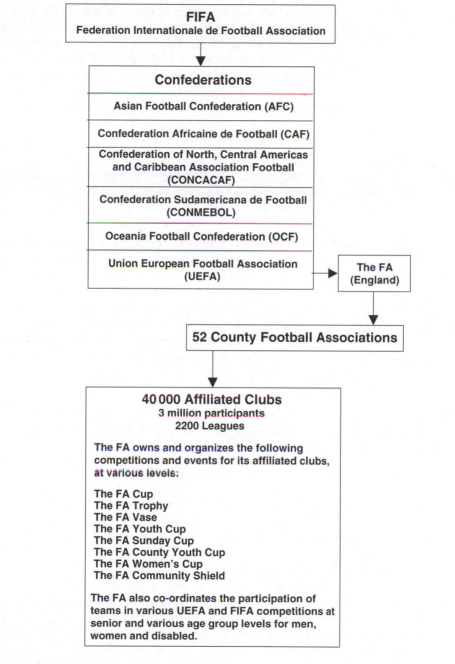

FIFA
Federation Internationale de Football Association

Confederations

Asian Football Confederation (AFC)

Confederation Africaine de Football (CAF)

Confederation of North, Central Americas and Caribbean Association Football (CONCACAF)

Confederation Sudamericana de Football (CONMEBOL)

Oceania Football Confederation (OCF)

Union European Football Association (UEFA)

The FA (England)

52 County Football Associations

40 000 Affiliated Clubs
3 million participants
2200 Leagues

The FA owns and organizes the following competitions and events for its affiliated clubs, at various levels:

The FA Cup
The FA Trophy
The FA Vase
The FA Youth Cup
The FA Sunday Cup
The FA County Youth Cup
The FA Women's Cup
The FA Community Shield

The FA also co-ordinates the participation of teams in various UEFA and FIFA competitions at senior and various age group levels for men, women and disabled.

Source: FIFA (2003), FA (2003)

1970s and 1980s there was also a very strong professional circuit for individual players in the US. The International Racquetball Federation (IRF) was formed in the late 1970s and remains a relatively smaller body with an executive member of USRA serving as its secretary. Another sign of early growth is the existence of more than one body purporting to be the NGB and racquetball again provides a good example. The growth of racquetball and the emergence of the sport's NGBs and IGBs are described in Case study 2.2. Similarly the International Stoke Mandeville Wheelchair Sports Federation (ISMWSF), the IGB for wheelchair sport operates a two-man office and is based at the newly

Case study 2.2

International and national governing bodies: the growth of Racquetball

IRF

The IRF, previously called the International Amateur Racquetball Federation (IARF), held its first World Championships and Congress in 1981 in Santa Clara, US where only six national teams took part. Since the second championships in Sacramento, US in 1984 the event has been held every 2 years and in 2002 featured 40 teams from six continents. The sport has been a medal sport for national and individual men's and women's entries at the World Games since they began in 1981 and since 1995 at the Pan American Games. The sport is now recognized by the IOC (International Olympic Committee) and is played in over 90 countries. This is a Federation that does have Olympic aspirations.

USRA

The USRA was founded some time before the IRF, in 1968, and has been at the forefront of the development of the sport including in the founding of the IRF. It has 25 000 members and there are nearly 7 million players in the US.

BRA versus GBRF

In Great Britain in the early 1980s various racket manufacturers and sports club managers discussed and founded the British Racketball Association (BRA). Their aim was to promote the sport in British squash clubs and on squash courts. The racquetball court is fundamentally different from the squash court in that there is no front tin, it is longer and racquetball shots can be played off the ceiling. There were commercial reasons for forming the body. These were to sell the game to an off-peak hours target audience. It consequently grew and still thrives today. In 1982 a number of British style racketball players were selected to represent Great Britain at the European Racquetball Championships in Holland. Having sampled the international game they returned and a new governing body was founded, the Great Britain Racquetball Federation (GBRF) for the promotion and development of that sport and it remains a member body of the IRF as the NGB for racquetball in Great Britain.

Source: USRA (2003).

developed Guttmann Sports Centre along with the much larger NGB, the British Wheelchair Sports Foundation (BWSF).

The importance of an IGB is not so much about its size but the role it can play in the development of its sport and the control of the development of a sport that is standardized. According to Thoma and Chalip (1996), the objectives for a typical IGB, or IF, include the development of competition between NFs under common rules. For example, USA Basketball is responsible for the selection, training, and fielding of US teams in FIBA competition and some national competitions (USA Basketball, 2003). This highlights the importance that is placed on events. On the one hand they are used to develop individual and team performance. On the other they are used to put the sport on show in order to encourage participation generally in that sport. Thereby they also become the mechanism by which governing bodies exert their control. The way in which even a local event is played to the same rules as an International Championship is down to the governance that is disseminated down through the structure of that sport.

The Olympic Movement

An understanding of Olympic sport and structure is key to an understanding of international sports governance generally. As indicated in the previous chapter the Olympic Games have played a significant historical part in the development of sport and sports events. Olympic sport has also served as a model for many sports in how they have structured themselves at all levels.

The IOC retains the rights to Olympic properties such as the five rings symbol and awards a host city the rights to use such in their organization of the Games. The Lausanne (Switzerland) based organization is not associated with any one country or government, is non-profit making and is governed by individual members who are elected by the organization itself. The funding it requires to exist is self-generated via its own marketing programme. An IOC member is a representative of the IOC in their respective country not a representative of that country. The ideals of Olympism are surrounded by debate but the IOC does maintain that it is concerned only with the development of the Olympic Movement.

The Olympic Movement is defined as consisting of the IOC itself, recognized IF's, NGBs and all those who belong to them including of course sportsmen and women. The Movement also consists of National Olympic Committees (NOCs) and Organizing Committees of the Olympic Games (OCOGs).

Each NOC is responsible for the development of the Movement within their country and this includes the encouragement of elite sports performance in that country and the leading of the national teams to Olympic Games. The NGBs that are Olympic recognized sports are affiliated to their own NOC and together they determine the teams that represent their country at Olympic Games. NOCs also have the right to determine which city from their country may bid to host an Olympic Games.

Following a successful bid, an OCOG is formed by the NOC and the host city concerned. The IOC members in that country, the President and Secretary General of the NOC, at least one host city representative plus municipal authority and other suitable members are sought to form what is the controlling body for the organization of a Games.

In addition the Movement also consists of regional organizations. These are the Pan American Sports Organization (PASO), Association of National Olympic Committees of Africa (ANOCA), Olympic Council of Asia (OCA), European Olympic Committees (EOC) and Oceania National Olympic Committees (ONOC). PASO, like the other bodies, is responsible for the development of the Movement, but is also responsible for other events, in this case the Pan American Games. OCA is responsible for the Asian Games. Both these multi-sports events feature Olympic recognized sports. This structure provides a model for many IGBs, particularly those that represent Olympic sports. One example is FIFA, as seen in Case study 2.1.

There are seven Winter Olympic sports and 28 Summer Olympic sports involving 34 different IFs/IGBs and up to 400 events in the whole Winter/Summer programme (IOC, 2003). In addition, the IOC recognizes other sports and has on occasion staged them as demonstration events at Olympic Games (but with no medal awards). Non-participating but recognized sports include climbing, bridge, golf, roller-skating and surfing (see Table 2.1 for a full list of Olympic sports and IOC recognized sports). In order to retain that sought after IOC recognition the IFs concerned are charged with administering their sports according to the Olympic Charter. This conformity includes for example, the application of the Olympic Movement Anti-Doping Code.

After every Olympic Games there are reviews of the sports programme and sports can be excluded as well as included. Tennis, for example, has achieved both by being excluded after the 1924 Paris Games and then being reintroduced at the Los Angeles Games in 1984.

The international events stage

Outside of the Olympic Movement there is plenty of life in the sports events industry. There are more sports not featured in either the Winter or Summer Olympics than are, and not all of those aspire to Olympic recognition. As well as the various events that are staged by, or on behalf of the NGBs of these sports, National Championships and international fixtures for example, there are several other movements that provide multi-sports platforms at international level.

Winter olympic sports	Summer olympic sports	IOC recognized sports
Biathlon	Archery	Air sports
Bobsleigh	Athletics	Automobile
Curling	Badminton	Bandy
Ice hockey	Baseball	Billiards
Luge	Basketball	Boules
Skating	Boxing	Bowling
Skiing	Canoe/kayak	Bridge
	Cycling	Chess
	Equestrian	Climbing
	Fencing	Dance sport
	Football	Golf
	Handball	Karate
	Hockey	Korfball
	Judo	Life saving
	Modern pentathlon	Motorcycle Racing
	Rowing	Netball
	Sailing	Orienteering
	Shooting	Pelote basque
	Softball	Polo
	Swimming/aquatics	Racquetball
	Table tennis	Roller sports
	Taekwondo	Rugby
	Tennis	Squash
	Triathlon	Surfing
	Volleyball	Tug of war
	Weightlifting	Underwater sports
	Wrestling	Water skiing
		Wushu

Source: IOC (2003).

Table 2.1

Winter and summer olympic sports

The Asian Games have historical roots nearly a century old but as a modern event they began in 1951 in New Delhi and are held every 4 years. In 2002 they were held in Busan, South Korea with over 37 sports being competed. The Games are sanctioned by the OCA and in 2006 in Pusan, Qatar 42 nations will be represented (OCA, 2003).

The World Games are also quadrennial and are held under the auspices of the International World Games Association (IWGA), a body that has 33 IF members. The IOC has now granted its patronage to these Games despite the fact that they are staged for non-Olympic participating sports and many of the IOC recognized sports feature at these Games. For example, Air Sports, Boules, Korfball and Racquetball. Other sports on the programme include Body Building, Fistball and Casting. At the first Games in 1981 in Santa Clara, US there were 18 sports contested by 1500 athletes (IWGA, 2001). The 7th Games will be in 2005 in

Duisburg, Germany and 4000 athletes will vie for medals at 17 different venues. The Games, under their IOC patronage, adhere to the principles of the Olympic Movement but do differ in one way. Host cities are not required to build any new facilities or infrastructure and must be staged in appropriate but existing stadia.

The first British Empire Games in 1930, Hamilton, Canada were the results of discussions that had started 30 years prior. In 1911 sporting competitions were a part of the Festival of the Empire held in London and several nations participated, England, Canada, South Africa and Australasia, a combined Australia and New Zealand team. The idea developed and then in 1930, 400 athletes from 11 nations competed in six sports. The Games are quadrennial and after the first four events the name was changed to the British Empire and Commonwealth Games for two more events and then to the British Commonwealth Games until 1974. The Commonwealth Games title was first used in 1978 in Edmonton, Canada and prevails today. In 1998 in Kuala Lumpur, Malaysia the team sports of Cricket, Rugby, Netball and Field Hockey were added to the programme for the first time, and at the 17th Commonwealth Games in Manchester 2002, 72 nations competed in 14 individual and three team sports (Manchester City Council, 2003).

Another quadrennial event, the Pan American Games began in 1951 in Buenos Aires, Argentina where 2500 athletes from 22 nations competed. The 2003 Games, though not without building difficulties, took place with 5000 athletes from all the 42 member nations from North, South and Central America. They competed in 35 sports. The PASO owns the Games and makes the award to the host city. The 2007 Games are due to take place in Rio de Janeiro (PASO, 2003).

The World University Games or the Universiade is another event that has changed its name more than once. They were originally called the International University Games, then the World Student Games and between 1947 and 1957 the Eastern and Western Blocs held separate events. In 1959 the Games in Turin, Italy were the first to use the term Universiade. Although there have been gaps, the Games are now held every 2 years and have separate Winter and Summer events. There are 10 Summer and six Winter sports and its large university/college competitor numbers make the Summer Universiade second only to the Olympics on those terms. In 1959 there were 1407 athletes and in Beijing in 2001 a total of 6675 students from 165 countries took part. The Games come under the auspices of the International University Sports Federation (FISU). The Federation also supervises the World University Championships where the sports are normally different from those of the Games. In 2000, World University Championships were held for 20 different sports at different venues and on different dates and involved 3623 students (FISU, 2003).

The Maccabiah Games are often referred to as the 'Jewish Olympics' and since they were first held in 1932 they have had a troubled history. After the Games in 1935 a large proportion of the 1350 athletes stayed in Israel and as a result, the 1938 games were cancelled for fear of a repeat (Maccabiah Games, 2003). They have always been staged in Tel Aviv, Israel although in 2001 Jerusalem was also used. This is another quadrennial event and in 997 they attracted 5500 athletes from 53 nations to compete in 43 events.

There are a number of other high profile sports events, either on the world stage or with global significance, the types of which are referred to throughout this text. Examples are featured in Case study 2.3. There are also other international events worthy of mention if only as examples of how diversified both the level of the sport is and the range of organizers/owners that are involved. These few examples can really feed the imagination: the Arctic Winter Games, Baltic Sea Games, Australian Corporate Games, Military World Games, Nat West Island Games, World Air Games, World Transplant Games, World Firefighter Games and X Games.

Case study 2.3

Major sports events

FIFA World Cup

The finals of this competition are held every 4 years. FIFA, the owners of the competition and the IGB for football, was founded in 1904. The first World Cup Finals were staged in 1930 in Uruguay. Since then France, Italy and Mexico have all staged the finals twice and Germany stages them for a second time in 2006. Brazil are the only team to play in all of the finals and have won the trophy the most times (1958, 1962, 1970, 1994, 2002).

Source: FIFA (2004).

Rugby World Cup

This competition is owned by the International Rugby Board, an IGB that was founded in 1881. The first World Cup was not until 1987 in New Zealand and Australia and it has a history of being shared by host nations. In 1991 it was hosted by the UK, Ireland and France and in 2003 was staged in Australia, and won for the first time by England. New Zealand (1987), Australia (1991 and 1999) and South Africa (1995) are the previous winners.

Source: IRB (2004).

ICC Cricket World Cup

The Cricket World Cup was first played in 1975 and is owned by the ICC. This IGB was founded in 1909 as the Imperial Cricket Conference and changed its name in 1965. The finals of this one-day cricket event feature the 10 Test playing nations, plus Kenya which has one-day playing status, plus three qualifying sides from the ICC Trophy which is for associate members. Australia has won this quadrennial event three times and the West Indies, who stages the event in 2007, has won it twice.

Source: ICC (2004).

NFL and Super Bowl

The National Football League (NFL) Championship was first decided on team win/loss percentage between 1920 and 1931. From 1932 a championship game was played to determine each season's champion team. Between 1960 and 1969 there was a rival league, the American Football League (AFL) and from 1966 an inter-league match was played between the two league winners. This was the start of the Super Bowl, first won by Green Bay Packers of the NFL. From 1970 the two leagues ran as one but with two conferences, the American Football Conference and the National Football Conference and the two conference champions play-off to determine the champion team in the Super Bowl. This annual event is played at a different football stadium and city each year.

Source: Pro Football Hall of Fame (2004).

NBA and Finals

The NBA Finals are the culmination of the US professional basketball season. They have been running since the 1946/1947 season when the Philadelphia Warriers beat the Chicago Stags 4-1. The finals are played over a best of seven match series to determine the winners.

Source: NBA (2004).

Baseball World Series

The World Series is the end of season play-off between the American and National Baseball leagues. This is also a best of seven series and in 2003 the Anaheim Angels beat the San Francisco Giants 4-3.

Source: MLB (2004).

The Open Championship

This first golf championship was inaugurated in 1860 at Prestwick. For 13 years it was by invitation only and then in 1874 it was declared an 'open' event. From 1894 several venues were used in rotation. The courses that have hosted The Open Championship most are St Andrews (26), Prestwick (24) and Muirfield (15). The competition is owned and staged by the Royal and Ancient Golf Club of St Andrews.

Source: The Open (2004).

IAAF World Athletics Championships

The IAAF was founded in 1912 by 17 national athletic associations and it now owns several key events including indoor, outdoor and youth World Championships. The 2003 World Athletics Championships are only the 9th to be staged and they are being hosted in Paris.

Source: IAAF (2004).

Event owners and organizers

Event owners are not always the organizers of their own sports events. NGBs in some sports contract event management organizations to run one-off events. In other cases many sports events can be a part of a series or tour where there will be any number of event organizations staging constituent events. The ATP for example, centrally administers a worldwide tour of men's tennis events at various levels for players of varying competence and/or age (Seniors, Challenger Series, Delta Series and Masters). They incorporate events in cities such as New Delhi, Atlantic City, Sau Paulo and Ho Chi Minh as well as the four events that make up the Grand Slam of tennis (Australian Open, French Open, Wimbledon and US Open). Each of these events is separately owned and administered locally. The US Professional Golf Association (PGA) and European PGA operate in a similar way with their tours. There are also governing body appointed host cities that set up sophisticated organizing committees and partnerships to manage their events. Independent and commercial promoters too can be authorized to manage sanctioned events.

Equally, all of these organizations can own and operate their own events. Governments, regional or local municipal authorities, educational institutions, clubs and commercial promoters can own and/or stage sports events and most will seek to run them according to the prescribed rules and regulations and often traditions of the relevant sport or sports. This can simply mean adhering to the printed rulebook or for events with greater profiles it can entail a more complex process of applying for official recognition, sanction or inclusion to the relevant sports governing body. Without such, it may be difficult to acquire the services, paid or unpaid, of officials and participants. This is why it is so difficult for entrepreneurs to set up rival events, tours or championships. The governing bodies maintain their control over their sports in this way and the intent is that by doing so the sport develops more successfully.

Host cities can bid to run an event by applying to events rights owners such as sports governing bodies or they can create their own and seek any necessary recognition or sanction required. For larger events this can involve the forming of organizing committees that can be made up of various stakeholders. There is more discussion on this elsewhere in this text and in particular in Chapter 6. The city of Manchester, UK bid for and won the rights to host the 2002 Commonwealth Games and put together an organizing committee that oversaw a new organization that had limited corporate liability to manage the event, Manchester 2002 Ltd. This organization employed nearly 500 people on short-term contracts including 25 Australian senior managers who had worked at the Sydney 2000 Olympics. There were clear links directly to national government through a select ministerial committee as well. Since the Games have closed, the city has further developed an events strategy and maintained its expertise and key personnel, resulting in the creation of brand new events such as the Manchester City Run.

Also in the UK, Sheffield has a municipal department that has staged over 400 events since its inception in 1991 following its hosting of the World Student Games. In the main, Sheffield Events Unit attracts interested events and their organizers to the city or bids to host events but it too has run its own events including a city marathon.

In Australia it is the individual states that are active in the development of event strategies and none more so than Victoria and its capital Melbourne. Their calendar of events is worth over AUS $500 million to the state economy and features the Australian Football League Grand Final, the Melbourne Cup and the Australian Tennis Open (SRV, 2003). The strategy is driven by the Sport, Recreation and Racing Division of the Department of State and Regional Development and operates under the title of Sport and Recreation Victoria (SRV). Utilizing the facilities at the Melbourne Sports Precinct, the previous focal point for the 1956 Olympics, the SRV Major Projects Department works with Tourism Victoria, the Victoria Major Events Company, sports governing bodies and promoters to identify, analyse and assist in planning events in the state (Victoria, 2001). The range of events is diverse with on the one hand the Australian Formula One Grand Prix at Albert Park and Ripcurl Pro on the Surf Coast. In 2003 it staged seven matches for the Rugby World Cup, and in 2006 will host the Commonwealth Games for 4500 athletes.

Most educational institutions such as schools, colleges and universities have sports events programmes. On the one hand they organize internal events in intramural competition and on the other they link into wider competition by selecting representative teams for all kinds of competitions at local, regional, national and international levels. The opportunities are broad and varied and need not necessarily be about elite performance. Many schools from all over Europe take up the opportunity to participate in rugby, field hockey and football tournaments for example. They are not representative sides of anything other than their school but these events allow non-elite performers to experience international competition. The tournaments are commercially promoted and teams pay to take part.

The college sports network in the US, is unlike any other. The National Collegiate Athletic Association (NCAA), constituted in 1906 and re-titled to its present name in 1910, is an association that administers 87 sports championships in 22 sports for its collegiate member institutions. Over 40000 students annually compete in these events for national titles. This voluntary association employs approximately 350 people and whilst there are similar associations in other countries, the British Universities Sports

Federation (BUSF) for example, the power, wealth and profile of the NCAA sets it apart. Many NCAA Championships are covered on network and cable television, radio and the Internet. Twenty-two NCAA Championship related events were featured on network television in the US in June 2003 alone (NCAA, 2003). In order to put this into further perspective the individual member institutions own their own broadcast rights for regular season fixtures and conference tournaments.

Sports Clubs vary in size, wealth and stature. Throughout the world local clubs are key developers of all kinds of sports. They can supplement the sports played in schools by providing another opportunity to play. They can also be a first provider of sport in that not all sports are taught or played in schools and so a club can be a one and only opportunity. They also provide a post-education link for those who wish to continue with, or at some time in their lives, take up a sport again. They can supply recreational opportunities as well as representative participation in competition of course and the vehicles that enable that are events. Intra club competitions are organized, from one-day knock-out events to club championships. These inter-club events are opportunities that are often provided not only by NGBs but also by volunteer organizers that set up and administer leagues, tournaments and other such competitions. For example, keen parents of participating children actively organize mini-leagues throughout many parts of the world.

There are larger clubs that have grown into significant organizations. Many of these emerged from humble and local beginnings into commercial entities with international profiles. Manchester United grew from a humble start and indeed another name. It was called Newton Heath LYR (Lancashire and Yorkshire Railway) and played matches against other LYR departments and then against other railway companies. It did not join the football league in England until 1892 and the more famous name was not used until 1902 (Manchester United FC, 2003). The club now plays in several sports event competitions, each are organized by a different body, the League Cup (Nationwide Football League), the FA Cup (The FA), the Premiership (Premier League) and when it qualifies, the UEFA Champions League (UEFA).

Sport is significantly important in the global economy and accordingly there are all kinds of commercial interests. This applies to the sports events industry where there are many organizations that own and operate their own events as well as win contracts to manage those events owned by other bodies. Many of the organizations discussed above are of course commercially orientated but there is a distinction to be made between those that make money and then distribute it amongst its member bodies and those that make a profit for shareholders. The IOC is non-profit making organization, as is Manchester City Council and the ATP is committed to the development of tennis and professional tennis players. On the other hand there are some high profile commercial organizations in the industry. Worthy of mention is International Management Group (IMG), founded by the late Mark McCormack in the early 1960s on the back of an association with the golfer Arnold Palmer. The Group was the first sports marketing organization and became a model for an industry that now has many of its clients on the world stage. IMG has 85 offices in 35 countries and employs nearly 3000 staff. It now has interests in sports, arts, fashion modelling, and television and as well as managing and representing many of the world's top sports stars it also owns and/or promotes some of the world's greatest sports events. It states that on any one day it is involved in an average of nine major events (IMG, 2003). IMG's own seven tennis events include the Pacific Life Open in Indian Wells for which it has built its own tennis stadium. It owns or partially owns several golf events including the World Match Play Championship and works as a marketing and television partner on many more including the Ryder Cup. Other television interests through its Trans World International (TWI) division include the Wimbledon Tennis Championships. IMG has worked closely with several IGB's and has done much for the development of sports other than tennis and golf. In X Sports it is a producer of 25 events, in motor sports it is managing partner of Champ Car Event (CART) in Australia, it sourced all of the funding for the founding of the Chinese Football League, and it helped to contribute towards the ICC's goal for the development of cricket outside of the traditional Commonwealth countries.

Summary

In order to identify the various types of event organizations that exist around the world this chapter has considered the basic structure of international sport. The optimum position of one IGB internationally and one NGB per country is an established princi-pal that has been encouraged and developed by the Olympic Movement in particular and has been generally adopted across sports whether they are a part of that Movement or not. Whilst the influence of the IOC is plain to see there are many more sports that thrive outside of the Movement.

Governing bodies at national and international level have used events to develop their sports. In establishing and developing events of all scales the members of these bodies have been able to increase their profile in order to increase participation. In add-ition the events prove valuable vehicles in maintaining gov-ernance whereby even the smallest IGB can control the standards of play through rule and regulation down through their structures to the most local of participation in their sport.

Through these structures it has been possible to identify those governing bodies that stage their own events and the relationships they develop in order to do that. It has also been possible to examine the relationships they have with other events organizers in maintaining their sports when the likes of governments, regional or local municipal authorities, educational institutions, clubs or commercial promoters seek to put on sports events. This highly centralized governance has no doubt caused and will cause issues but it has at the very least provided events that are linked, whatever their scale, in a worldwide calendar of sport. The fact that a school sports event is generally played to the same limitations as any Olympic or World Championship final makes the sports events industry important.

Questions

1 What concerns do you have for the future governance of sport? Evaluate the roles of sports governing bodies and the dilemma they face in the development as well as the control of their sports in the light of these concerns.

2 Evaluate the issues and challenges that independent commercial organizers might have to face in the development of events at three different levels: local, national and international.

3 Identify a country that is currently not a member nation of FIFA and a relevant confederation. Analyse the steps that would need to be made in order to develop the game in that country.

4 Evaluate the potential promotion of racquetball from a World Games sport to an Olympic sport. What issues and criteria might be involved?

References

FA (2003). www.thefa.com (accessed 12 June 2003).
FIFA (2004). www.fifa.org (accessed 27 January 2004).
FISU (2003). www.fisu.net (accessed 10 June 2003).
IAAF (2004). www.iaaf.org/insideIAAF/history (accessed 27 January 2004).
ICC (2004). www.icc.cricket.org (accessed 27 January 2004).
IMG (2003). www.imgworld/areasofbusiness (accessed 11 June 2003).
IOC (2003). www.olympic.org/uk/sports/index (accessed 10 June 2003).
IRB (2004). www.irb.com/events/worldcup (accessed 27 January 2004).

IWGA (2001). *The 6th World Games Guide Book: World Games 2001 Akita*. Akita, The Organizing Committee for the World Games 2001.

Maccabiah Games (2003). www.internationalgames.net/maccabia (accessed 10 June 2003).

Manchester City Council (2003). *The impact of the Manchester 2002 Commonwealth Games*. A Report by Cambridge Policy Consultants. Executive Summary. Manchester, Manchester City Council.

Manchester United FC (2003). www.manutd.com/history (accessed 11 June 2003).

MLB (2004). www.mlb.com (accessed 27 January 2004).

NBA (2004). www.nba.com (accessed 27 January 2004).

NCAA (2003). www.ncaa.org (accessed 12 June 2003).

OCA (2003). www.ocasia.org (accessed 7 January 2003).

The Open (2004). www.opengolf.com/history (accessed 27 January 2004).

PASO (2003). www.cob.org.br/pan2007/ingles/jogos_historico (accessed 7 January 2003).

Pro Football Hall of Fame (2004). www.profootballhof.com/players (accessed 27 January 2004).

SRV (2003). www.sport.vic.gov.au April, 2003 (accessed 12 June 2003).

Thoma, J. and Chalip, L. (1996). *Sport Governance in the Global Community*. Morgantown, Fitness Information Technology, Chapter 3.

USA Basketball (2003). www.usabasketball.com/general/index (accessed 9 June 2003).

USRA (2003). www.usra.org (accessed 12 June 2003).

Victoria (2001). *2001/2002 Sport and Recreation Industry Directory*. Melbourne, Sport and Recreation Victoria.

The sports event planning process

After studying this chapter, you should be able to:

• understand the importance of following a planning process for the organization of sports events.

• recognize the need for the process to consider short- to long-term objectives.

• recognize the need for a staged and iterative process that allows continuous alignment with objectives.

Introduction

This chapter considers the case for a new model for the sports event planning process.

The importance of sports events in terms of their impacts and benefits, particularly major international events, is well documented and also well covered in the media. In the main it is the economic benefits that receive the most attention, due mainly to the fact that they are more easily quantified (Jones, 2001; UK Sport, 1999). However, it is the other less quantifiable benefits, those that involve regeneration, physical legacies, cultural, social, environment, tourism and sports development which may be of more significant value over the long term.

In 2001, a lack of planning led to the loss of the 2005 World Athletic Championships for the UK. The government promised a London venue in its bid with Picketts Lock intended as a long-term legacy for the sport. Upon discovering the costs would be too high, the government tried to offer an alternative location away from London. This resulted in the International Amateur Athletics Federation (IAAF) deciding to put the event out to bid again. Whilst it is commendable that an uneconomic project was aborted, a potentially beneficial event and its stadium legacy might have been better planned for. Alan Pascoe, who runs Fast Track, the organization that is responsible for UK Athletics' commercial activities, estimated the loss for athletics at £15–20 million but recognized that it was not just about the financial loss. The world championships could have helped the development of the sport as well the creation of the legacy of a national stadium for future athletics events (Hubbard, 2002).

Much of the theory that underpins the teaching of event management in higher education is centred on how important the event planning process is for organizers of events. An evaluation of the theories of Allen et al. (2002), Bowdin et al. (2001), Getz (1997), Shone and Parry (2001), Torkildsen (1999) and Watt (1998) shows that they propose that event planning is a staged process. Others such as Catherwood and Van Kirk (1992), Goldblatt (1997) and Graham et al. (1995) propose a less formal approach to event planning.

These theories and models generally accept that event organizations should strategically plan for the long term including there being a responsibility for the ongoing and long-term management of the financial and physical legacies of major events. Getz (1997) maintains that long-term gains and losses should be assessed at the feasibility stage of the planning process. Allen et al. (2002) and Bowdin et al. (2001) follow a similar approach. Hall (1997) stresses the importance of long-term planning with the acceptance that it is the long-term legacies of an event that have the most consequence. Several of the theories also consider wind-up or shutdown (Allen et al., 2001; Catherwood and Van Kirk, 1992; Getz, 1997; Shone and Parry, 2001). The latter recognizes that some thought should be given to intended legacies in the formation of objectives at the beginning of the planning process.

The theory that is offered however, appears to be more appropriate for the short-term benefits that events can bring rather than for the long-term value that major international events can be strategically planned for. What the models do not cover is where the development of strategies for successful long-term legacies should sit in the event planning process. There is a need for the inclusion of specific long-term strategies when planning major international sports events and strategies that will extend beyond the end of the event itself. Secondly, it is accepted that current event planning theory and models adequately cater for the implementation of events, though not specifically for major sports events. What is required, therefore, is a more comprehensive process that can encompass the needs for sports event planning, a process that can accommodate sports events of all scales and intentions and thus enable the event to provide benefits in the longer as well as the shorter term.

A new approach to the event planning process

It is essential that any potential long-term benefits intended as attributable to the event be comprehensively covered by strategies that ensure that long-term success. Firstly, the inclusion of a cost–benefit forecast at the feasibility stage of the event planning process would enable organizers to not only forecast the extent of the benefits of their events and budget accordingly, but through that forecast gain support for the event at an early and appropriate stage.

Secondly, implementation strategies for the use of any new facilities and/or regeneration projects need to be built-in to ensure their long-term futures.

Thirdly, assessing the impact of such an event requires not only an evaluation of short- and medium-term economic and cultural benefits. It also requires a long-term evaluation, possibly even 10 years on or more, of the sustainability and durability, in other words the success, of the regeneration and the legacies that were created as a result of staging the event.

Fourthly, in order for objectives to be met there is a case for the inclusion of mechanisms in the process that will allow continuous alignment with short-, medium- and long-term plans.

What follows, is a new event planning process that encompasses both short-term requirements for the implementation of the event and the long-term objectives that become the legacies of the event (Masterman, 2003a,b; 2004). The model put forward here is intended to address the planning process that is required for all scales of event and whilst this text is concerned with the management of sports events it is proposed that this process is universally

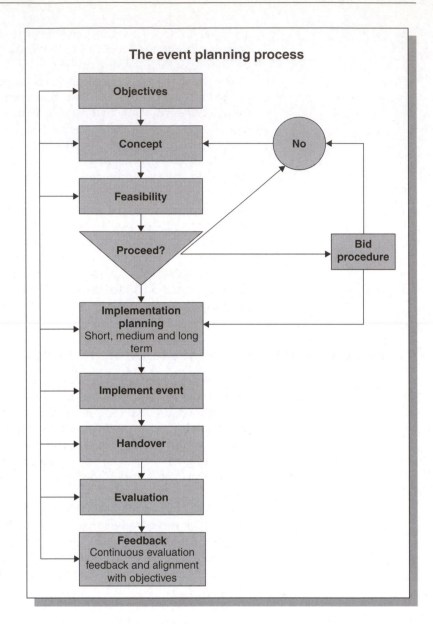

Figure 3.1
The event planning process
Source: Masterman (2003a;
2003b; 2004)

applicable across the events industry (see Figure 3.1 and Event management 3.1).

Staged process

The event planning process model consists of up to 10 different stages.

There is justification for a staged process where progression through the planning process is made step by step. Manchester for example decided on urban regeneration objectives before it decided to bid for both the 2000 Olympics and the 2002 Common-wealth Games (Bernstein, 2002; Department of Environment,

Event management 3.1

The event planning process – in progression

Objectives

Determine why the event is to be held, what it is to achieve, who is to benefit, and how they are going to benefit; are there political, social, cultural, environmental and/or economic benefits and over what timespan?

Any briefs or bidding processes should be considered as early as this stage.

Concept

Determine what the event is and what it looks like? Design the outline by completing a situational analysis, and a competitor analysis (particularly if there is a bid involved).

Consider scales of event and operation, timings, locations and venues, facilities required and available, target markets, etc.

Identify strategic partners: local and national government, national and international governing bodies, event owners and promoters, charities, sponsors, participants and after-users.

Identify all internal and external decision-makers.

Identify the stakeholders and organizers: determine if there is to be limited company status, the after-use for any facilities and infrastructure, and the publics that are affected?

Ensure the design is in alignment with the objectives – short to long term.

Feasibility

At the feasibility stage the event design is tested:

- Identify who is responsible for the delivery of the shorter- and longer-term objectives.
- Identify resources required: human resources (HR), facilities, equipment, marketing, services, etc.
- Consider the co-ordination of any bidding process, the event's implementation and the handover of legacies and returned facilities/venues/equipments.
- Specifically consider long-term usage of facilities and the continued management of such.

- Determine the nature and timing of partnerships to be involved including those required at this stage of the process, that is, bidding finance if applicable, any finance required to underwrite the event, any handover agreements or operational strategies required for the long-term usage of the facilities used for the event.

- Identify any partners not previously identified, particularly those that can provide financial support.
- Budget according to these requirements.
- Perform a costs versus benefits analysis not just for the event but also for any long-term legacies.
- Determine the critical path required – shorter and longer term, see Event management 8.1.
- Ensure alignment with shorter- and longer-term objectives.

Proceed?

All of the identified decision-makers are involved in deciding if the event is feasible and will achieve the objectives …

If the answer is *no* then evaluate and feedback to the concept stage to reshape and begin the process again and/or *abort* the project …

If the decision is to *proceed*

… and if there is a *bid procedure* … prepare, market and present the bid,

… if the bid is not won *abort* the project but evaluate the process and feedback for future use,

… if the bid is won or there is no bid procedure then move onto the next *key* stage …

Implementation planning

It is at this stage where often only the short-term requirements of the event are considered.

Determine all the operational strategies: financial, HR, partnerships, suppliers, services, facilities, equipment, sales and marketing – include in those: the requirements for after-use, the identification of after-users and their requirements (gained by involving them in the process), and what the handover arrangements will be, including how the evaluation over the long term will be completed.

Develop the critical path and the performance indicators to incorporate all the fine detail involved in executing the event in the shorter term and for realizing the benefits in the longer term.

Alignment with the short- and long-term objectives can then be made.

Implement event

The implementation plans are then executed and the event staged. Having completed this implementation there are still key stages of the event planning process remaining.

Handover

The handover of facilities or even equipment is key for all scales of event. The planning for this has already been conducted in previous stages and now managers implement the handover of facilities to the identified or contracted organizations for their continued operation and/or development.

In addition there is the handover of the responsibility for the evaluation of the legacies/facilities over the long term – to determine the level of success according to the long-term objectives.

Evaluation

Post-event evaluation is performed against original objectives, short and long term:

- Short-term evaluation: of the costs, benefits, impacts of the event itself and performed immediately after the event.
- Medium- and long-term evaluations: of the costs, benefits and impacts after a predetermined time and in particular of the legacies to see if they are achieving the objectives set for them.

Continuous evaluation

By using performance indicators (budget targets, deadlines for contracts to be achieved, etc.) in evaluation at all stages of the process, continuous alignment with the objectives is achieved.

Feedback

The evaluation is not complete without feedback:

- The process is iterative by conducting evaluation at all stages thus ensuring feedback is continuous throughout the life cycle of the event.
- Post-event feedback following the evaluation, short or long term, includes recommendations that feed into the process for the next event whenever or whatever it is.

Source: Masterman (2003a; 2003b; 2004)

1993). It then looked at the feasibility of the latter being able to successfully deliver the objectives over the long term. On deciding to proceed the city then went to bid for the event. There was then the development of strategies prior to the event, so that the event would deliver over the long term: for example, the building of the venues and the ensuring of their after-use prior to construction. The policy to only build permanent facilities when after-use and users were secure demonstrates that the city was not only planning for the long term at a pre-event stage but it was also not prepared to progress to the next stage in its planning until these requirements had been met (Bernstein, 2002).

Sydney also decided on its long-term objectives first and then developed the concept for the 2000 Olympic Games (Adby, 2002). Feasibility was next assessed, albeit not to the same level as in Manchester, prior to submitting a bid. Sydney did not, for example, have secured after-use for its new facilities in place prior to the construction of building.

A handover stage followed the implementation of each event and then similarly evaluation and feedback followed as the final stage.

A review of literature pertaining to the event planning process also supports a staged model (Allen et al., 2002; Bowdin et al., 2001; Getz, 1997; Hall, 1997; Smith and Stewart, 1999; Shone and Parry, 2001; Torkildsen, 1999; Watt, 1998) with the remainder of the literature demonstrating no arguments against such (American Sport Education Programme, 1996; Cashman and Hughes, 1999; Catherwood and Van Kirk, 1992; Goldblatt, 1997; Graham et al., 1995). The main advantage of a staged process being that it is an efficient way of not advancing too quickly and finding out that effort and budgets have been committed unnecessarily.

There is also justification for each stage to be completed prior to progression to the next in order to maintain efficiency in both time and finance. This is also advocated by Allen et al. (2002), Bowdin et al. (2001), Getz (1997) and Shone and Parry (2001).

A description of each stage in the process now follows with the 2000 Olympics in Sydney, the 2002 Commonwealth Games in Manchester and the 1991 World Student Games in Sheffield used to exemplify key points.

Objectives

It is important to identify why the event is to be staged prior to deciding what the event will be or what it looks like and so objectives are the first stage in the process. The objectives determine the nature and scale of the event. In the case of major international sports events host cities may well have regeneration objectives such as the redevelopment of derelict lands for new facilities, housing and business opportunities. The event in effect becomes the catalyst for the achievement of such objectives. Therefore for this scale of event it is important to consider how event objectives might fit into wider urban plans. For all scales of event, of international or local importance, the objectives are concerned with what the event itself is to achieve. These could be for monetary profit, to develop participation in sport, to determine winners via competition and to engage communities. Whatever the objectives are, they are what the event will be evaluated against in order to determine whether it has been a success or not.

The use of objectives is not necessarily widespread in the industry. Emery (2001) for example, researched 400 major sports event organizers and found that whilst 64% of the respondents maintained that they used aims and objectives, they were generally a single general aim and/or lacked detail. There may be a number of reasons for this. One may be management complacency, but it may also be due to a perception that setting objectives is too difficult a task due to the diverse nature of the various stakeholders involved. Setting objectives for a long planning process may also be seen to be too inflexible an approach when so much can change in the meantime. Also, because objectives are used as the eventual benchmark for an event, there may also be a reluctance to use them politically. After all, not many people want to be seen to fail.

The argument in favour of the use of event objectives is that they provide the direction for planning and execution. Event management texts agree that the use of objectives is necessary for the production of a successful event (Allen et al., 2002; Bowdin et al., 2001; Getz, 1997; Goldblatt, 1997; Graham et al., 1995; Hall, 1997; Shone and Parry, 2001; Smith and Stewart, 1999; Torkildsen, 1999; Watt, 1998). However, not all agree that they should be ahead of the development of the event concept in the planning process. Some describe a process that begins with the concept, and include an intention to bid for an event where appropriate (Allen et al, 2002; Getz, 1997), or an idea and a proposal (Torkildsen, 1999; Watt, 1998). Getz (1997) and Watt (1998) propose that scanning the internal and external environments is necessary prior to setting the vision and goals for the event. Shone and Parry (2001) at least wraps all of these elements into one initial stage that includes the setting of objectives, and Allen et al. (2002) and Bowdin et al. (2001) agree that objectives are required before any situational analysis. The process in Figure 3.1 and Event management 3.1 recognizes the necessity for objectives to be the first stage in the planning process. The concept is the vehicle that is designed to achieve the objectives and can only be designed once objectives have been set.

Much is made of objectives being SMART, where they are specific, measurable, achievable, realistic and timely. For them to be achievable and realistic for sports events, the next stage in the process, feasibility, is key. That they are specific, are to be achieved in a certain timeframe and have performance indicators that can be measured, aids the penultimate stage of the process, evaluation.

In order that objectives can be determined it is necessary for all stakeholders to be identified and their requirements considered in this first stage so that they can be incorporated into the planning of the event. This includes considering potential partners and linked strategies. The basic questions that should be asked at this stage include, why is the event to be held, what is to be achieved, who is to benefit and how? Whilst it is not necessary to categorize sports event objectives in order to determine them, in analysis they may well be political, social, cultural, environmental or economic in nature. Such a categorization may well assist in determining who the people and/or organizations are that have an influence on the staging of the event; in other words its stakeholders.

Stakeholders . . .

- *Customers*: Seat and corporate ticket buyers, sports players or competition participants, advertisers, corporate package buyers such as those for franchised space, sponsors, merchandise buyers.

- *Suppliers*: The organizations that are used to supply equipment, services or goods in connection with the event, for example tournament equipment, legal advice, food and beverages, transportation and emergency services.

- *Partners*: Many sports events are not possible without the sanction of the relevant regional, national and international governing body and these bodies also run their own sports. Other partners may well be local, regional or national government or their agencies. Separate event management organizations may well combine forces to execute an event. Sponsors are often referred to as partners both in their title rights and because of the longevity and/or closeness of the relationship, as too are those media organizations that purchase event rights.

- *Investors*: Some of the above partners may also be investors in that they have a vested interest as a result of providing funding either monetarily or via services/goods in-kind. This interest may result in a monetary return on investment but not always. Municipal or agency investment may require non-financial returns such as sports, cultural or social development.

- *Staff*: Permanent staff, short-term event hired personnel, those that are sub-contracted, and volunteers can fall into this category.

- *External influencers*: These include the event publics that are important for the success of the event and therefore influence any decision-making even if they are not directly connected to the event in any of the above terms. For example, the local community in which the event is delivered, pressure groups, local and national governments from legislative, economic, health and safety, cultural and social perspectives, individual politicians and the media.

At this stage it is also important to consider any briefs that have been received for the event. Competition to win the right to stage an event for example is increasingly in use by event owners. In the corporate world, pitching against others in order to run a sports event on behalf of event owners is growing. A sports management agency will need to discuss, negotiate and fulfil the latter's stipulated conditions and targets. Even if there is no competition there is likely to be such a brief. In the same light bidding is also being increasingly used by event owners where host cities compete for the right to stage major events. Again various stipulated conditions or criteria will have to be met by any bid in order to be successful.

It is important that the planning process has built-in alignment mechanisms that ensure that objectives are evaluated throughout all stages of the planning process. Sydney was able to change its 2000 Olympic masterplan on three occasions (Adby, 2002; Sydney 2000,

2001) and Manchester conducted independent reviews of its performance at various stages of the planning process undertaken for the 2002 Commonwealth Games. Alignment can be achieved with the identification of performance indicators and targets. For example, in setting objectives that include the long-term success of facilities and a resultant economic gain from the staging of an event, the planning process automatically gains performance benchmarks. For all scales of sports event, the setting of deadlines for the achievement of certain levels of income, prescribed levels of media coverage or the signing of appropriate contracts ensures that the process gains its own integrated indicators. Incorporating mechanisms and operational systems throughout the implementation planning stage and thus allowing for further thinking on how a project can be improved, will also ensure that ultimately the event achieves what it is supposed to achieve.

Concept

Having determined the objectives the concept for the event can be designed.

The previous stage identified all the stakeholders that could or should be involved. Now the decision-makers need to be identified. In designing facilities that were to be used after the 2002 Commonwealth Games, Manchester found it critical to involve the after-users so that they could contract them at an early stage and in some cases receive funding in order to proceed. Indeed without an identified and signed after-user any new facility would have been of only temporary build (Bernstein, 2002). Sydney was also able to involve relevant municipal agencies at the concept stage with the design of its facilities and Sydney Olympic Park incorporated as part of the strategy for the development of Homebush Bay.

The key questions asked at this stage of the process are what is the event and what does it look like? A situational analysis, including an evaluation of competition, is required in order that the concept can be fully developed to achieve the objectives. The contrasting example of the 2000 Olympics and the 2002 Commonwealth Games provides a reason why Sydney failed to fully consider the competition that existing venues would exert on Stadium Australia. Manchester researched the need for a stadium that could house athletics and field team sports for the Commonwealth Games and the long-term contracted use by Manchester City Football Club (FC) and itself in bringing other major events to the city. Other stadia in the area could not provide such use.

Consideration of the scale of the event, how it will operate, the timing involved, locations and venues, the facilities and equipment required and already available are all key issues at this stage. The identification of potential strategic partners, possibly local or national government, sports governing bodies, event owners, and promoters and charities are also early considerations in forming the concept.

Consideration should also be given at this stage to the show. Sports events are entertainment and can be expensive to stage. It may be tempting to keep the event at its bare bones and not add interval entertainers, extra floral decoration, ceremonies with pomp and style and it will always be a cost versus benefits decision, but the perspective needs to be long term. For those events that want to view their customers in terms of life asset value there is a need to evaluate the event experience and how it will attract them next time. The National Basketball Association (NBA) spends $1 million on research to help its teams find out what its fans want and in particular what will make season ticket holders renew year after year. In the top 10 reasons for renewing seat tickets, fans indicated that they viewed in-game entertainment and gifts as the seventh and eighth highest motivations, respectively. A clean arena was placed sixth, and the attitude and behaviour of neighbouring fans in your seat area was placed fourth (Cann, 2003). It can be argued that if it is customer orientated, in other words if the customer values it, then it is a part of the show and such items become important budget considerations. How much extra cleaning and how many more floral bouquets is clearly a subjective managerial decision but the NBA shows that such decisions can be aided by customer research at this stage of the planning process. Setting a budget for these elements is the solution so that as the planning develops and certainly after the decision has been made to go ahead, there is a cost centre to use and the flexibility to respond to changes in requirements nearer to the implementation of the event.

One of the key findings in the NBA research was the dependence of fans on their neighbours in the stands. It showed that one of the most influential aspects on an event experience is the person that sits next to you. You and they are part of the show. Individual experiences on this level would appear to be beyond the control of the event manager but in at least making sure the seat is occupied, the atmosphere for spectators and participants can only be enhanced. Making sure that each and all are entertained becomes a key aspect of the delivery of the event. At the 2002 Commonwealth Games for the 7 a'side rugby matches, fans for each of the participating national teams were sat side by side. They sang together and entertained themselves with humorous banter. The organizers had done their homework and their knowledge of rugby fans was sufficient to ensure that not only was it safe for fans to sit together it was actually preferable for the most conducive atmosphere. A host announcer, music and screen video footage was used to ensure that this was encouraged.

There are two further decision areas that should be highlighted for this stage. The first is that of after-use. Whatever the scale of the event there is use of the facilities, equipment and venues after the event has concluded, unless it is temporary. Even then a temporary structure may be used or moved on for use elsewhere. For major events this may include handing over newly built sports stadia and for locally important events it may be the handing back of the venue to the owners for everyday use. Either way there is a need to consider how this handover will be achieved at this early stage of the planning process.

The second concerns target markets. If it has not already been done as part of the previous stage, it is important to identify who the target customers for the event will be. This will include targets of participants or sports competitors as well targets for sponsors, advertisers and ticket sales. For instance, the sportsmen and women who take part in the event may or may not bring in revenue in participation or entry fees but they are nevertheless clearly critical. There is no concept without them. It is important that they are identified as a realistically achievable target and this is often decided in tandem with all the other considerations above. Are the two exhibition tennis players available on the right date, how many ticket buying fans will be able to be seated, what ticket sales price strategy will be appropriate for the audience demographics? The answers to these questions can help determine what the event is.

Whilst the next stage of the planning process is concerned with deciding if and how the concept can run, as long as there is enough flexibility, the concept can be revisited until it is made feasible.

Having determined the objectives at the outset, all of the subsequent stages of the planning process require the implementation of a system of constant alignment with those objectives. Whilst not this is simple to achieve in reality, if alignment with all the objectives at every stage of the event planning process is made, the event has to be a success. More practically, being aware of the objectives throughout the planning and execution of the event should be considered the best event management practice.

Feasibility

Feasibility is a key stage that is recognized by the majority of event theory (Allen et al., 2002; Getz, 1997; Smith and Stewart, 1999; Torkildsen, 1999; Watt, 1998). Having determined the concept for an event and what it is to achieve, it needs to be tested to see if it will work. This does not entail a dress rehearsal but for major events it may involve the delivery of one or more events that are used as learning curves. In Manchester prior to the 2002 Commonwealth Games the city ran a series of events that were significant in their own right but were still used to test various event management aspects not least the performance of new venues. One such example was the delivery of national swimming championships in the newly built aquatics centre. In a 2-year period, 2000–2002, the city delivered major championship events in such sports as squash, table tennis and cycling, and used them as part of their learning process for the management of the 2002 Commonwealth Games.

Whatever the scale of event the feasibility stage needs to include a cost–benefit evaluation in order that the budget can be set. This will enable organizers to forecast the extent of the benefits. Through that forecast they can gain important stakeholder's support for the event and by determining costs versus benefits prior to any proceed decisions, organizers can also ensure that unnecessary costs can be kept to a minimum. This may involve the identification of long-term after-use and users or the need for handover of legacies at the end of the event that come with an advantageous financial position. In order to conduct the cost side of this exercise a number of considerations are required:

- Identify who is responsible for the delivery of the objectives (short or long term) and the timings involved.

- Identify the resources required and sources where possible, including financial, personnel, facilities, equipment, marketing, services, etc. and the timings for payment involved.

- Any bidding process criteria and finance required, and the capacity to write that off or benefit from a losing bid.

- Event implementation, execution and evaluation requirements and timings.

- Legacies handover and any requirements of long-term after-use of facilities.

These considerations lead to the forming of an event budget and therefore provide a view on the cost at which the event benefits will be achieved. The budget goes onto act as a performance indicator and means by which alignment with the objectives can be continually assessed.

Getz (1997) agrees that long-term gains and losses should be assessed at this stage but maintains that it should also concern an assessment of social, cultural and environmental factors. He sees feasibility as a comprehensive evaluation that also includes 'fit' whereby matters of track records in events, the interests of the community, the availability of personnel, and local politics and ideology are all considered.

At this stage it may be difficult to give any due credence to non-economic-related criteria simple due to the fact that these issues tend to dominate. Most stakeholders are interested firstly in the economics of whether the event will pay its way. Jones (2001) goes one stage further and suggests that even a balanced economic analysis of whether to host an event may get overshadowed by the political objectives of event organizers, and local and national politicians. Hall (2001) supports this and discusses the lack of feasibility assessment in what he terms 'fast-track planning.' This is where government reaction to short timeframes in hosting events results in the pushing through of proposals without due economic, social or environmental evaluation procedures. Clearly, unbiased feasibility assessment would appear to be critical in aiding the decision of whether to go ahead or not.

Next, it is important to determine a critical path whatever the scale of event. This should include the short- and long-term implementation of the event and any handovers and management of after-use and legacies, physical or non-physical. The importance of this at this stage is to ensure that the timings that are considered necessary are mapped out to see that they can indeed deliver. This is covered in greater detail in Chapter 8.

The benefits an event can achieve should be inherent within the objectives and if these objectives are specific and measurable they can be compared with the costs and therefore determine if the event is of value.

In many cases cost–benefit exercises involve subjective views and forecasts. The greater the scale of event perhaps the greater the need is for a more objective view due to the increased need for accountability. Independent evaluations can entail further expense. For example, the Arup Report produced in May 2002 (Arup, 2002) commissioned jointly by the Greater London Authority, the UK Government and the British Olympic Committee (BOC) reported on the feasibility of London staging the 2012 Olympic Games. It included a forecast of costs and an estimation of the extent of possible benefits. Whatever the scale of the exercise, and whether or not it is an internal or external audit, the expense does need to be included in the costs for the event.

The essential focus of the feasibility stage is to determine if the event can deliver the objectives. Only through continuous alignment of the planning process with the objectives this can be assured.

Proceed?

The decision whether to proceed or not is dependent upon the objectives being feasible and this requires the involvement of all decision-makers. Both Allen et al. (2002) and Getz (1997) include this as a stage in the planning process models.

The reason why it is necessary to separate this stage from the previous one is that when the event is deemed unfeasible there may well be a case to revisit the concept stage using feedback from the cost–benefit exercise to reshape the event. There is also the decision to completely abort the event.

If the event is feasible then the decision to proceed can be made.

Bidding

If there is a bid procedure the bid needs to be prepared, marketed and presented, and clearly there are costs involved (Allen et al., 2002; Getz, 1997). The decision to progress from feasibility to one of proceed must identify the sunk costs that are involved in not winning the bid. If these are not acceptable then the decision not to proceed should also include relevant feedback for future decisions. Manchester was able to feed its experience of its failed 1996 and 2000 Olympics bids into the process by which it won the bid to host the 2002 Commonwealth Games.

It may also be the case that the bid itself can deliver a number of objectives and that a successful bid concerns a further set of objectives. This makes the bid both a means to an end and a worthwhile project in its own right. Torino, for instance, in its bid for the 2006 Winter Olympics formulated a bid that would achieve a set of objectives, win or lose. This is discussed in greater detail in Chapter 7.

Implementation planning

The next stage, bid process or not, is the planning for the implementation of the event concept. This involves the determination of strategies that can achieve the objectives. It is at this stage where often only the short-term requirements of the event are considered in depth.

For the delivery of the event itself there are operational strategies. These entail the considerations for the delivery of the event, such as the requirements for finance, human resources (HR), partnerships, services and suppliers, venues, facilities, equipment and marketing.

If the event has no long-term objectives it is implemented via relatively short-term strategies. However, if there are long-term objectives it is important that long-term strategies are implemented at this stage. Sydney intended that its 2000 Olympics facilities would be of long-term use for the cultural and sporting development of its residents and of national tourism importance. Whilst it had long-term benefits in its sights, its strategies are to date failing with Stadium Australia in serious financial plight. Sheffield saw the importance of an events strategy over the long term as a legacy of its investment in the facilities it built for the 1991 World Student Games. The objectives were to regenerate an urban area that had been stricken with unemployment. The Sheffield Event Unit, a city authority department, was set up accordingly and was to attract new events to make use of the new facilities and as mentioned earlier, over 400 to date have been delivered, (Coyle, 2002). The cost of building the facilities however is still a financial millstone around the city's neck and it will continue to pay off its debt until 2025 (Wallace, 2001). On the other hand, it would appear that Manchester was only going to build its new 2002 Commonwealth Games facilities if they could be a catalyst for regeneration, with jobs, tourism, sports and cultural development the intended impact over the long term (Bernstein, 2002). In order to achieve this it implemented a strategy that entailed the commencement of building only when the long-term facility after-users were in place. The identification of Manchester City FC as the user of a new stadium was made as early as 1993 in the city's 2000 Olympic bid (Department of Environment, 1993). In failing with that bid the strategy came to fruition with the subsequent bid for the 2002 Commonwealth Games.

The strategies that are required to deliver the event and its short- and long-term objectives need to be tied into the further development of the critical path. This stage of implementation planning is closest to the delivery of the event itself and whatever the length of period, it is necessary to add all the fine detail that is required in order to deliver a successful event. Day-to-day item-ization is needed in this lead-up time and so the staffing, catering, equipment requirements for example are mapped out to deadlines and costs, as are the receipts of ticket, hospitality, entrant fees and sponsorship revenue to deadlines and income. At the same time, as is noted above, the negotiations with the likes of after-users concerning handover dates and other issues need to take place.

The alignment of these strategies with the event objectives is again a key element and the re-addressing of the budget require-ments and the assessment of performance indicators throughout this stage of the process can help to assure this.

Implement event

The successful delivery of the event involves the implementation of the strategies that ensure that the short-term objectives of the event are met. The success of these short-term objectives is also of critical importance for the success of any long-term benefits. The attraction of future events to a new stadium will be influenced by how successful the event was and the long-term objectives of sport development may well be dependent upon how successful the spectacle was for example.

Handover

This stage involves the shutdown of the event and as highlighted earlier this needs to be considered at the concept and feasibility stages. Whilst several authors consider this an important stage in the planning process (Allen et al., 2002; Getz, 1997; Shone and Parry, 2001) they do not highlight the nature of the planning that is required for the handover of legacies that are to be managed in the long term. If there are facilities to be handed back to owners, or new venues to be divested or handed over to after-users, the strategies that ensure this is to be achieved are dealt with early in the process. In Manchester's case, no construction of new facilities was undertaken until the after-users were in place and so hand-over actually involved strategies that had been implemented at the concept stage. In contrast, Sydney's after-use strategies for Stadium Australia were considered after the bid had been won and then when these strategies failed the venue was left with financial issues. Earlier consideration of the competition and a more effective cost–benefit analysis may have led to more success for the latter.

Shutdown involves clearing out and clearing up, and a strategy has to be in place so that this is a seamless activity. This is therefore a stage of the process that when reached, has already been diligently prepared for at the implementation planning stage. Equally important for event managers at this stage is the need to prepare for and execute the handover of the facilities and equipment used. This could involve a hand-back to owners of a building that was overlaid for the event, or a handover of a new legacy to new operators.

There is one further aspect that may require handover too. If there are long-term objectives the handover of the responsibility for the evaluation of the legacies and facilities over the long term is necessary if the event managers/owners are not going to perform it themselves. Sydney Olympic Park was a resulting legacy of the 2000 Olympics and entailed the handing over of facilities to a new organization in 2002 and their strategy for the Park's future management and development involves evaluation after 15 years of operation (Adby, 2002).

Evaluation

The role and place of evaluation in the process is generally agreed. In one form or another theories and planning models identify that evaluation of the event, and then feedback to aid future practice, is a key component. There is agreement in that evaluation is performed after the event, but there is little consideration for longer-term evaluations. Getz (1997) does make the point about event objectives being measurable targets with various timeframes but for major sports events there is a need for specific planning for longer-term measures. Assessing the impact of an event may require both short- and long-term evaluation. In the longer term it is the sustainability and durability, in other words the success, of the regeneration and the legacies that were created as a result of staging the event that are to be measured. In Manchester there is the intention of regular evaluation against objectives, possibly every 2 years and with a 60-year contract in-place for the use of its stadium it has its performance indicators already in place. The Sheffield Event Unit evaluates its events prior to agreeing to host them and also assesses how each event will impact on its overall event strategy. It regularly reports the accumulative impact since the 1991 World Student Games for example.

It is therefore evaluation at the end of the process, rather than at the end of the event itself, that is required. However, evaluation is not just necessary at the end of the process. If continuous alignment with the objectives is to be achieved than evaluation is required throughout the process. This is important no matter what the scale of the event but it is critical for the planning process for major international sports events. The planning for such events extends over a number of years and it is necessary to adapt to new business, social, cultural and political expectations and conditions. Continuous reassessment of how the objectives are going to be met is therefore required and consequently evaluation has a role throughout the process at all stages as well as over various time-frames after the event.

Whatever the scale of the event, performance indicators, such as budget targets or deadlines for completion of contracts, can be used to continually evaluate whether alignment with objectives is being achieved. Sydney and Manchester both had sets of targets as part of their objectives and were and are able to measure against those. For example, by how much their employment, economies and tourism should grow. Evaluation methods include the use of economic impact analysis, employment statistics and tourism data but may also include the use of participation data in order to measure sports development. Similarly, data regarding the continued participation in community activities following an event may be used to assess cultural impact in the long term. Sheffield set no such targets and consequently cannot assess how successful or not it has been against its original objectives for the 1991 World Student Games. Evaluation requires specific and measurable objectives. These need to be set as part of the first stage of the process, in order that success can in fact be evaluated at whatever point, during or at the end of the planning process.

Feedback

Evaluation is only of use if the results are fed back into the decision-making process. At whatever stage the evaluation is being done it is critical that future plans incorporate why and how previous strategies worked and failed and so feedback is necessary. This is equally true of short- and long-term evaluation periods, as the next event should always benefit from the feedback from a previous event.

Feedback after a 20-year evaluation period for the legacies of a major event would clearly be too late for any follow-up events that occur earlier, but that is where regular evaluation and alignment throughout the process is appropriate.

Thus evaluation is conducted at all stages and therefore feedback is also continuous throughout the process.

A formal overall evaluation report is required at the end of the process. This enables the managers of the next event to easily refer to how the new event should be delivered. A small-scale event for example, may be an annual occurrence, but memories for detail fade. However, the use of such reporting is uncommon in the events industry and the sports sector is no better even at the highest levels. It was only in 2002 for example, that the International Olympic Committee (IOC) finally incorporated a feedback system for Olympic hosts with its Transfer of Olympic Knowledge (TOK), whereby current hosts can access evaluation reports from previous games (Felli, 2002).

Summary

There is a case for a new event planning process model. A model that particularly addresses the long-term legacy needs for the planning of major international sports events.

A staged process is important so that clear progression can be made without unnecessary action being taken too early. Attempting to complete each stage prior to progressing to the next is good management practice though it is only common sense to realize that the boundaries between each stage can be less than clear at times. Consistent alignment with the objectives of the event is important and this is made more effective via evaluations of such at each stage. Thus the process is iterative in nature allowing adjustments to be made where necessary as a result of evaluation feedback. Objectives that are Specific, Measurable, Achievable, Relevant and Timely (SMART) have built-in performance indicators and will make this continuous monitoring easier.

The setting of objectives prior to any concept development allows the whole planning process to be driven towards the event's intended goals and in many cases these two stages can be delivered at minimal expense. Testing the feasibility of the event next is critical thus ensuring that any expenditure of time or money is not going to be superfluous. The assessment of costs versus benefits here will determine whether it is worth pursuing the objectives and a particular concept at all.

The next stage of strategy implementation is where there are cases in the industry of neglect. If there are long-term objectives and legacies requiring post-event development, management and after-use, then the strategies that will ensure this need to be inherent at this stage. Much of current literature also fails to consider this relationship.

Despite this being an iterative process there is still a clear need for an evaluation of the event after it has been executed. However, it is important to understand that an event is only a success if it has achieved its objectives and post-event evaluation against such can reveal to what degree this has been the case. Therefore the timely nature of the objectives is a key factor in determining when this evaluation is performed. The success of achieving sales and expenditure targets is a short-term task but the success of the after-use of a new arena may require evaluation over a much longer period. Whenever evaluation is completed it is its use of feedback for future performance that is important here.

Questions

1 Consider the implications of not setting objectives and designing an appropriate event concept? Support your analysis with your own researched examples.

2 The success of an event can be identified at any point during the event planning process. Identify how this can be effectively achieved by applying appropriate management techniques. Relate your answer to specific event examples.

3 Evaluate the arguments for and against the use of short- and long-term objectives for events.

4 Long planning periods require flexible management. What issues if any do you see being important considerations for the success of long-term planning?

5 Analyse the role of evaluation and feedback in the planning process, both as an iterative and final stage tool.

6 What issues do you envisage with the evaluation of long-term objectives?

References

Adby, R. (2002). *Email Questionnaire: Director General, Olympic Co-Ordination Authority 2000 Olympics*. 9 July.

Allen, J., O'Toole, W., McDonnell, I. and Harris, R. (2002). *Festival and Special Event Management*, 2nd edition. Queensland, Australia, John Wiley & Sons, Chapters 2, 5 and 13.

American Sport Education Programme (1996). *Event Management for Sport Directors*. Champaign, Illinois, Human Kinetics.

Arup (2002). *London Olympics 2012 Costs and Benefits: Summary*. In association with Insignia Richard Ellis, 21 May. www.olympics. org.uk/library/boa (accessed 11 November 2002).

Bernstein, H. (2002). Interview: Chief Executive, Manchester City Council at Chief Executive's Office, Manchester City Council, Town Hall, Manchester. 3 p.m., 28 June.

Bowdin, G., McDonnell, I., Allen, J. and O'Toole, W. (2001). *Events Management*. Oxford, Butterworth Heinmann, Chapters 2, 4 and 12.

Cashman, R. and Hughes, A. (Eds) (1999). *Staging the Olympics: The Event and Its Impact*. Sydney, University of New South Wales, Chapter 16.

Catherwood, D. and Van Kirk, R. (1992). *The Complete Guide to Special Event Management: Business Insights, Financial Strategies* from Ernst & Young, Advisors to the Olympics, the Emmy Awards and the PGA Tour. New York, John Wiley & Sons, Chapters 1 and 11.

Cann, J. (2003). *NBA Research Overview.* Presentation by NBA Senior Manager for Market Research and Analysis, NBA Store, New York, 2 December.

Coyle, W. (2002). Interview: Manager, Events Unit, Sheffield City Council at Events Unit, Sheffield City Council, Sheffield. 12 noon, 19 July.

Department of Environment (1993). The Stadium Legacy. In *The British Olympic Bid: Manchester 2000*, Section 12, Vol. 2. Manchester, Department of Environment.

Emery, P. (2001). Bidding to host a major sports event: strategic investment or complete lottery. In Gratton, C. and Henry, P. (Eds), *Sport in the City: The Role of Sport in Economic and Social Regeneration.* London, Routledge, Chapter 7.

Felli, G. (2002). Transfer of Knowledge (TOK): A games management tool. A paper delivered at the *IOC-UIA Conference: Architecture and International Sporting Events*, Olympic Museum, Lausanne. IOC. June.

Getz, D. (1997). *Event Management and Tourism.* New York, Cognizant, Chapters 3 and 4.

Goldblatt, J. (1997). *Special Events: Best Practices in Modern Event Management.* New York, John Wiley & Sons, Chapter 2.

Graham, S., Neirotti, L. and Goldblatt, J. (1995). *The Ultimate Guide to Sport Event Management and Marketing.* Chicago, Irwin, Chapter 13.

Hall, C.M. (1997). *Hallmark Tourist Events – Impacts, Management and Planning.* London, Bellhaven Press, Chapters 3–7.

Hubbard, A. (2002). The Interview: Alan Pascoe: A sport stabbed in the back, a nation and its youngsters badly let down. In *The Independent on Sunday.* London, The Independent, 6 January.

Jones, C. (2001). Mega-events and host region impacts: determining the true worth of the 1999 Rugby World Cup. *International Journal of Tourism Research.* **3**, 241–251. London, John Wiley & Sons.

Masterman, G. (2003a). The event planning process. In Moragas, M., de., Kennett, C. and Puig, N. (Eds), *The Legacy of the Olympic Games 1984–2000.* Lausanne, IOC.

Masterman, G. (2003b). Major international sports events: planning for long-term benefits. In Ibbetson, A., Watson, B. and Ferguson, M. (Eds), *Sport, Leisure and Social Inclusion.* Eastbourne, LSA.

Masterman, G. (2004). Sports events: a new planning process. In McMahon-Beattie, U. and Yeoman, I. (Eds), *Sport and Leisure: A Services Operations Approach.* London, Thomson Learning/ Continuum, Chapter 13. (In press)

Shone, A. and Parry, B. (2001). *Successful Event Management: A Practical Handbook.* London, Continuum, Chapters 6 and 12.

Smith, A. and Stewart, B. (1999). *Sports Management: A Guide to Professional Practice.* Sydney, Allen & Unwin, pp. 249–261.

Sydney 2000 (2001). www.gamesinfo.com.au/Home/Sydney 2000OlympicGamesReport (accessed 4 July 2002).

Torkildsen, G. (1999). *Leisure and Recreation Management*, 4th edition. London, E & F N Spon, Chapter 15.

UK Sport (1999). *Major Events: A Blueprint for Success.* London, UK Sport.

Wallace, S. (2001). Behind the headlines. *The Telegraph.* London, Telegraph. 15 June.

Watt, D. (1998). *Event Management in Leisure and Tourism.* Harlow, Addison Wesley Longman, Chapter 1.

Impacts and legacies

After studying this chapter, you should be able to:

- understand that the importance of the role sports events can play as catalysts for the achievement of short-term benefits and long-term legacies.

- recognize the various forms of impact that can be gained from sports events.

- demonstrate how the positive impacts of sports events can be maximized.

- demonstrate how the negative impacts of sports events can be minimized.

Introduction

The impacts of sports events on their immediate and wider environments can be both negative and positive, and the key to minimizing negative impacts and achieving potential positive impacts is in the effective planning of the event. Impacts can have effect over the long term as well as during and immediately after the event and so the planning needs to reflect an understanding of the different strategies that are therefore required. Even in some of the highest profile sports events this has not always been the case.

Long-term impacts as a result of staging events are referred to as the event's legacies and as discussed in the previous chapter there is a necessity to include long-term strategies in the planning of events at appropriate early stages in order to achieve successful legacies. The long term is the point at which the physical and non-physical legacies begin, generally referred to as after-use. The medium term is concerned with the impacts that occur post-event after the original event has closed down. The short-term impacts are those that take place during the event, and may also refer to those impacts that occur prior to and immediately after the event. Generally speaking there is no defined timeline used to identify when short-, medium- or long-term impact periods begin or end other than those that might be specified by an event itself. The difference in the nature of shorter- and longer-term impacts is that more often than not the latter, the legacies, are not managed or developed by the original event organizers. At some stage after the event, a handover of some kind has been implemented, and the expectation of success over that term is passed to new users. It would only be good managerial practice, therefore, for these after-users to want to be involved in those parts of the planning process that bear influence on those legacies.

Spilling (2000) lists the main potential long-term impacts of events as falling into four categories: enhanced international awareness, increased economic activity, enhanced facilities and infrastructure, and increased social and cultural opportunities. Whilst the political impacts of events are acknowledged by Spilling, the research he has conducted is focused on what are termed, the long-term 'industrial' impacts. Getz (1997) makes distinctions between various economic impacts including those of tourism whereby the event acts as a marketing mechanism for the host city as a destination. UK Sport (1999) identifies three main impacts, winning performances and the social effect that has (the development of sports) and economic benefits. Allen et al. (2002) split the impacts into four spheres: social and cultural, physical and environmental, political, and tourism and economic. Therefore, there is general agreement on what the main impacts are, with the only difference being the way they are grouped or categorized.

What is intended in this chapter is an overview of the potential benefits that are attributed to both larger and smaller sports events. Examples are used to identify where events have been used as catalysts for the achievement of short-term benefits and longer-term legacies. In addition the chapter considers the negative impacts that can occur as well as the strategies that can be undertaken, as part of the event planning process, to ensure that they do not.

Land regeneration

There is some agreement amongst other authors on the capacity for major international sports events to produce physical legacies in the form of built facilities, that can ultimately bring economic benefit (Allen et al., 2002; Bowdin et al., 2001; Getz, 1997). However, Hall (1997) goes further and maintains that the decision to bid to stage a major international sports event will depend on more than just potential budgeted economic benefits. The wider benefits that can be gained by incorporating regeneration projects and new facility provision can lead to critically important local community support as well as political and financial assistance to ensure the bid goes ahead. An event that necessitates the development and utilization of land that would otherwise not be used, can then leave physical legacies for future social, cultural and economic benefit, and for some these can help the initial event staging costs. Indeed without such support the bid may not even get off the ground.

Cities that have made bids for the right to stage major sports events in recent years have included plans to build new facilities. In many cases these plans have had to look to the regeneration of land and buildings due to the scarcity and cost of utilizing prime inner-city development sites. In the cases of Sydney and Manchester this has necessitated the development of land beyond inner-city boundaries; the Homebush Bay area in Sydney Harbour, for the 2000 Olympics, and Sports City, on the east side of Manchester, for the 2002 Commonwealth Games. This not only allowed for the development of disused and derelict land but also the opportunity to create a central site and focus for each event. The municipal justification in each case being that the regenerated land would have remained derelict if it were not for the opportunities given by the requirement to have new state-of-the-art sports facilities for these events. Further examples include the 1996 Atlanta Olympics which revitalized downtown areas with the creation of Centennial Park, a new stadium, college sports facilities and residential housing (Roche, 2000). In Melbourne the revitalization of its Docklands area featured in Olympics and Commonwealth Games bids at various stages throughout the 1990s (Hall, 1997; 2001). Also in Australia, there was the development of Fremantle for the 1987 America's Cup.

There were clear regeneration objectives set by Manchester that were a part of first of all their 2000 Olympics, and subsequently their 2002 Commonwealth Games planning. The objectives were concerned with the regeneration of an inner-city area for the development of jobs and economic growth. The city concluded that these objectives would be best delivered via a sports-led strategy that included the building of major new facilities. In what it entitles it is 'Sustainable Strategy,' Manchester 2002 Ltd (1999) declared that the new sporting facilities for the 2002 Commonwealth Games were to provide an important legacy for future improved health, jobs and the regeneration of derelict urban land.

Facilities and services

Buildings that are newly erected and redeveloped to house major sports events are generally seen as long-term legacies, and the appropriate city authorities have to look to justify their investment by looking to their usage beyond the end of the event. They can look for two types of usage, sports, leisure and recreational use by the local community and/or the further staging of more events. Roche (2000) had recognized that the 1992 Barcelona Olympics were a part of a wider long-term city strategy for modernization. The strategy, 'Barcelona 2000' was implemented in the mid-1980s, and included new sports stadia, an Olympic Village on the waterfront, a new airport and communication towers. Two distinct organizations were created to manage the legacies. One was to attract and run major events and the other was for the development of public sports participation. Roche (2000) maintains that this strategy assisted in ensuring after-use by the general public and the development of public and private sector initiatives to manage the facilities in the long term was achieved.

The redevelopment of the Faleron Bay is another example. This area in Athens had been a municipal regeneration objective since the early 1960s and formed the basis of the Athens proposals for their candidature for the 1996 and 2004 Summer Olympic Games. Having been awarded the 2004 Games the city is currently using the event as a catalyst to provide a number of new facilities that were desired long before they intended on bidding for either games. These include a water plaza and esplanade, nautical sports complex and the post-games transformation of the beach volley arena into an open-air amphitheatre (Marcopoulou and Christopoulos, 2002).

Melbourne provides an example of the sustainability of legacies. The Melbourne Sports Precinct was originally built for the 1956 Olympics, as discussed in Chapter 2, and now provides a home for a host of important national and international events such as the Australian Open Tennis Championships. This represents 47 years of after-use.

The importance of planning after-use has already been highlighted but the after-users themselves should also play a key part. Those that will be using a facility in the long term are going to be interested in how it is designed and there is therefore an argument that they should be involved at the stages of the event planning process when this input is the most useful. Meinel (2001) maintains that in practice after-users are involved mainly after the facility has been designed. He maintains that 50–80 per cent of subsequent operating costs are determined at the planning stage of a facility. He argues therefore that for a facility to be a long-term success there should be consideration of the needs of both the after-use and the users.

A question arises here. At what point in the event planning process should a host city of a major international sports event devise and then implement a strategy that will achieve a successful legacy. Torino planned the building of several new facilities for the 2006 Winter Olympics, and has already determined their after-use some 2 years prior to their games. However, the design and therefore the after-use of their ice sports stadia for example, were not considered until after the city had been awarded the games. The International Olympic Committee (IOC) had to advise them, a year after the awarding of the games in 2001, to consider leaving a legacy for ice sports in a city (Felli, 2002).

Athens planned the use of its facilities prior to its bid for the 2004 Olympics because they were a part of a wider municipal strategy. However, not all cities have ongoing strategies and some use the hosting of major events to create new plans of this nature. Furthermore, not all cities look this far ahead. The Millennium Stadium in Cardiff, built to stage the 1999 Rugby World Cup was designed to ultimately house different events and not just sports. The proposed location for the venue was very accessible to central Cardiff and there was a good case that argued for the need for a national venue. However, according to Cardiff City Council (2000) the urgency of the task in building the stadium meant that there was little time to consider future usage at the planning stage, and that bookings were acquired after the event via post-event marketing. Similarly, the planning of the Stade de France for the 1998 Federation Internationale de Football Association (FIFA) World Cup consisted of a complicated process in order to justify the build in Paris where there were many other stadia. At one point this included the moving in of a top-flight football club as one of several solutions to a long-term after-use problem. Even there was thought given to creating a brand new club for that purpose when there was no agreement on which existing club should go in (Dauncey and Hare, 1999). The thoughts as to future usage were retrospective to the already done deal to build the stadium.

An important factor to consider is the danger of obsolescence in planning early. For example, where even the most advanced facility designs may not be socially or legally acceptable in 10 years because of new standards in health and safety or for the environment. Sports too may become less popular over time. This is something Japanese architect Isozaki (2001) suggests is a concern to some sports architects and that they therefore consider sustainable design for sports facilities as an insurmountable problem. Far from advocating that long-term planning is not necessary, he suggests that the answer lies in adaptability of design, where good design will allow for change of use over time. Such design would necessitate the early planning of after-use and identification of after-users.

Negative impact mainly comes in the form of superfluous physical structures. The term often used is 'white elephant' and host cities and supporting governments are keen to avoid such obsolescence and drains on further funding. The Olympic Stadium built for the Montreal Olympics in 1976 is a famous example and is often and still referred to as a white elephant. The cost of the building of the stadium left the city with enormous debt. The stadium was unfinished at the time of the Olympics and cost overruns and engineering problems meant that it was not completed until 1987. In order to pay off the debt, the government used national lotteries, taxes on tobacco products and property to diffuse the cost onto Quebec citizens.

In addition to new facilities and venues there is also the need to plan for the infrastructure that is required to serve these facilities. In building facilities in disused and outer-city areas there arises the need to provide adequate transportation if only for the event itself. High on the list of any scrutiny of Olympic bids are the provisions made for people flow (IOC, 2002). For example, intended for Athens 2004 are, 120 kilometres of new roads, an expanded metro system, a new traffic management centre and a new international airport (Athens 2004, 2002a). The planning for the provision of transportation infrastructure clearly goes hand-in-hand with the facility plans. The Homebush Olympic zone in Sydney also required considerable new transport infrastructure to provide links to the city. However, if the facilities that this type of infrastructure serves become underused then the knock on effect can be that they too become white elephants.

Another important and related legacy here is the event management expertise that is gained in staging an event. If the facilities are intended to stage further events, then such management expertise not only serves as an attractive asset in future event bids but also gives the city itself an internal understanding of what it is capable of. This will of course enable it to improve its performance. The dedicated municipal department in Sheffield was set up in the city in 1990 to make full use of the facilities built for the 1991 World Student Games (Coyle, 2002).

The development of local facilities is important too, despite their less significant profile. The raising of funding via one or more sports events can and has resulted in the provision of facilities in many community-led sports and leisure provision. Including new courts, clubhouses, pitches and the like. Case study 4.1 considers physical legacies in the surfing sector.

Case study 4.1

Fistral Beach, UK

August 2002

The Ripcurl Boardmasters festival takes place on Fistral beach, in the UK county of Cornwall and is the British leg of a world tour. It is a 9-day event featuring professional surfers and in 2002 attracted an estimated 100 000 visitors to the town of Newquay.

The surf industry is important to Cornwall's economy and is estimated to be worth £40 million per year.

Year round Newquay attracts 2 million visitors and most visit the mile long beach. However, the facilities are basic with only two cafes, kiosks and lavatories. The municipal authority, Restormel Council, is planning to use the surfing industry as a catalyst for regeneration projects. In particular they plan to attract surf-related industries and future international events by building new facilities.

Britanic Industries won the tender as the preferred developer and are investing the bulk of the money required but investment partners also include Restormel and Cornwall County Council. A grant has been awarded in the form of European 'objective one' funding. The investment will provide a £1.8 million international surf centre with retail, restaurant and changing facilities. The centre will also house the British Surfing Association, Newquay Life-Saving Club, lifeguards, creche, and event competition and training quarters.

In an attempt to capitalize on the buoyant impact of the surfing industry, Restormel Council is seeking to invest in legacies. The new facilities will be the focus for future beach visitors including event tourists, and the staging of international events. It is hoped that will lead to increased economic impact as well jobs, business investment and sports development.

Source: Benjamin (2002).

What these examples show is that there need to be changes in the way long-term benefits are strategically planned for. It is necessary to consider their after-use at the concept stage of the planning process. In determining if the objectives are feasible, the identification of after-use and the involvement of after-users become critical. Furthermore, the involvement of those who are responsible for the design of facilities that are expected to be successful over 30 years or more is also critical at this stage.

Social regeneration

The regeneration and legacies of events are not always of the built environment. The benefits of city renewal programmes can create a new focus for social activities whilst new sports facilities, as a result of an event, can clearly provide longer-term benefit. Hall (1997) also maintains that events can improve the cultural identity of a host city, develop community involvement and integration, and instigate local economic benefits. Event tourists also benefit from this (Getz, 1997).

The regeneration of land, the building of new facilities and the planning of events provide employment opportunities prior to the event. The implementation of the event also provides short-term event jobs but as it can be seen in Sheffield, in the Events Unit, major sports events can also lead to the employment of personnel in the long term. If the facilities are going to be legacies they require manning with teams that will plan their economic futures either to provide local community services or to attract further events which in themselves provide further employment opportunities. The origin of Sheffield's plans to bid for the World Student Games was focused on a solution to the downturn in its economy due to the steep decline of the local iron, steel and coal industries in the late 1980s. Unemployment was as high as 20 per cent in some areas of the city and an event-led strategy offered a way forward (Gratton and Taylor, 2000) and still provides employment today. In Manchester there were clear long-term targets for increased employment as a result of staging the 2002 Commonwealth Games and these were set to come from the prescribed local area around Sports City. There are also a number of key event management roles that have emerged as permanent jobs in city departments where the focus is firmly on ensuring the games legacies are sustained over the long term.

On the negative side there are issues concerning how local the social benefit can be. In building new facilities in a regenerated area there may well be objectives concerning the improvement of housing, job opportunities and facilities for those that are local to that area. That being the case it is important that the economic status of such residents is considered and that the new opportunities are financially within their reach.

Political development

The improved profile of government at national and international level as a result of staging a successful major international sports event is considered of value. The extent to which profile and prestige can be improved though is clearly difficult to assess but economic development as a result of the improved profile is perhaps more quantifiable, and can result in an enhanced political image if successfully achieved.

Individuals as well as larger bodies can benefit at both collective and individual levels (Hall, 1997). The frequenting of key sports events by politicians can gain them much desired exposure to their target publics. President Chirac and Prime Minister Jospin despite their different political persuasions, showed higher poll results at the time of the 1998 FIFA World Cup in France (Dauncey and Hare, 1999). Administrators too can achieve certain political credibility as a result of perceived success. Peter Uberroth is an example of an event manager who is now credited with the mantle of having turned Olympic Games finance around with his success in directing the first Olympics to make a considerable profit in Los Angeles in 1984 (Catherwood and Van Kirk, 1992). In the UK both the Chairman and Chief Executive of the Manchester Commonwealth Games received the Queen's New Years honours and the Chief Executive of Manchester City Council, Howard Bernstein, received a knighthood.

Political impact is thus perceived as being of benefit at both the micro- and macro-levels. Hall (1997) maintains that despite the fact that some events generate negative impact, more commonly, individual politicians and governments view them as being of benefit, due to their capacity to promote an attractive image that can lead to increased investment and tourism.

Another recent example in the UK serves well here. The government, in its embarrassment over the loss of the 2005 Athletics World Championships, as detailed earlier in Chapter 3, decided to give British athletics a £40 million injection. Out of that grant several new indoor stadiums are, to date, still to be built and ironically they include the site of where the 2005 event will be staged, Picketts Lock in North London. The Culture Secretary Tessa Jowell used her 'political weight' to ensure that this went through and saw it as due compensation for the way that government let athletics down (Mackay, 2002a). The government saw the granting of funds as a way of retrieving its political face and indeed the same might be said of the individuals concerned. This level of political impact is arguably short term.

National and cultural identity is also claimed to be affected by events and therefore available for political manipulation. It is claimed that the 1992 Barcelona Olympics were used to enhance the Catalan regional profile, identity and pride, and not just the Spanish national profile (Roche, 2000). Three consecutive Summer Olympic Games were boycotted over political standpoints. In 1976 African nations did not go to Montreal in a protest over New Zealand's rugby tour of South Africa and in 1980 the US and allies did not go to Moscow in protest over the then Soviet Union's invasion of Afghanistan. In 1984 Warsaw Pact Nations including the Soviet Union did not go to Los Angeles with accusations of US violations against the Olympic Charter, and it should be said, amongst accusations of retaliatory activity against the US for their previous boycott. The lengths individuals will go in order to maintain their political standpoints through sports events have also been remarkable in many ways. The silent statements made by two black athletes, Tommie Smith and John Carlos, on the medal rostrum at the 1968 Mexico City Olympics over American civil rights issues, and the Zimbabwean cricketers, Andy Flower and Henry Olonga, over human rights issues in their country at their opening match in the 2003 Cricket World Cup, were undoubtedly political in their nature. Keeping politics out of sport may be seen as a distant utopia when individuals and governments seek to put their politics into events in these ways, but this point aside, such activity is testament to the powerful political profiles sports events can have.

Cultural development

Major sports events can offer wider programmes that are seen to be culturally and socially beneficial. The Spirit of Friendship Festival, part of the overall 2002 Commonwealth Games programme, was planned by Manchester to offer more than just sport to its local community. They saw the opportunity to provide food, drink and music events that would be entertainment for incoming event tourists, participating teams and businessmen, as well as the local community (Manchester City Council, 2000). The long-term benefit of this will be difficult to measure but the importance of the effect it has on attracting future tourists to a city that tries hard to be an attraction should not be overlooked. The IOC recognizes the importance and requires cultural events to be an 'essential element of the celebration of the Olympic Games,' and a required provision by any bidding host city (IOC, 2002). The Winter Olympics hosted by Salt Lake City in 2002 staged 60 performances, 10 major exhibitions and 50 community projects in its Olympic Arts Festival (Salt Lake City, 2002). Hall (1997) argues that the success of major sports events should not just be measured in economic and tangible terms but also in social and cultural impact.

MacAloon (2003) maintains that culture is not just one form of an Olympic legacy it is the source of all the other forms. This view proposes that all tangible benefits such as stadia, transport infrastructure and tourist facilities and intangible benefits, such as sports history making, rituals, national profiles and political developments are accumulated cultural capital. He says that the most important thing an Olympics can leave behind is systems that can contribute to the increasing of the accumulated cultural capital. He goes further and states that these local legacies can then be transformed into global legacy. The international perception held of Sydney 2000 for example is already well developed, although it is not necessarily one universal perception.

Smaller-scale events can also offer opportunities for different cultural groups to come together in sporting competition and the like. Programmes consisting of such events are also arguably required in order that the initial short-term cultural impact and impetus created by major events is sustained over the long term. Manchester for example has developed 112 'Cultureshock' projects in an attempt to capitalize on the benefits of the 2002 Commonwealth Games. Sixty-eight of these projects have specific links to ethnic groups from Commonwealth countries (Manchester City Council, 2003). If there is no follow-up development then the memory of being a volunteer at the Sydney Olympics in 2000 is all that remains and whether this is a useful legacy is difficult to determine. MacAloon (2003) argues that anything that is not repeated, renewed in performance, ceremony or other representations is in danger of being forgotten.

One way of enabling events to achieve such success is to embody existing local culture into them so that when the event has passed the legacy is contributing to what is already there. Garcia (2003) maintains that this can also maximize the marketing of an event because an understanding of the local cultural contexts and values will provide opportunities for event promotions. By including arts and cultural programmes that are representative and distinctive of the local community, a sports event can more successfully appeal to a key customer base.

This does raise an important point concerning the evaluation of events. A legacy is something that is simply left behind. As MacAloon (2003) maintains, for a legacy to develop and become culturally significant will take time. Its evaluation then is something that can only be implemented in the long term.

Sports development

Another area of benefit that is difficult to measure is the level of development a sport can achieve as a result of being showcased by a major event. National and international governing bodies are aware of the importance of exposure via the likes of the Olympics and of course the profile television brings to any potential participants in their sports. UK Sport (1999) states that hosting events can lead to the winning of more medals and a greater stage for sports. This benefit is one a sporting organization might be more interested in than the event host. The IOC is an example of a body that is concerned with the broader goals of competitive sport including the provision of facilities that become legacies for sports and actually advises thus (Felli, 2002). Although it should be pointed out that IOC President Jacques Rogge in his official opening of the 2002 IOC Annual Symposium, stated that this is not an IOC responsibility (Rogge, 2002). The important point though is not who benefits or who most benefits, it is that the planning for the event would be incomplete without such provision.

The Paralympics in Athens in 2004 will feature four new sports that are popular in Greece, boccia, goalball, powerlifting and wheelchair rugby (Athens 2004, 2002b) which will help develop the profile of those sports by providing them with important national exposure through the media. The profile of paralympic sport in general will be further enhanced by the fact that the Paralympics and Athens Summer Olympics will be run for the first time by one organizing committee (Athens 2004, 2002c).

Manchester has estimated that take up of new and existing sports facilities since the 2002 Commonwealth Games is 250 000 visits made up of new and existing users. The new facilities are expected to provide over 31 500 places on sports development courses (Manchester City Council, 2003). The strategy has been put in place to capitalize on the interest in sports following the 2002 event.

It is not just large-scale events that can perform as shop windows for the development of sports. Any event that offers participation opportunities, particularly for new starters, can potentially be used for grassroots sports development. This short-term impact requires considerable thought and planning if it is to be developed into long-term legacy. The ongoing management of further opportunities for watching and participating in sport requires strategies that follow up on the initial initiatives. For example, at a local level the opening up of tennis clubs in the UK to non-members and new players as part of the Lawn Tennis Association's National Tennis Day initiative is only the first step. It is incumbent upon the clubs to then offer further opportunities to those that attend in an effort to develop their interest in playing tennis.

Environmental development

In an age of concern about our environment, major sports events can play a key role in incorporating operational policies that can not only be efficiency conscious for the event itself but also lay down environmental legacies for the host city for the future.

Sydney has possibly played what may well turn out to be an important role in the development of this area with a comprehensive 'green' approach for the 2000 Olympics. Athens 2004 for example, plans to leave behind a cleaner, healthier environment that has improved environmental awareness and performance, and a lasting legacy (Athens 2004, 2002a). Its programmes include new planting, building with environmentally friendly materials and improved waste management. Torino has similar objectives for the 2006 Winter Olympics and as a result a new type of feasibility study has been introduced. Strategic environmental assessment (SEA) verifies the compatibility of the environmental and economic works to be implemented before they are carried out and in effect puts long-term strategies for the protection of the environment into place (Torino 2006, 2002).

David Chernushenko has served on the IOC Sport and Environment Committee since 1988 and maintains that to create successful legacies out of sports facilities they need to be designed with conservation and environmental protection in mind and not just because this is now more socially demanded, but because it can also be of benefit economically too (Chernushenko, 2002). He maintains that too few designs for new stadia consider the importance of reducing resource consumption and eliminating waste.

This is possibly because of a perception that it is more costly to make such considerations and then implement appropriate processes in the building of facilities. However, whilst designing for sustainability can be more costly, the implementation of energy and resource saving processes can be made to be cost effective in the long term. The Lillehammer Olympic ski jumps were designed to follow the contours of the hills for example. This not only made them less obtrusive it also kept construction material costs low.

Negative environmental impacts, certainly in the short term, include the non-disposal of waste and the destruction of the habitat. In order that such impacts are avoided event managers need to plan for the post-event handover of sites and facilities that are not disturbed and are returned in their original state. Event shutdown is not complete without comprehensive clear-up systems being in place and ready to be implemented at the right time.

Economic development

The economic impact of major sports events is of critical importance when it comes to justifying the investments made. The impact, if negative, can be a lasting and costly legacy for local taxpayers but if positive, can bring important revenue to bolster municipal budgets. Uberroth's Los Angeles Olympics achieved a £215 million surplus (Gratton and Taylor, 2000) but for some host cities, achieving revenue from the operation of a major sports event that exceeds the initial investment is not as important as the long-term economic benefits that will come from tourism and future usage of the facilities.

The 1976 Montreal Olympics left the city with a debt of £692 million (Gratton and Taylor, 2000) and Sheffield too has a not too insignificant negative legacy as a result of its 1991 World Student Games, as mentioned in Chapter 3. The mortgaging of its debt will have taken 25 years to pay off at a rate of £25 million per year by 2025 (Wallace, 2001).

The staging of major sports events may incur losses for those that make the investment. However, host cities and governments may well be looking for not much more than a break-even position from the actual operation of the event itself as the wider benefits to the community in additional spending are a higher priority. The 2002 Salt Lake City Olympics is reported to have produced a relatively small surplus of $40 million but there are significant expectations for the future return on the original investment through inward investment, new business and tourism (Mackay, 2002b). Larry Mankin was the President of the Salt Lake City Chamber of Commerce at the time of the games and recognized the importance of the event delivering in the long term (Mankin, 2002). The event managed to pay back the State of Utah's original loan and also achieved surplus monies that were put into funds that were to ensure that the facilities would continue to be operated, maintained and developed in the long term. It is expected that the economic growth experienced during the games would slow but the impact of further inward commercial investment into the city would impact positively on tourism and convention business in the long term.

The results and indeed the forecasts of economic impact are often the focus of attention when it comes to the questions raised over whether to stage major sports events or not. The media will use it to extol or berate the event and those who are responsible for selling an event to stakeholders will be looking for all that is positive both in the short- and long-term economy. The measurement of economic impact however can be an abused process (Coates and Humphries, 2003). Multiplier analysis is commonly used in order to assess costs versus benefits both in feasibility studies and post-event impact analysis. However, the fact that there are a number of different multiplier calculations that can be used leaves the industry in need of a standard that can be used for fair comparison from event to event.

This point aside the general focus for multipliers in this context is a calculation of the additional expenditure into the local economy as a result of staging an event. The calculation includes the discounting of the expenditure that does not remain within the economy, such as the income generated by those that are not resident in that area, for example, suppliers. After these 'leakages' are accounted for, what remains is the monetary benefit that has been achieved. The more sustained this benefit, the more the likelihood of improved employment. It is clear therefore that economic impact and forecasts are a key factor in the decision-making of event hosts. The greater the case is for a return on investment, the greater the case is for staging the event.

Case study 4.2 focuses on Sheffield and provides an insight into the long-term impact gained from the staging of sports events in the facilities built for the 1991 World Student Games. Case study 4.3 considers the 2002 Commonwealth Games in Manchester. It compares the forecasted impact of the event (1999 feasibility study) with the impact data from the first post-event evaluation report in early 2003. The report shows all targets being exceeded and a predicted 2009 target achievement for gross value added. Case study 4.4 shows a number of sports events and economic impacts data in the US, Australia and the UK.

Tourism

Event tourism is one of the current key phrases and as can be seen from the previous section, is a key aspect of economic impact. Events are seen as catalysts for driving tourism but not just for the event itself. Major sports events can develop high profiles for host cities, particularly if they are televised and are claimed to be

Case study 4.2

Additional expenditure generated by sports events 1990–1997

The table shows the event that generated the greatest economic impact each year (not including 1991 World Student Games).

Year	Event	Actual gross expenditure generated
1990	McVities Invitation International Athletics	£248 991
1991	Yorkshire versus West Indies versus Rest of World Floodlit Cricket	£649 697
1992	UK Athletics Championships and Olympic Trials	£353 854
1993	European Swimming Championships	£1 271 454
1994	AAA Championships and Commonwealth Trials	£590 010
1995	All England Womens Hockey Centenary Celebrations	£207 655
1996	FINA World Masters Swimming Championships	£3 333 875
1997	English Schools Track and Field Championships	£346 951

Source: Kronos (1997).

Economic impact of sports events by financial year 1991–2001

Year	Number of events	Actual gross expenditure	Additional visitors to Sheffield	Full time equivalent job years created
1991/1992	55	£217 7000	57 000	67
1992/1993	30	£2 398 000	72 000	74
1993/1994	47	£3 477 000	83 000	104
1994/1995	49	£2 444 000	67 000	73
1995/1996	41	£1 502 000	34 000	42
1996/1997	43	£11 444 000	127 000	291
1997/1998	30	£2 370 000	43 000	62
1998/1999	30	£2 070 000	35 000	49
1999/2000	34	£2 900 000	25 000	73
2000/2001	36	£2 822 000	33 000	66
Total	395	£38 232 000	576 000	901
Average per year	40	£3823.000	58 000	90
Average per event	N/A	£97000	1460	2.00

Source: Kronos (2001).

Case study 4.3

Event economic impact: 2002 Commonwealth Games

A comparison of the economic impacts in the City of Manchester predicted and gained as a result of staging the 2002 Commonwealth Games

Impact	1999 Feasibility forecast	2003 First impact study
Total direct permanent and 10-year equivalent jobs	4494	6100
Net additional direct permanent and 10-year equivalent jobs to Manchester	988	2400
Regenerated land area	40 ha	60 ha
Regenerated employment floor space (square metres)	51 223	72 000
Gross value added	£110 million (1998–2009)	£22 million to date, plus a forecasted 300 000 additional visitors per annum spending £12 million per annum

Source: Manchester City Council (1999, 2003).

Case study 4.4

Event economic impact: an international perspective

US Sports Council events

Atlanta Sports Council

- 2000 Super Bowl XXXIV $292 million
- 2000 Major League Baseball All-Star Game $49.6 million

Los Angeles Sports and Entertainment Commission

- 1999 FIFA Women's World Cup $30 million

Minnesota Amateur Sports Commission

- 2000 ISI World Figure Skating Championships $3.58 million
- 2000 National Junior Wrestling Championships $497 000

Sources: Atlanta Sports Council (2003), LASEC (2003), MASC (2003).

Nashville Sports Council

2001/2002 year

- $24 million impact
- 56 hours of network television coverage

- 100 full pages of print media coverage
- 116 391 participants – spectators, volunteers, media and competitors

Source: Nashville Sports Council (2002).

Perth, Western Australia

- 2000 Telstra Rally Australia   AUS $23 million
- 2000 Quantas Triathlon World Champs   AUS $16 million
- 1999 Australian University Games   AUS $10.3 million
- 2001 Heineken Classic Golf Tourney   AUS $7.1 million
- 1999 Pan-Pacific Masters Swimming   AUS $2.6 million

Source: EventsCorp (2000).

Hockenheim

1997 German Grand Prix

- DM 87 million local economy impact
- 70 per cent (DM 61 million) spending by non-locals
- 258 000 spectators spending on average DM 336 per day on tickets, parking, lodging, food and drink, tourist retail

Source: FIA (2004).

good for attracting future tourists after the event has been staged. How long term this impact can be is disputed.

It is clear that host cities regard it as an important objective. Many of the objectives and criteria set out by Sheffield's Event Unit in deciding on the staging of an event are linked to how much media attention it can gain and hence improve its tourism profile. Tourists are also attracted to future staged events and can therefore potentially improve the local economy that way too.

Research was undertaken in Wales following the 1999 Rugby World Cup. Three hundred and thirty thousand people were estimated as having visited Wales because of the event and only 20 per cent had been to the country before. Seventy per cent thought that they might return on holiday and 25 per cent of those who watched the event on television thought they were more likely to go to Wales as a result. The research estimated that Welsh tourism might benefit by £15 million over the 5 years after the event (Cardiff City Council, 2000).

The Sydney 2000 Olympics bid documentation claimed that there would not only be event tourism but also national tourism growth up to 2004 (Brown, 1999). Sion's failed bid for the 2006 Winter Olympics was seen as important for the host city, the Valais region and for Switzerland generally. The Swiss saw this as an opportunity to reposition the national brand for increased tourism growth.

Whilst some authors agree that tourism is a benefit of events (Getz, 1997) and that every destination should formulate an event tourism plan to enable it to contribute to the national economy (Keller, 1999), others doubt whether the growth levels achieved in the short-term out of event tourism are sustainable over the long term (Hughes, 1993) and that tourism therefore cannot be viewed as a potential event legacy.

For any event tourism growth to become sustained it would have to be strategically planned as with for other event benefits. This would include pre-event as well as post-event strategies. Chalip (2003) refers to the need to leverage an event in order to achieve tourism legacy. In Sydney's case this included four pre-event strategies that focused on visiting journalists, event media programmes, sponsors and industry programmes, respectively. This involved the provision of background information and support to enable Sydney to be used and featured as an attractive destination. This suggests that awareness of and interest in a destination that increases as a result of an event, requires further strategic consideration if they are to be converted into longer-term benefits. This can be achieved by further marketing. The difficulty however, lies in the likelihood that budgets for this will be reduced after the event.

Summary

The potential impacts of staging sports events fall into several categories. Major international sports events can be used by municipal authorities as catalysts for the regeneration of key areas of their cities. The redevelopment of disused or contaminated lands and buildings in inner or outer urban areas is an important first stage for many, though not all, host cities. The second stage is the choice of strategy for the achievement of the objectives set for the development of the economy through increased business investment, tourism and employment. Event-led strategies that provide new facilities and venues for long-term use have proved popular choices. The same applies to smaller-scale redevelopment and the relative impacts that they can have.

Such choices can also prove of great value politically to those that are involved in the decision-making process. Social benefits in the form of jobs, cultural and environmental development, increased community value and quality of living are clearly important political decisions as well as objectives of worth in their own right.

Sports events also offer the potential for sports development that again bring enhanced opportunities for both participants and spectators. The profile gained via the media and in particular television helps a sports event to put its sport into a shop window though just as important are local events that encourage newcomers to take up the sport.

For any long-term impact, there is a need for strategies to be put in place, at the appropriate stage of the planning process. These strategies must plan the handing over and/or development of short-term benefits so that they can be realized into sustainable legacies.

Questions

1 Identify the main types of positive- and negative-event impact with the use of your own researched examples. Evaluate the extent and nature of the short- and long-term impacts involved.

2 Research and analyse how one city of your choice has used sports event-led strategies to achieve wider municipal objectives?

3 Identify the event management that is required to ensure that risks are minimal and benefits are optimal.

4 Consider how Restormel Council will make a success of the intended new developments at Fistral Beach.

References

Allen, J., O'Toole, W., McDonnell, I. and Harris, R. (2002). *Festival and Special Event Management*, 2nd edition. Queensland, Australia, John Wiley & Sons, Chapters 2, 5 and 13.

Athens 2004 (2002). www.athens.olympics.org (accessed 24 April 2002): (a) /Home/Legacy; (b) /Home/Paralympic Games/Sports; (c) /Home/Paralympic Games.

Atlanta Sports Council (2003). *Economic Impact Studies*. www.metroatlantachamber.com/macoc/sportscouncil/economic-studies (accessed 26 February 2003).

Benjamin, A. (2002). Storm warning. *The Guardian*. 7 August. London, Guardian Newspapers.

Bowdin, G., McDonnell, I., Allen, J. and O'Toole, W. (2001). *Events Management*. Oxford, Butterworth Heinmann, Chapters 2, 4 and 12.

Brown, G. (1999). Anticipating the impact of the Sydney 2000 Olympic Games. In Andersson, T. (Ed.), *The Impact of Mega Events*. Ostersund, Sweden, ETOUR, pp. 133–140.

Cardiff City Council (2000). *The Economic Impact of the Millennium Stadium and the Rugby World Cup*. Report by the Economic Scrutiny Committee, Cardiff City Council. Edinburgh, Segal Quince Wicksteed Ltd and System 3.

Catherwood, D. and Van Kirk, R. (1992). *The Complete Guide to Special Event Management: Business Insights, Financial Strategies from Ernst & Young, Advisors to the Olympics, the Emmy awards and the PGA tour*. New York, John Wiley & Sons, Chapter 1.

Chalip, L. (2003). Tourism and the Olympic Games. In Moragas, M., de., Kennett, C. and Puig, N. (Eds), *The Legacy of the Olympic Games 1984–2000*. Lausanne, IOC.

Chernushenko, D. (2002). Sustainable sports facilities. A paper delivered at the *IOC-UIA Conference: Architecture and International Sporting Events*, Olympic Museum, Lausanne, IOC. June.

Coates, D. and Humphries, B. (2003). *Professional Sports Facilities, Franchises and Urban Development*. University of Maryland, Baltimore County, working paper 03-103. www.umbc.edu/economics/wpapers/wp_03_103.pdf (accessed 7 January 2004).

Coyle, W. (2002). *Interview: Events Unit*, Sheffield City Council, Sheffield. 12 noon, 19 July.

Dauncey, H. and Hare, G. (1999). *France and the 1998 World Cup: The National Impact of a World Sporting Event*. London, Frank Cass Publishers.

EventsCorp (2000). www.eventscorp.com.au/history/index (accessed 5 March 2003).

Felli, G. (2002). Transfer of Knowledge (TOK): a games management tool. A paper delivered at the *IOC-UIA Conference: Architecture and International Sporting Events*, Olympic Museum, Lausanne, IOC. June.

FIA (2004). *The Economic Impact of the European Grands Prix. A Study*. www.fia.com/Etudes/F1_Impact (accessed 25 January 2004).

Garcia, B. (2003). Securing sustainable legacies through cultural programming in sporting events. In Moragas, M., de., Kennett, C. and Puig, N. (Eds), *The Legacy of the Olympic Games 1984–2000*. Lausanne, IOC.

Getz, D. (1997). *Event Management and Tourism*. New York, Cognizant, Chapters 3 and 4.

Gratton, C. and Taylor, P. (2000). *The Economics of Sport and Recreation*. London, Spon, Chapter 10.

Hall, C.M. (1997). *Hallmark Tourist Events – Impacts, Management and Planning*. London, Bellhaven Press, Chapters 3–7.

Hall, C.M. (2001). Imaging, tourism and sports event fever. In Gratton, C. and Henry, I. (Eds), *Sport in the City: The Role of Sport in Economic and Social Regeneration*. London, Routledge, Chapter 11.

Hughes, L. (1993). Olympic tourism and urban regeneration. In *Festival Management and Event Tourism*, Vol. 1. USA, Cognizant, pp. 157–162.

IOC (2002). www.olympic.org/uk/organisation/missions/cities (accessed 13 March 2002).

Isozaki, A. (2001). Designing an Olympic City. A paper delivered at the *IOC Conference: Olympic Games and Architecture – The Future for Host Cities*. Olympic Museum, May, Lausanne, IOC.

Keller, P. (1999). Marketing a candidature to host the Olympic Games: the case of Sion in the Swiss canton of Valais (Wallis), candidate for the Winter Olympics in the year 2006. In Andersson, T. (Ed.), *The Impact of Mega Events*. Ostersund, Sweden, ETOUR, pp. 141–156.

Kronos (1997). *The Economic Impact of Sports Events Staged in Sheffield 1990–1997*. A report produced by Kronos for Destination Sheffield, Sheffield City Council and Sheffield International Venues Ltd. Final report, December.

Kronos (2001). *The Economic Impact of Major Sports Events in Sheffield, April 1991–March 2001*. A report produced by Kronos on behalf of Sheffield City Council Leisure Services Department, August.

LASEC (2003). *Economic Impact of Major Sporting and Entertainment Events*. www.lasec.net/econimpact (accessed 26 February 2003).

MacAloon, J. (2003). Cultural legacy: The Olympic Games as 'World Cultural Property'. In Moragas, M., de., Kennett, C. and Puig, N. (Eds), *The Legacy of the Olympic Games 1984–2000*. Lausanne, IOC.

Mackay, D. (2002a). Picketts Lock to get indoor track. *The Guardian*, 30 April, Manchester, The Guardian Media Group.

Mackay, D. (2002b). Tainted games hailed a success. *The Guardian*, 26 February, Manchester, The Guardian Media Group.

Manchester City Council (1999). *2002 Commonwealth Games: Background Information and Overview*. A report produced by KPMG, 16 June.

Manchester City Council (2000). *Spirit of Friendship Festival Executive Summary*. Manchester, Manchester 2002 Ltd.

Manchester City Council (2003). *The Impact of the Manchester 2002 Commonwealth Games*. A report by Cambridge Policy Consultants, Executive summary. www.manchester.gov.uk/corporate/games/impact (accessed 25 February 2003).

Manchester 2002 Ltd. (1999). *Manchester 2002 Commonwealth Games: Corporate Plan*. Manchester, Manchester 2002 Ltd., October.

Mankin, L. (2002). Cited in 'Keeping the winter alive'. In Britcher, C. (Ed.), *Host Cities: A Sportbusiness Guide to Bidding for and Staging Major Events*. London, Sportbusiness Group.

Marcopoulou, A. and Christopoulos, S. (2002). Restoration and development of the Faleron Bay, Athens. Paper delivered at *IOC-UIA Conference: Architecture and International Sporting Events*. Olympic Museum, Lausanne, IOC. June.

MASC (2003). *Major Championship Events: Minnesota Hosts the World's Best*. www.masc.state.mn.us/events/championship (accessed 26 February 2003).

Meinel, K. (2001). Sustainability: management issues for the design – the involvement of the future manager of a new competition facility during planning and design phase: an indispensable prerequisite for sustainability. A paper delivered at the *IOC Conference: Olympic Games and Architecture – For Future Host Cities*. Olympic Museum, Lausanne, IOC. May.

Nashville Sports Council (2002). *Nashville Sports Council Announces a Total Economic Impact of $24.2 Million during the*

2001–2002 Year. 22 October. www.nashvillesports.com/nsc/impact_release102202 (accessed 4 March 2003).

Roche, M. (2000). *Mega-events and Modernity: Olympics and Expos in the Growth of Global Culture*. London, Routledge, Chapter 5.

Rogge, J. (2002). Opening address at the *IOC Annual Symposium: Legacy*. Olympic Museum, Lausanne, IOC. November.

Salt Lake City (2002). Olympic Arts Festival. www.saltlake2002.com/sloc/cultural (accessed 24 April 2002).

Spilling, O. (2000). Beyond intermezzo? On the long-term industrial impacts of mega-events – the case of Lillehammer 1994. In Mossberg, L. (Ed.), *Evaluation of Events: Scandinavian Experiences*. New York, Cognizant, Chapter 8.

Torino 2006 (2002). www.torino2006.it/Venues (accessed 24 April 2002).

UK Sport (1999). *Major Events: A Blueprint for Success*. London, UK Sport.

Wallace, S. (2001). Behind the headlines. *The Telegraph*. 15 June. London, Telegraph.

Financial planning and control

After studying this chapter, you should be able to:

- understand the importance of assessing financial feasibility in the planning process.

- identify key practices in the planning and control of sports event finance.

- understand the importance of financial risk assessment and identify key risk management practices.

Introduction

This chapter considers the importance of implementing financial planning and control at the feasibility stage by describing the process involved. The role of budgeting and targets are discussed as a key part of this process. The complimentary area of income generation, also a key activity at this stage of planning, is covered in the next chapter. Event finances have to be managed on an on-going basis and throughout the process however, and so the central focus here is on how that can be achieved. Key areas such as the acquisition of funding and the control of expenditure are considered, as well as the need for financial risk management emphasized.

Event feasibility

A decision to go ahead with a sports event is a managerial one and can therefore be subjective, but this decision-making process can be made more reliable via planning. The purpose of determining if an event is feasible, prior to a decision to go ahead, is needed to ensure that expenditure or effort is not wasted. Therefore, the importance of the feasibility stage in the event planning process cannot be underestimated. The model, proposed in Chapter 3, in the main considers an iterative process but is cautious about early progression from stage to stage. At the feasibility stage, progression should not occur unless the event can be successfully implemented to achieve its objectives. This is achieved by considering if the event concept does indeed meet objectives and whilst it is improbable that a dress rehearsal of the event is practical, the determination of the financial status of the project is a pre-requisite. This involves financial planning and in some cases may require implementation of those plans prior to any decisions to go ahead with the event. It may also require other forms of planning and in particular the implementation of key partnerships that make the event feasible, and the assessment of financial risk in determining plans for its on-going management.

Financial planning

This text does not consider generic financial planning and business accounting in great detail but does focus on the aspects that are pertinent to the strategic planning of sports events. There are however, a number of texts recommended at the end of the chapter that will serve well for theory and practice of event financial management.

There are a number of stages in the financial planning and control process that need to be considered (Berry and Jarvis, 1999).

Stage 1: Objectives

There are two levels of objectives involved in the management of events. Firstly, there are the organizational objectives that are desired by the event owners for the future direction of the organization. Then there are the objectives for individual events. The first level of objectives will have wider implications for the organization as a whole and will impact on the objectives that are set for any event it owns and/or organizes. Whether there are one or more events, the objectives set for each event need to be aligned with the organization's objectives. This congruence of goals will become a greater issue the larger an organization becomes, and as the aspirations of managers may conflict with those of others and the organization itself. The issue here in the events industry is that many events are run by event management organizations on behalf of event owners and the lack of goal congruence between the two may be a critical factor in the running of the event and the company's success.

Secondly, there are business objectives that are set for events, for example the maximization of sales, the maximization of profits, the improved return on investment through dividends to shareholders or the re-investment of profits into the business for growth. These are all quantitative objectives and are therefore quantifiable with targets that can be set and importantly, easily assessed.

Non-financial objectives may also be set and for organizations involved in non-profit events these can be an important aspect. For example, local authorities may be most concerned with objectives that ensure that their sports events deliver an amount and quality of service. Even with non-financial objectives however, there are implications for the financial planning and control of the event.

Stage 2: Strategic decisions

For the organization as a whole there are strategic decisions to be made regarding the future of the business that will be in accordance with the organizational objectives. For event owning organizations this may well involve the divestment of properties, or the investment in other areas of business either for security purposes or to develop and grow. These decisions are long-term decisions and are made at a senior level. Consequently they may impact on the management of individual events.

The decision to create a new business that would open up opportunities for the development of International Management Group (IMG) was taken by Mark McCormack, when Trans World International (TWI) was formed. This new division was to explore the television opportunities for both IMG and its clients' events, and claims to be the world's largest independent producer, packager and distributor of televised sports programming (IMG, 2003). One such client is the Association of Tennis Professionals (ATP) Tour and for them this assisted in the delivery of two objectives, one financial and one non-financial, growth in worldwide coverage and the achievement of increased broadcast revenue, and the development of the sport of men's tennis, respectively.

Stage 3: Operating decisions

Operating decisions are mainly concerned with pricing and the level of service to be offered (Berry and Jarvis, 1999). These decisions need to be aligned with the strategic policies that have been set previously in order for them to be effective and are the basis of the short-term financial plan for the event. This short-term plan is referred to as the event budget.

Budgets differ according to the requirements of the organizations involved but will typically represent the duration of the event planning process. Depending on the size of the event an event budget can cover a very short period of hours or days or be run over a number of years. For example, a cycle road race organized by a local club may be advertised to its members, entry fees collected and catering supplies and a trophy purchased only a week in advance of the event. The club treasurer will operate a very simple budget covering that period and those types of revenue and expenditure. In contrast, the winning bid for the 2000 Olympics in Sydney necessitated an accounting period that lasted from 1993 and an operational budget that involved divestment and handover elements that lasted well into 2002 when Sydney Olympic Park Authority eventually took over the Olympic facilities (Adby, 2002).

Stage 4: Monitoring and correction

In the setting of the budget, personnel are individually made responsible for revenues and costs and therefore should have contributed to the formulation of the budget and its targets initially. As the planning for the event progresses the budget can serve as a valuable tool in the measurement of performance for individuals as well as organizations as a whole. A reporting system is required so that individuals and teams who are financially accountable can report on actual performance against the budget so that deviations or variances can be identified. This is commonly referred to as a process of responsibility accounting. Through this monitoring of performance, causes for variance can also be identified and the necessary management decisions can be taken.

Budgeting

A budget can be beneficial in a number of different ways. First and foremost, in order to prepare a budget there needs to be a degree of forecasting and this at least gets a management team to look ahead. The preparation and research required engages an organization in planning. Budgets also serve as communication tools by identifying what is required of the event and its managers. Regular updates on performance against budget also serve as control mechanisms and as a means to inspire improved managerial performance. The larger the organization the more a budget can serve as a catalyst to increase inter-team or departmental cooperation in both its preparation and in the application through the achievement of targets.

Budgeting for events consists of identifying where revenue will derive from, determining costs and the setting of performance targets that will realize the objectives set. These targets also aid the on-going control of performance against this budget and therefore act as a means of ensuring alignment with objectives. The key contents of an event budget are summarized as follows.

Revenue targets

Revenue can derive from funding and/or income generation and targets for each will be set as a part of the budgeting process. Funding is associated with investment in the event and the securing of monies with or without any return on investment. Whereby income generation is associated with the exploitation of the event and its assets. Each of these areas of revenue is represented in the budget line by line so that the value of funding and generated income sources can be separately identified.

Expenditure targets

The expenditure for an event has to be off set against the revenue raised in order to calculate profit or loss. Each area of expenditure is referred to as a cost centre and can be related to management or programme aspects of the event. For example, typical cost centres would be expenditure on staffing, participants, transportation and marketing. These centres consist of individual line costs such as wages, prize monies, accommodation, limousines, fuel and printing. This makes both the identification of detailed expenditure line by line, and reviewing centre by centre, an easier process.

Costs can be direct and variable in that they are clearly identified with the event and can be allocated to a specific centre. Variable costs are those that may increase or decrease according to the size of attendance by audience or participants, or numbers of events and performances. Typically, these might be accommodation, subsistence or participants appearance fees and they would increase for every extra participant that takes part in the event. Another variable cost might be the employment of a predetermined number of extra catering staff for every predetermined number of extra corporate hospitality packages sold. It is important that events provide an adequate level of service as the revenue increases and this means identifying the levels at which this will occur within the budget so that the costs can be identified as they become active.

Costs can also be indirect, sometimes referred to as fixed or overheads, where they may not be as clearly allocated and may need to be apportioned to one or more centre. They are costs that are paid regardless of the revenue gained. Typically, they could be capital costs such as equipment or buildings, or venue rentals fees and guaranteed prize monies. They may also be costs that extend over a longer period than the event and are therefore not easily allocated, for example those that are associated with the running of the organization on an annual basis such as office rental and utilities. Such indirect costs require management to decide where they will be allocated and if they can be apportioned to different costs centres.

For many events the costs are predominantly fixed and this has significant implications for pricing strategies. An over reliance on non-guaranteed revenue that comes in on the day of the event, such as for tickets, merchandise and programmes, can leave the event exposed and financially at risk. Pre-event revenues that are guaranteed and can cover fixed costs are one solution. Another is to set prices so that those sales that are confidently expected cover fixed costs.

For many businesses the budget will remain fixed but for events there is a need for flexibility. The longer the event planning period the more this becomes a necessity. A plan that runs over a number of years will be faced with increased costs over those years as economic influences on suppliers take effect. The costs for the 2000 Olympic Games in Sydney exceeded original fore-casts and in order for the same objectives to be realized the rev-enue earning operations had to respond accordingly (SOCOG, 2001). Case study 5.1 demonstrates how the budgets were revis-ited at various points in the long planning period for that event. External forces can dictate, not only that events remain flexible in their budgeting, but also that they either adapt to new constraints or they do not run. After the New York terrorist attacks of 11 September 2001, insurance premiums and security provision for events became major financial issues. Prior to the Federation Internationale de Football Association (FIFA) 2002 World Cup there was concern over the increase in premiums by AXA, the insurance company, that at one point jeopardized the taking place of the event (Shepherd, 2001). The staging of the Winter Olympics in Salt Lake City only months after the New York catastrophe also presented new budgeting issues for the organizers. These exam-ples emphasize the importance of continuous monitoring in the on-going financial control of the event, and the need for flexibil-ity in allowing for adjustments.

Getz (1997) identifies that in the budgeting process there are a number of key stages. These include the involvement of oper-ational managers, or committee chairs, in the research, preparation and even negotiation of the budget. Essentially there must be agreement on event objectives and financial planning by all

Case study 5.1

Financial management: Sydney Olympics, 2000

The pre-bid budget for Sydney's staging of the 2000 Olympic Games was prepared by Sydney Olympics 2000 Bid Ltd (SOBL) in 1992. It forecast a surplus of AUS $25.9 million.

Despite winning their bid in 1993, the Sydney Olympic Project Management Group had focused and restricted their activities to programme planning and observation of the 1996 Atlanta Games. The pre-bid budget was therefore still in play until the first post-bid budget, set in 1997.

The Sydney Organizing Committee for the Olympic Games (SOCOG) reported in to the New South Wales (NSW) State Treasury and undertook four formal major budget revisions throughout the planning of the Games.

- April 1997: The first post-bid budget revision following observations at the Atlanta 1996 Games.
- June 1998: A total reforecast of the budget.
- June 1999: A budget rebalancing due to the identification of shortfalls in sponsorship revenue.
- February 2000: Only months prior to the Games a second budget rebalancing due to further shortfalls.

The major revisions were as a result of consistent monitoring and review, including activities such as staff level rationalization in 1999 and monthly financial reporting and accounting, bi-monthly forecast updates following input from each of the SOCOG departments.

Allowances were also required for inflation as the planning period covered such a long period. A factoring process was installed whereby projected annual inflationary factors were applied to the then current year values.

Contingencies were required in order to cover cost risks and sponsorship revenue shortfalls but whilst contingencies were built in to each budget revision, it still took AUS $70 million from the NSW Treasury to cover shortfalls in June 2000, and another AUS $70 million to cover expected increased operating costs.

Source: SOCOG (2001).

involved if an event is to be successful. For an operational budget to be successful managers have to be in support of the budget and so their input into its preparation is required. Managerial input into the preparation of budgets is a requirement. In practice however, this is not always the case as individual managers may have conflicting agendas in submitting the revenue targets when they may affect the achievement of their bonuses. The problem of goal incongruence increases the larger the organization (Berry and Jarvis, 1999) and this is especially the case when it comes to the budgeting for major events. Budgets are often a fundamental part of business plans and the presentations made to acquire funding and political support. They can also form a distinctive part in the determination of event feasibility.

Flexibility for revision is therefore clearly required when sources for funding and income generation can change accordingly. Issues also arise at a later point when the budget has been revised and then set for an incoming and newly appointed team of event managers. Whilst accountants may be contracted to supply the preliminary budget in the determination of feasibility the event managers that are eventually appointed are not a part of that preparation. The 2002 Commonwealth Games appointed a team of commercial managers that struggled to respond to the unrealistic income targets that were set. Over the planning period these targets were changed and as costs also escalated funding requirements were also stretched. A government commissioned report in 2001 revealed that the organizers were £110 million short in funding. The result was further injection of funding by the government, Sport England (via its National Lottery distribution) and Manchester City Council. Funding that was not originally planned (Chaudhary, 2001).

Financial control

The financial planning of an event is a key component in the objectives set. The budgeting process clearly allows for an alignment with the objectives at the outset but ultimately the financial control of an event involves further key elements.

It has been established that a budget can be used as a performance indicator in that its targets can be reviewed to identify any deviation from revenue or expenditure forecasts. Management accounting practices involve the formulation of internal reports at prescribed times so that performance can be reviewed and thus aid decision-making. Books for further reading on this are recommended at the end of this chapter.

Cash flow can also be used as a performance indicator and for the financial control of an event it is a key tool. Events have common revenue streams that are realized nearer to the execution of the event that are prepared for at the front end of the planning process, for example ticket income, sponsorship instalments and broadcast royalties. As stated earlier however, expenditure seldom follows the same pattern and payments are often required in advance of the event. Even the costs involved with ticket sales, sponsorship recruitment and broadcasting, as well as venue deposits, equipment rentals and overheads can all be due for payment prior to the event. A review of the budget at this point can indicate a healthy position in that a break-even or better financial position is forecasted. However, it is imperative to look at the position of cash flow and the capacity to pay bills at required points throughout the accounting period and these could be prior to sufficient revenue being available. The production of regular cash flow reports, throughout the planning of an event are therefore, essential for the financial control of an event.

Cash flow shortfalls are a common occurrence in the events industry, but they need not be insurmountable problems. The shortfalls can be made up and there are various solutions on both sides of the budget. Cash flow can be made more fluid through the negotiation of payment dates and arrangements. Costs centres can be reduced, possibly by limiting the levels at which variable costs will increase, and possibly through the reduction or elimination of fixed costs. On the revenue side, arrangements for both funding and greater income generation can be made to reduce exposure to risk of cash shortfalls.

The reduction of financial risk can also be addressed in the planning of revenue as well as expenditure with the use of strategic partners. For some events the involvement of key partners is critical if the event is to succeed and such partners can be used to generate revenue as well as reduce expenditure. It is therefore often a requirement for such partnerships to be not just planned for, but negotiated and even implemented at the feasibility stage. Joint ownership of an event can alleviate the risk by sharing the financial accountability. This accountability might be in the form of equal shares on expenditure and the resulting profit. It might also be made up of partners with responsibility for certain areas of expenditure, funding and revenue generation. The London bid for the 2012 Olympics involves a joint partnership between the Greater London Authority (GLA), the British Government and the British Olympic Committee (BOC). With London as the host the financial onus lies with the GLA but the Government has approved the use of the national lottery for the selling of new and specific tickets that would raise funds if the bid were to be successful. The plans by Camelot, the organization that operates the lottery, include a daily lottery draw and other games that are to contribute as from 2004. If London were not to be successful the funds raised thus far would be transferred over to the general lottery sports fund (Kelso, 2003).

Similar risk reduction might also be achieved for an event owner with the appointment of agents to recruit sponsorship, advertising, ticket and hospitality revenue. For larger events this can involve the agreement of guaranteed payments whereby the agent will pay a fixed amount to the event and try to acquire sufficient sponsorship deals that realize more than that amount in order to make a business profit for themselves. Clearly the recruitment of agents in these cases needs to be done early in the planning process but if arranged prior to the decision for the event to go ahead then the event will be that much more feasible. Octagon are one such organization and they are involved in raising commercial revenue for a number of event organizations including Cricket Australia, the European Rugby Cup, International Badminton Federation, The English and Scottish Premier Leagues, USA Track and Field, and the US Youth Soccer Association. Octagon has worked with the latter organization since 1994 and has helped build a new brand in a very competitive field. Between 1998 and 2003 they were able to increase sponsorship revenue 10-fold and bring in 11 partners. Following an asset audit that revealed there were over 3 million registered youth players they created two key tournaments, the Tide America Cup and the Uniroyal TopSoccer Programme. The key asset was their capacity to reach what the organization refers to as the 'Soccer Mom' and the involvement of a domestic product like Tide shows how the agency was able to attract an appropriate sponsor (Octagon, 2003).

'Supply-in-kind' arrangements can also alleviate financial risk in the same way but on the expenditure side of the budget. The supply of essential as opposed to non-essential equipment, goods or services means that much less expenditure is incurred therefore reducing financial risk. Similarly, media partners can supply some or all of the events promotional needs. Clearly the risk is not reduced in such circumstances if the budget is still fully spent on further promotion. The decision here is whether the risk can be covered elsewhere and the event gain through the added promotional value through increased sales or the achievement of other objectives.

Financial risk management

Whilst risk management is required to be an on-going concern throughout the planning process it is also a major aspect of feasibility assessment and is a required part of the financial planning and control process. The sections above addressed the reduction of cash flow risks via the strategic use of partners and innovative revenue attainment but there are other areas of risk that affect the financial planning for events. Getz (1997) maintains that event financial risk management is a process that consists of anticipation, prevention and minimization and that would indicate that it is a necessary consideration at an early stage of planning and therefore strategically important.

There are two key factors. On the one hand, there is a requirement for an event to be safe and there are minimum levels of event health and safety that are governed in most countries by law. This will involve the planning of expenditure that will be incurred in the provision of security and medical services for example, and these will be different at every event. The unique nature of the event will determine the provision required and so the risk management process is a necessary inclusion as early as when the event is first conceptualized. The very numbers and nature of the audience and participants, and their likely behaviour, may well impact on the financial outlay for the event and for sports events there are particular considerations to be made. The provision of safety glass at ice hockey, for example, will require expenditure on special facilities and the monitoring of no go zones at motor racing will additionally incur special stewarding and zoining, both of which have necessary financial implications.

On the other hand, there is the production of entertainment and a spectacle. This may also require expenditure that was not spent at last year's event, or is not spent by a competitor to exceed customer expectation and gain competitive advantage. It is just as important to make these decisions early in the planning process. The unreliability of weather is a common risk for sports events and contingencies for the provision of cover against foul weather can include insurances against financial loss and the provision of extra facilities such as marquees. There are often greater risks in not taking such precautions of course and it is therefore a dangerous gamble not to be fully prepared. Additionally, in order to gain competitive advantage there are financial considerations that may appear to be superfluous at the outset and will require the event manager to assess cost versus benefit. The decision of whether to spend more on extra facilities, equipment and entertainment for example will require an assessment that may well require research. The provision of half-time entertainment for the crowd or better changing facilities for participants may not be directly benefiting revenue but may in the long run attract greater target market take-up. Only target market research will effectively support such decision-making.

Summary

Financial management and control, and the exercise of such throughout the planning process, are clearly recognized as being essential elements for the successful delivery of an event. However, it is perhaps the stage at which the planning for such has to be first implemented that is less widely acknowledged. Certainly the agreeing of a workable budget is intrinsic to the determination of feasibility. However, the strategic importance of assessing not only the financial feasibility of an event, but also the maximization of finances prior to event execution cannot be underestimated. Whereas for many events the acquirement of funding, the generation of revenue and the recruitment of partners in order to limit risk are an essential requirement prior to the decision to go ahead. It is however, the use of cost controls and the generation of income that is possible at this stage that can be the deciding factor in the gaining of competitive advantage.

The focus in the following chapter moves on to the complimentary area of revenue generation.

Questions

Select a sports event, and:

1 Analyse the strategic importance of financial planning at an early stage.

2 Identify the key practices exercised in its financial management by identifying any cost controls.

3 Identify and analyse the key areas of financial risk, how successful the event was in this risk management and suggest ways in which the event could have been more successful.

Recommended reading
Finance

Davies, D. (1997). *The Art of Managing Finance*, 3rd edition. Maidenhead, McGraw-Hill.

Dyson, J. (2001). *Accounting for Non-accounting Students*, 5th edition. London, Pitman Publishing.

Glautier, M. and Underdown, B. (2001). *Accounting Theory and Practice*, 7th edition. Harlow, Financial Times.

Lumby, S. and Jones, C. (2000). *Investment Appraisal and Financing Decisions*, 6th edition. London, Chapman Hall.

References

Adby, R. (2002). *Email Questionnaire: Director General, Olympic Co-ordination Authority 2000 Olympics*. 9 July.

Berry, A. and Jarvis, R. (1999). *Accounting in a Business Context*, 3rd edition. London, International Thomson Business Press, Chapters 14 and 19.

Chaudhary, V. (2001). Why Manchester may rue the day it won the Commonwealth Games. *The Guardian*. 25 July. Manchester, The Guardian Media Group.

Getz, D. (1997). *Event Management and Tourism*. New York, Cognizant, Chapter 10.

IMG (2003). www.imgworld.com/areas of business/twi/default.htm (accessed 12 September 2003).

Kelso, P. (2003). 1p lottery ticket to help fund Olympics. *The Guardian*. 25 May. Manchester, The Guardian Media Group.

Octagon (2003). www.octagon.com/diverts/rights_owner_case_study.php (accessed 12 September 2003).

Shepherd, R. (2001). World Cup in crisis. *Daily Express*. 13 October. London, Express Newspapers.

SOCOG (2001). www.gamesinfo.com.au/postgames/en/pg000329 (accessed 12 September 2003).

Event revenue maximization

After studying this chapter, you should be able to:

- further understand the importance of assessing financial feasibility in the planning process.

- understand the value and critical nature of strategic exploitation of commercial opportunities.

- identify the role and use of an event asset audit for income generation.

- consider the key income generating areas of media rights and partnerships, ticket and hospitality sales, space sales, merchandising and licensing.

Introduction

To achieve the greatest competitive advantage, an event needs to fully exploit its revenue potential and much can be achieved at the feasibility stage. Indeed, so much does have to be achieved at this point if the event is to be successful. If an event can be financially underwritten as early as this in the event planning process then there is every chance of it achieving its objectives. However, it is not apparent that all events can, do or indeed attempt to attain such a status before progressing.

This chapter continues with the theme of the last by highlighting the need for early strategic financial planning. Whilst the focus of the last chapter was on expenditure and control mechanisms, the focus here is on maximizing revenue.

Revenue planning

Event external funding

Event operational financial objectives may include the acquisition of income in the form of external funding. The sources that are available for the funding of events differ from country to country. In the US, UK and Australia funding for events can be gained via both commercial enterprise and government support. Funding in the UK for larger sports events is provided by the National Lottery, via funds that are allocated for sport and distributed by sports councils, such as Sport England. In all three countries there are provisions for the support of major events by regional government. However, there is one difference between these countries that is worthy of note. In the US, public money is used more commonly for building stadia than elsewhere. Typically there are cities that have built a stadium in order to attract a major league sports team. The competition between cities is intense and so they offer their stadia at peppercorn rents as inducements (Gratton and Taylor, 2000). The only way for a city to then recoup its outlay is via stadium event sales and marketing programmes that do not include any team rights. Clearly the demand for major league sports by cities is high.

The new stadia that have been built in the past 10 years contain premium price seating areas and corporate boxes, swimming pools, restaurants, hotels and theme park type amusements and represent a much more diverse entertainment centre than did their predecessors. The revenue earning potential has been extended beyond the more traditional ticket, food and beverage, and vehicle parking commercial return (Coates and Humphries, 2003).

Research into this area is growing and it currently offers no support to the idea that US sports stadia are important catalysts for economic growth. Despite this, proposed stadium construction projects continue to go ahead. In their working paper, Coates and Humphries (2003) identify that on average, public funding accounted for 65 per cent of the costs of the 26 major league sports stadia that were built between 1998 and 2003. On average the amount of public spending was $208 million per facility. They maintain that these facilities have been sold to communities on the basis that they will provide economic growth, development and urban renewal and the projections have been calculated using multiplier techniques. They recommend that further more reliable empirical methods be used to help taxpayers make more informed decisions on subsidies for sports facilities.

In the UK, the National Lottery provides funding for sport at various levels and is also used to provide funding for special events. The 2002 Commonwealth Games received lottery funding and a special lottery ticket sales programme will be utilized to provide funds to help support London host the 2012 Olympics if the city wins its bid, as mentioned earlier. One of the issues for sport in general in the UK is that the lottery is suffering from decreasing revenue and contribution to worthy causes such as sport decrease proportionately. Since a 1997 high at £5514 million, UK annual lottery ticket sales have decreased each year to a 2003 figure of £4575 million (The Guardian, 2003).

Income generation

Other operational financial objectives could be to grow income through the acquisition of specific revenues. Event operations are considered in Chapter 8 where the focus is on the implementation of plans that have been devised prior to and during the event at an operational level. The focus in this chapter however, is on what can be planned prior to the event and the degree to which it can be implemented prior to the event in order to secure feasibility.

Rather than simply identify, list and describe the various categories of income generation that exist for sports events, this section seeks to demonstrate that income generation involves a strategic process that requires innovation and sales skills. Whilst the implementation of ticket and corporate hospitality sales, sponsorship, merchandising, and licensing programmes is conducted after it has been decided to go ahead with the event, the planning for this exploitation of the events assets is performed at the feasibility stage in the attempt to financially underwrite it. Some revenue may be secured prior to a go-ahead decision and indeed some may need to be secured in order for the event to go ahead.

The process consists of determining what the event has that it can sell. This can be a simple exercise, but if considered in greater depth may be very productive. As this exercise can be the deciding factor in the achievement of competitive advantage, the need for innovation is clearly critical. In the North of England in County Durham there is an established tennis club in the village of

Lanchester, founded in 1911 but with few assets and currently only 50 members. In 2003 the club decided to sell corporate hospitality packages locally. Local businesses were attracted by the club's picturesque setting of three grass courts, clubhouse, stream and leafy surroundings and not unimportantly, the package of champagne, strawberries and a tennis tournament. Corporate hospitality is an established area of income generation and is not new in sport. However, in this case the process of determining what would generate income was innovative considering the size of organization. The club identified its assets, an offer was created and a market was targeted. An event was created in order to maximize the commercial potential.

A lot of income generation for events involves the use of sponsorship, and in order to produce a sponsorship programme an audit of the event's assets is required (see Chapter 11 and in particular Event management 11.1 for a greater exploration of this). In addition, the audit can provide many more opportunities. With an innovative approach this task may be able to assist in the maximizing of the event's income.

An event's assets can be categorized into the following areas.

Media rights and partnerships • • •

An event can sell or give the right to use its assets to interested parties. These rights can include the use of logos, a particular status with the event in terms of a title, or sponsorship rights. There are also the much sought after media rights.

The media generally are important stakeholders as events always seek positive public exposure, but media organizations are also important as partners. The selling or giving of media rights to a broadcaster clearly achieves media exposure that is of value to sponsors and for the promotion of the event in the short and longer terms. In addition, and if secured early enough, the rights can therefore become valuable assets in the selling of the sponsorship programme. Thus it would be advantageous for media rights to be agreed prior to negotiations with sponsors, as the benefits via the media rights will be of value to them.

Television broadcasting

If the event is powerful enough it can sell its rights to home and international broadcasters. This brings in media rights income and promotes the event via either live or delayed scheduling of the event. The securing of such sales in advance of the devising of the sponsorship programme allows for more leverage when it comes to recruiting and developing sponsors.

It can also be beneficial in another way. If the broadcaster values the event sufficiently it will agree to promotional traffic prior to the event. The timely and regular promotional slots that are produced to attract a television audience for the media organization can also act as important promotions for the event.

Pay-per-view is a more recent broadcasting format that has been used in particular with boxing in the US. UK satellite broadcasters have also been covering football in this way since 2000.

Not all events are going to achieve such a status and have attractive television rights but there are other opportunities if the broadcaster is interested at all. It may be of benefit for the event to supply the rights for free or even produce and supply edited tapes itself. It is a cost versus benefit decision. Will the costs in producing broadcast standard material and the supply of it for free be recouped via the securing of sponsors or other generated income as a result?

There are also ownership issues here. Professional sports teams in particular often have restricted rights to sell as their membership to leagues and other competitions provide limitations. This is the case throughout most of the major sports in the UK but does differ in the US. Some major league teams in North America can currently sell their television rights to local TV stations and yet national television rights are centrally administered by the leagues. Premiership clubs in the UK may not directly sell their rights in their country under the current contract between the Premier League and BSkyB. However, there are some developments in this area with the emergence of Manchester United Football Club television channel (MUFC TV) and Chelsea Football Club television channel (Chelsea TV) and their programming of action highlights that may be part of long-term strategies in preparation for when this may be possible. Manchester United also have an agreement with the New York Yankees baseball club and their television channel, the Yes Network, where Premiership games get airtime in the US.

Radio broadcasting

The same advantages apply to radio broadcasting but are usually less rewarding in terms of actual revenue and audience reach.

However, radio can be a great event friend. Pre-event promotional exposure is often readily available at national as well as local radio stations and whilst it is not directly earning revenue it can be achieved at no cost and can therefore be a saving on promotional expenditure whilst providing a vehicle for promoting event partners. The latter may therefore provide greater funding as a result. The presence of live radio broadcasts at events can also add to the spectacle and therefore competitive advantage. The use of radio as a means for promotion is considered in greater depth in Chapter 10.

Press coverage

It is possible to secure exclusive rights to press coverage for events. For example, insights into the lives of celebrity sports stars seem to be of particular interest to popular magazines, however there are dangers. Exclusivity for one written medium means a limitation on coverage for the event. In the UK when the Today national newspaper launched, it sponsored the Football League and it was this sponsorship that helped lead to the demise and liquidation of the organization. Neither the newspaper nor the League could have been too happy at the lack of coverage of the sponsor's name by other media when publishing football reports and league tables. Perhaps it should not have been a surprise that other media would have been unlikely to promote a rival organization.

There are however, more innovative ways of making press coverage a more attractive proposition and these are considered in depth, again in Chapter 10.

Internet broadcasting

The technology that is available for webcasting sport offers many opportunities including the development of virtual fans. This began to emerge in the late 1990s and involves rights ownership restrictions wherever there are television contracts. The MUFC example cited earlier is indicative of this. Some of the early webcasts of sport include the first live National Basketball Association (NBA) game on the Internet between the Dallas Mavericks and the Sacramento Kings in April 2001 (RealNetworks, 2001). The Epsom Derby and eight other races were also webcast live in July of the same year, (BBC, 2003). Webcasting in Asia began earlier, and Showei.com, a Chinese sports web site, webcast the Union European Football Association (UEFA) Euro 2000 matches and then the Sydney 2000 Olympics live in 2000 (Turbolinux, 2000). The selling of these new forms of broadcast rights have added greatly to the income generation potential for events.

Ticket sales • • •

Many events are dependent upon the revenue derived from ticket sales. In budgeting such revenue it is important to correctly predict the times at which tickets will be sold and the revenue collected. The ticket sales life cycle lasts from the point at which the decision for the event to go ahead is made, through to the end of the event. There is often a need to expend before any of this revenue is realized, not least on promoting the event, and so it is for this reason that so many of the other areas of revenue, if they can be generated early, play such an important role. The problem in selling tickets at any other stage than after a decision to go ahead is that if the event does not go ahead it becomes a costly and time-consuming job to organize refunds.

This is not to say that ticket sales strategies are an unimportant aspect of the assessment of an event's feasibility. The planning of ticket sales income is a fundamental part of the budgeting process but in order to ensure that revenue is generated as early as possible it is necessary to be creative.

The encouragement of ticket purchase as far in advance of the event as possible can be the key to this process and this can be achieved in a number of ways. The successful use of event communications to create a sense of urgency in ticket buyers is desired by all events but customers are not easily taken in by an event that communicates that tickets are selling fast or even selling out. The introduction of early purchase discounts at least offers the customer value and something tangible to encourage early purchase. To succeed in getting large amounts of revenue from ticket sales there needs to be effort in achieving sales volume. Compared with other forms of revenue such as sponsorship for example, individual tickets carry relatively small prices and so a focus on sales targets where there is potential for block bookings can be both effective and efficient. These might include use of event databanks and sales to previous event attendees, the attendees of other events, members, participants families, sponsors and the personnel of other partner organizations.

Selling tickets for the next event whilst staging the current one may be possible, and certainly offering first refusal via a deadline to purchase is one way of reaching previous event attendees. The freezing of prices up to that deadline can help too.

Ticket pricing policies are an important aspect of financial planning. Ticket income, for admission or participation, can make up the bulk of intended revenue but the more income streams there are in addition, the more flexible the ticket pricing policies can be. With more flexibility in how much is charged there can be greater focus on the requirements of the target markets and, in the long run, as a result, greater revenue. The policies available to sports events are:

1 *Standard price*: One price for all.

2 *Differential prices*: Prices that alter according to the age of the buyer such as for senior citizen and children's admission, the time they purchase such as lesser cost for those who purchase by a deadlines in advance, lesser cost pro-rata for group numbers, lesser cost pro-rata for individual multi-visits or season tickets/passes.

3 *Admission plus*: Either free or standard priced admission alongside premium charges for specific sub-sections to the event such as for special matches or seat reservation at Wimbledon, or for charges for other requirements such as car parking.

The process by which decisions are made as to which pricing policies to follow is commonly a subjective one for sports events. As Getz (1997) maintains, traditional pricing analysis via the determination of price elasticity and marginal costs is inherently difficult. The problem being that one more person at an event is not necessarily going to affect the costs for that event. The staging of publicly provided events can often mean that there are political motivations behind the choice or pricing policy, take for example free admission. At the opposite extreme there are commercial events that appear to have both comparatively high admission prices as well as premium charges and a success can be made of both of these extremes if there is sufficient knowledge of the target market and the decision is made in relation to the planning of the budget as a whole. For example, the New York Yankees has a waiting list for season tickets and the San Francisco 49ers have been sold out since 1981 (Berridge, 2003).

Corporate hospitality ● ● ●

The success of different ticket price structures and premiums can be extended via the packaging together of further elements that add to customer value. Adding food and beverage to a ticket price leverages more income from that ticket but corporate hospitality packages are by no means a new concept. The creation of audience hierarchies has been a common practice since ancient times. For example, we only have to look to the Roman Empire and the differences between senatorial seating and the provision for the common citizen at gladiatorial events. Indeed, the more recent origins of sponsorship lie in the enhancement of simple corporate hospitality.

The creation of such ticket packages adds further customer value. In addition to the main event there is the benefit of a meal in good company and possibly entertainment via dinner speakers. For some events these packages can raise more revenue and can therefore be potentially more important than ordinary ticket sales. The selling of corporate hospitality in the 120 boxes at the Royal Albert Hall for the annual Nabisco Masters Doubles tennis championships for example, meant that 20 per cent of the audience (1000 people) were paying for food, drink and programmes as well as tickets, and mostly well in advance as a result of renewing their box directly after the previous championships. This not only raised more revenue for the event owners, World Championship Tennis (WCT) Inc, it also ensured revenue well in advance of the event giving an improved cash flow.

The financial planning for such packages clearly needs to be implemented at the feasibility stage. The costs involved in all the package elements plus the much sought after extra profit level, are required information for the budgeting process. By identifying and securing early corporate hospitality sales the revenue cash flow can be improved as the costs to be incurred for food and beverage will not be due until much closer to the event. It is therefore only practical sense to determine as early as possible where new and perhaps not so obvious areas for corporate hospitality might exist and providing that they can be sold they will provide innovative opportunities for revenue. The audit of an event's assets may reveal new areas for the provision of corporate hospitality facilities, a disused room or building or simply an area where temporary facilities can be erected.

Sponsorship • • •

The art of placing the right sponsorship with the right organization is the key to the development of an event sponsorship programme (see Chapter 10). But this too is another form of the packaging of an event's assets into saleable bundles. The beauty of a sponsorship package is that it contains elements that often have no cost. Those events that have built sufficient equity into their brand will command greater sponsorship fees.

There are dangers to be aware of in this process and they need to be highlighted in this chapter. Those elements that are bundled together that do have costs need to be accounted for and so they need to feature as expenditure budget lines. Equally if the total sponsorship fee is accounted for as an income line in the budget it is important not to double count it. For instance, if the packages include elements such as tickets, corporate hospitality packages and advertising then it is important to apportion the sponsorship fee revenue into those individual income lines or into the sponsorship line, not both.

Space sales • • •

There is always more space at an event than you think. This section is concerned predominantly with space at the event site, in printed form, and via Internet and mobile telecommunications opportunities.

On-site

The audit can also reveal dead areas that are either disused or non-revenue earning. These can be external or internal concourse areas for example, and if they are situated on regularly used routes they may be of interest to organizations as exhibition, demonstration or sales space. There are dangers as with most of these considerations such as over-commodification and the resultant loss of credibility with event stakeholders for the sake of increased revenue. The process therefore involves another assessment of cost versus benefit. The ambience, aesthetics and image of an event are important considerations and even if it is determined that there will be no negative impact, the occupants who pay to go into these spaces need to be appropriate for the event. It may simply be a case of dictating the look of signage so that it complies or matches that of the event or it may be a more sophisticated audit of their merchandise stock and the satisfying of predetermined quality controls. For even the smallest event the image and quality of produce created by the burger, drink or ice cream concession is crucial. If an organization is to occupy space at the event it will become a part of the event and its inclusion is therefore an important decision for the event manager.

Available space can also be two-dimensional with opportunities to sell advertising hoarding. There are the commonly sold areas that are within event audience and/or television audience sight lines, such as around the pitches, courts and halls that are used for the main spectacle. In addition there are other discreet areas that are frequented by event audience traffic such as concourses, seating aisles and even car parks. For the 2002 Commonwealth Games the prospect of handling event visitors arriving by car, was of concern in a city where there were already existing vehicle congestion issues. This is a common event planning issue that requires various agencies to come together to provide solutions. Manchester 2002 Ltd worked with a local public transport provider, First. Two car parks were created in open green-belt areas to the north and south of the city near to motorway networks. First then created bus terminals at both sites. No customer parking was provided at any of the events venues, and park and ride tickets were sold. The logistics for the operation were sufficiently complex for First to have to also work with other transport organizations for the provision of loaned personnel and busses at peak times.

Many events realize the potential of their directional signage and sell advertising opportunities to interested organizations. For smaller events this enables them to approach smaller local companies with opportunities to reach target markets at smaller costs. The 2003 US Open Tennis championships sold space on its hoardings, located in the stands, to IBM, Heineken and Wilson as part of its' sponsorship agreements with those organizations and at the 2002 Flora London Marathon the mile indicator placards carried the logos of Adidas jointly with the title sponsor.

Space is not just available via on-site physical fixtures. Events also use their people and their clothing to create advertising opportunities. Tennis ball boys and girls have long worn sponsored clothing but now stewards, if there are enough of them, can become an important way of reaching target audiences. As part of their agreement to sponsor the 2002 Commonwealth Games, Asda, the UK supermarket chain, provided tracksuit uniforms for all of the 12 000 plus volunteer helpers. The tracksuits carried the Asda-owned brand logo for George clothing and were also predominantly purple in colour, the brand colours for Cadbury's, another Games sponsor.

The fee for advertising space of any kind can be set according to prominence and frequency of sightings. For other space sales, occupancy agreements can be a straightforward rental per size of space. For events that are keen to raise such extra revenue and need to try harder to convince potential occupants, there could also be a share-of-profits but this requires more work in auditing sales for an accurate settlement.

Printed form

Space can also be sold in and on printed event paper materials. Selling space in the event programme is common as is space on event tickets, flyers, posters, organizational headed paper, score sheets, retail and giveaway bags, and media information packs.

Internet opportunities

Similarly there are now opportunities for events to sell advertising space on their web sites. The value of which lies largely in their longevity as they can operate year round as opposed to just around event time. However, as this is an event asset it is also available to partners and sponsors and as a result, managers must first identify the needs of the latter before entering any potentially conflicting agreements with additional advertisers.

The use of web sites is a relatively new opportunity and in this early stage of such usage there are various differing industry examples of commercial practice. In many cases event-related web sites have evolved as public relations (PR) tools. The Internet provides a relatively easy way of supplying frequent and updated information to target customers about the event. This can keep adopted fans hooked on an on-going basis. A web site can then become a highly productive e-tail vehicle for tickets and merchandise. Unfortunately some events even use their sites to advertise sponsorship opportunities and even provide application forms by which prescribed packages may be purchased online. This latter application rather defeats the objective of building mutual sponsorship arrangements and the attempt to identify a sponsors needs before proposing their involvement with an event. Nevertheless, the key to getting target customers to hit an event web site is utilizing information about the event and in particular content pertaining to participants. This is a key driver of site traffic and needs to be sustained for successful ticket and merchandise sales.

Sites can also earn revenue via advertising or sponsorship sales. Creative sites can produce regular promotions, games, auctions and editorial features that can be endorsed by organizations. These may be sold independently of the events sponsorship programme but run the danger of cluttering both the events and its sponsors' massages. The San Francisco 49ers web site provides an example of a site that is highly creative in generating revenue. 49ers.com has two key revenue sources merchandise and sponsorship that are producing income in the low seven figures and to get on-site it typically costs a minimum of $50 000 00, (Berridge, 2003) (see Case study 6.1). The site was predominantly a PR function when it was first taken back in-house from CBS Sportsline in 2001. The objective of controlling whilst extending the brand is still paramount as the site is where most 49ers fans experience the brand other than via television. One of the concerns, even for Kirk Berridge (2003), the 49ers

Senior Manager for Corporate Sponsorships, is that whilst the site imparts news and stories about the team it has in the past been constrained by an editorial process that has not broken or covered news on controversial topics. In 2002 when the 49ers released a team coach there was no coverage of that story on 49ers.com. The concern is that such policies may drive fans to visit other sources and that would impact on web site traffic and therefore sponsorship sales.

Case study 6.1

Web site income generation: 49ers.com

The San Francisco 49ers took the operation of its web site back in-house in 2001 and by utilizing a number of key partnerships with suppliers was able to invest as little as $15 000.00 into its development.

In November 2003 the site was delivering 3 million visitors a day and as a vehicle for extending the brand, the management evaluate it as being more lucrative than stadium, radio or publishing activities.

Some of the strategies that have been adopted include no use of banners, pop-up or under advertisements, and use of the 49ers colours (red, gold with black and white) as possible, including for the re-design of corporate advertisements and identities using. Other strategies include limits on the numbers of sponsors for less clutter, a minimum level of investment for entry on to the site, national brand targeting and no-use of cost-per-click models. The focus is on maximizing customers' brands. The following commercial opportunities are available with 49ers.com:

- *My 49ers ENews*: Established in 2002, fans get e-mail notification via pre-selected personalized alerts such as breaking stories, injury updates, ticket availability, new arrival merchandise, auctions and special events. Over 100 000 fans receive ENews. There are 12 sponsors attached to various elements of the service.

- *Business partnerships*: Launched in 2003 this consists of a rotating advertisement on the homepage that cost only $4000.00 to develop. It has achieved a return of $100 000.00 (November 2003).

- *49ers store*: Launched in 2001 this service is operated by a partner. Footlocker distributes 49ers merchandise to online customers and has six-figure annual sales revenue.

- *49ers marketplace*: This is a private label auction for the 49ers profit. One-of-a-kind 49ers merchandise is auctioned online. In 2003 the pom-poms used by a player in a touch down celebration were auctioned for $800.00. Players cars have also been auctioned.

- *49ers fan travel*: Another partner, Prime Sport Travel, operates this away match travel service that produces six-figure revenue annually. The 49ers receive a share-of-profit.

- *Games*: Games such as Pigskin Pick Em 'consist of free, weekly access to 3550 online fans (November 2003). Levitra are the sponsors at $50 000.00 per year and this particular product involves fans predicting wins across the National Football League (NFL) in sweepstakes.

- *49ers photos*: This product was launched in November 2003 in time for the Holiday season in the US. It offers 49ers photos, framed or unframed, on a limited-edition basis via partners Pictopia.

Future projects for the 49ers include the development of 49ers.comTV, an Internet radio station, wireless subscription services, foreign language versions of 49ers.com (Chinese, Spanish and Japanese), 49ers dating club and ticket exchange services.

Source: Berridge (2003).

Mobile telecommunications opportunities

The advent of wireless communications via mobile telecommunication handsets is an exciting development that has yet to be fully developed. In the UK there are mobile telecommunication carriers that are providing premiership football match highlights to their customers via their handsets. According to the National Hockey League (NHL's) Director of New Media Business Development, Ryan Hughes (2003), this application and provision in the US market is possibly 2 years away and this despite NHL's market leadership in the exploitation of wireless opportunities in the sports industry. Currently the bandwidth does not have sufficient capacity. However, in 2002 the NHL did begin servicing ice-hockey fans with scores, downloadable logos, ringtones, games, teams statistics and ticket information via mobile handsets. One of these services includes last-minute ticket availability alerts for teams of the fans choice. As well as providing traffic-related revenue from the carrier to the NHL there is also revenue from the sponsorship of the service by Nextel. The NHL distributes its revenue according to which of its member teams drive the income streams. Hughes (2003) has conducted research that indicates that by 2007 there will be a total of 456 million mobile handsets worldwide and indicates that he believes this offers considerable revenue opportunities for many sports teams.

Merchandising • • •

The event T-shirt is a memento that is popular with event participants and at some sports events selling to those that compete is an important revenue stream. At international racquetball tournaments the memento to collect is a pin badge, something that the International Olympic Committee (IOC) has also recognized as a key part of its merchandising programme. The latter has clearly a sufficiently powerful brand it can create and sell a range of items at Olympic events as well as out of its popular Olympic Museum in Lausanne. Not all events have this kind of power of course, but the T-shirt example shows that smaller events also have the opportunity to think about where sales might derive.

The development of sophisticated merchandise product lines is achievable for some events and there are also merchandising organizations that will design, produce and sell event merchandise. The more common arrangement will be to pay a commission to the event after an agreed audit of sales. The advantage of contracting external agencies being that there is no event expenditure, only revenue. Handling the programme in-house of course may offer more potential profit but a lot will depend on the retail expertise available.

Licensing • • •

The more powerful events brands can evolve one stage further into licensing programmes. The All England Lawn Tennis Club, the owners and organizers of the Wimbledon tennis championships, have a range of goods available via its web site and all around the world as a result of a carefully monitored licensing programme. The NFL also operates a sophisticated licensing operation whereby it is able to command license fees in the US as well as other world regions such as Europe and the Far East. Different manufacturers can buy these licenses and produce agreed products according to the conditions of the license. The more powerful the brand the more manufacturers will be interested and thus the more revenue will be earned. The key again is in the quality of the products produced as they are depicting the image of the events and organizations involved. Quality assurance and control by the rights owner is made all the more complex when the manufacture of the products concerned is conducted by a license holder, or even a third party, and so strict license conditions and their policing are required.

Case study 6.2 describes how the IOC has identified and packaged its assets. Clearly the Olympic offering is a sophisticated programme that has necessitated innovative management in the layering of the partnerships and supplierships available. This is a model that other events have mirrored in an effort to present credible benefits to commercial parties from all types of diversified industries and yet still place them to work effectively together on the same event.

Case study 6.2

Revenue maximization: the Olympic Marketing Programme

The Olympic Marketing Programme consists of a number of key elements that are either managed or overseen by the IOC. Firstly there are three tiers of Olympic sponsors and secondly three tiers of supplierships that together account for 40 per cent of IOC marketing revenue. Broadcasting (50 per cent), ticketing (8 per cent) and licensing (2 per cent) make up the remainder of revenue; 2001–2004 figures (IOC, 2003). The IOC retains 8 per cent of its revenue for the upkeep of its administration with the remainder distributed to the Organizing Committee for the Olympic Games (OCOGs), National Olympic Committees (NOCs) and International Federations (IFs).

Olympic Sponsorship

- *The Olympic Partner (TOP) Programme*: This programme consists of exclusive sponsor-ships that offer worldwide rights year-round and on an on-going renewable basis directly with the IOC: Current partners include:
  - Coca-Cola: Non-Alcoholic Beverages rights
  - John Hancock: Life Assurance rights
  - Kodak: Film rights
  - McDonald's: Retail Food Services rights
  - Panasonic: Audio Visual rights
  - Samsung: Wireless Communications rights
  - Schlumberger Sema: Information Technology rights
  - Sports Illustrated Time: Publishing rights
  - Swatch: Timing rights
  - Visa: Consumer Payment rights
  - Xerox: Document Publishing rights.

- *Olympic Games Sponsorship Programme*: This programme consists of exclusive agree-ments with sponsors for rights to any current Olympiad and are negotiated directly with the host city OCOG.

- *NOC Sponsorship Programme*: These programmes are negotiated by each NOC and can be on-going renewable agreements.

Olympic Suppliership

- *Olympic Supplier Programme*: Exclusive supplierships that offer worldwide rights year-round on an on-going renewable basis directly with the IOC. Current supplierships include:
  - DaimlerChrysler: Rights to supply transport outside of the host country
  - Mizuno: IOC clothing supplier rights
  - Pfizer: Pharmaceutical rights to the IOC Medical Commission
  - Schenker AG: Freight forwarding and customs service supplier rights.

- *OCOG Supplierships*: Exclusive agreements with suppliers for rights to any current Olympiad that are negotiated directly with the host city OCOG.

- *NOC Supplierships*: Agreements that are negotiated by each NOC that can be on-going renewable agreements.

Source: IOC (2003).

Summary

There are increasing pressures on event managers to be creative in generating revenue. Whilst the traditional methods of selling media rights, agreements with media partners, ticket and hospi-tality sales, selling space, merchandising and licensing are still appropriate, it is now a necessity for managers to look at these areas for new vehicles that can attract both audience and corporate customers alike. An event audit can reveal new mechanisms and vehicles for commercial properties that if managed carefully will not clutter the event but rather enhance it and income figures. As with most businesses today, the dynamic introduction of new technology offers a wealth of new opportunity for the event manager. The evolving Internet offers events a year-round opportunity to sell and communicate with its customers and wireless technology may prove to provide instant access to customers almost round the clock. However, these vehicles can only be as effective as there is care and thought in finding out what the customer wants. The event asset audit can reveal potential products and the event manager can bundle up innovative benefits, but the focus must be on what the customer will buy and that requires market research. The marketing planning process is considered in greater detail in Chapter 9.

Questions

Select a sports event, and:

1 From a revenue earning perspective, analyse the strategic importance of financial planning at an early stage.

2 Audit the event and identify the key areas available for revenue generation.

3 Identify the key practices exercised in generating revenue whilst highlighting specific examples.

4 Suggest new ways in which the event might generate revenue in the future.

5 Now consider the IOC model of revenue maximization and compare and contrast it with other events.

6 Critically analyse the costs and benefits of implementing new technology for event revenue maximization.

References

Berridge, K. (2003). Marketing and enabling technology: beyond content, turning a team web site into a profit center, paper delivered by Senior Manager of Corporate Partnerships, San Francisco 49ers, at *Sport Media and Technology 2003*. November 13–14, New York Marriott Eastside, New York. *Street and Smith's Sports Business Journal*.

BBC (2003). www.bbc.co.uk/sport1/hi/in_depth/2001/epsom_derby/1362059.stm (accessed 12 September 2003).

Coates, D. and Humphries, B. (2003). *Professional Sports Facilities, Franchises and Urban Economic Development*. University of

Maryland, Baltimore County, working paper 03-103. www.umbc.edu/economics/wpapers/wp_03_103.pdf (accessed 7 January 2004).

Getz, D. (1997). *Event Management and Tourism*. New York, Cognizant, Chapter 10.

Gratton, P. and Taylor, P. (2000). *Economics of Sport and Recreation*. London, E & FN Spon.

Hughes, R. (2003). Marketing and enabling technology: expanding the fan experience with wireless applications, paper delivered by Director, New Media Business Development, NHL at *Sport Media and Technology 2003*. November 13–14, New York Marriott Eastside, New York. *Street and Smith's Sports Business Journal*.

IOC (2003). www.olympic.org/uk/organisation (accessed 15 September, 2003).

RealNetworks (2001). www.wnba.com/news/webcast_announcement_030529 (accessed 12 September 2003).

The Guardian (2003). http://image.guardian.co.uk/sysfiles/Society/documents/2003/07/03/4329/lottery.pdf (accessed 7 January 2004).

Turbolinux (2000). www.turbolinux.com/news/pr/olympicwebcast.html (accessed 12 September 2003).

CHAPTER 7

The bidding process

After studying this chapter, you should be able to:

- identify the planning and management processes required in the bidding for sports events.

- identify the key components for successful bids.

- understand how losing bids can be winning strategies.

Introduction

This chapter is concerned with the process undertaken in bidding for the right to host sports events. Before the Los Angeles Olympics in 1984, the terminology used in bidding today was unheard of. The hosting of major sports events, in particular the Olympics, was seen to be a financial millstone (Gratton and Taylor, 2000) until the unprecedented surplus income generated at those Ueberroth led games. The result is a calendar full of events that require host cities to bid, and a calendar that does not just consist of only high profile events. Now, international events like the World Masters Games, European Wheelchair Basketball Championships and the World Badminton Championships are much sought after, as well as a host of national events in many countries (Kronos, 1997). In this chapter the requirements of the International Olympic Committee (IOC) and the Olympic bidding process will be used as a model to be applied as appropriate to other sports events. The key factors required for successful bidding will be identified as well as an assessment of the strategic use of bids do not succeed and still gain benefits. A key focus will be on the bidding cities for the 2012 Olympics.

The bid process

The preparation and implementation of a bid to host a sports event are an intrinsic part of the event planning process. Whilst the preparation and submission for event candidature requires specialist expertise and project management, it is essential that the process is aligned into the overall event planning mechanism. For example, it is necessary for the feasibility of the event to be assessed prior to a decision to go ahead and submit a bid. Getz (1997) proposes that a bid is based on at least a pre-feasibility study where preliminary figures for the costs and benefits are assigned. For some events this can be a relatively low cost and therefore of small financial risk. However, for larger events the cost of assessing impact can be high but is nevertheless a critical undertaking if all potential stakeholders are to be convinced that the benefits of the event outweigh the costs. For major events such as the Olympics there are planning costs that are entirely at risk, for example. In 2002 London commissioned Arup to conduct a study prior to any decision to bid for the 2012 Olympics.

The preparation of any required bid therefore does not begin until event feasibility has been assessed and a decision has been made to go ahead with the event. Clearly any earlier assessments can then be used and the costs incurred can be included in the budget for the bid.

That then raises a question about bids that fail and how the costs associated with that failure are justified. There are two answers. The first is that the funds raised to finance a failed bid get written off. The loss is accepted as a calculated risk. This further highlights the need for stakeholder support in going to bid because in Olympic cases the costs can be now as high as £13 million, as for London and its 2012 bid (Arup, 2002). The second is that a bid can be a means to end, and this is discussed at the end of the chapter.

Getz (1997) proposes that a further detailed feasibility study be conducted after the bid has been accepted in order to begin planning the implementation of the event. However, there are dangers here. There is no doubt that this indeed is common practice but for major events that identify new cost factors that are widely apart from the event budget then any feasibility exercise prior to a decision to go ahead was futile. As mentioned earlier, Sydney Organizing Committee of the Olympic Games (SOCOG) formally readjusted its event budget on four occasions after it had decided to go ahead, and its costs escalated way beyond their original forecasts (SOCOG, 2001). See Case study 5.1 in Chapter 5. The message here is that the feasibility stage is perhaps even more critical than currently the industry accepts.

The Olympic bid process involves two main stages. The IOC awards its games to cities not countries and in some cases there are national competitions for interested host cities to win the nomination of that nations National Olympic Committee (NOC). The NOCs are given 6 months warning by the IOC, approximately 9.5 years ahead of an Olympic Games to decide to nominate a host city (Thoma and Chalip, 1996). Six months is clearly too short a time for interested hosts to consider a bid and so they are in contact with their respective NOC long before. Only an NOC can nominate a host city to the IOC for the bidding competition. For the 2012 Olympic Games the United States Olympic Committee (USOC) ran a competition between San Francisco, Houston, Washington and the eventual winners New York. In contrast the British Olympic Committee (BOC) selected London outright. For some countries with limited resources the decision of which city requires a simple selection procedure (Thoma and Chalip, 1996), take Cuba and its nomination of Havana for example. However, the decision by the BOC to select London was more contentious, with rivalry from Manchester and Birmingham in previous years. Manchester had already received national nominations and failed in its bids for the 1996 and 2000 Olympics, as did Birmingham in 1992 and the BOC identified London as the UK's best opportunity to win.

The process for nominated cities then becomes more clearly defined and timetabled. The IOC's Bid Process, which came into effect on 20 February 2003, can effectively be divided into four distinct steps. These are discussed below in particular reference to the awarding of the 2012 Games (IOC, 2003).

The Olympic Games bidding process

Pre-applicants

This phase is for interested host cities to contact their respective NOC and partake in selection procedures in order to be chosen for nomination to the IOC.

NOCs, if they so wish, may inform the IOC of their nominated Applicant City. This is to be done by 15 July 2003 in writing (9 years out from the event).

An application fee of $150 000 is to be submitted no later than August 2003. This fee entitles cities to use a 'mark' of their city name and the Olympic year '2012.' It also allows them access to the IOC's Olympic Games Knowledge Management Programme and accreditation for the Applicant City Seminar.

Candidature acceptance procedure

NOC nominated cities remain classified as Applicant Cities until accepted as candidates by the IOC. Applicant Cities initially answer a questionnaire in writing, submitted by 15 January 2004. This is then assessed by the IOC Administration and recruited expertise under the governance of the IOC Executive Board. No formal presentations take place at this stage but city visits by experts may or may not take place. The IOC Executive Board then informs the Applicant Cities which ones will be accepted as the Candidate Cities to go forward to the next stage. It does this by the 18 May 2004 (8 years out from the delivery of the event).

Applicant Cities are assessed on the following:

1 The potential of the cities, including their countries, to host a successful multi-sports event.

2 Their compliance to the Olympic Charter, code of ethics (which includes the right to promote their candidature in their respective NOC territory but not on an international level and the banning of all giving and receiving of gifts by Olympic parties), anti-doping code and other conditions concerning the candidature as set by the IOC.

The questionnaire is concerned with providing the IOC with an overview of the concept using the following seven themes:

1 *Motivation, concept and public opinion*: This section includes the request for maps that show new versus existing infrastructure and an explanation of the motivation behind new build, post-Olympic use and long-term strategies.

The section is also concerned with gauging public support and asks for polls to be undertaken and reported. Detail of any opposition to the bid is specifically required.

2 *Political support*: Information on the status of the city's Governmental support is requested and who would be involved in the future management of the event if won. Letters from the Government, NOC and City authorities are required as testimony to their support of the bid. Details of any forthcoming political elections are also required.

3 *Finance*: Details are required on the Games Budget from each Applicant City and in addition they are to inform the IOC of how the phases of candidature will also be funded. The amount of Government contribution is a required information here too.

4 *Venues*: Details on existing and planned venues are required including whether they are to be temporary overlay or permanent. Specific plans for an Olympic Village, International Broadcast and Press Centres are requested.

5 *Accommodation*: The status regarding hotel provision and media accommodation at the time of the event are required here.

6 *Transport infrastructure*: Information on existing and planned transportation is requested and for new facilities construction timelines are also needed. This section concerns most forms of transportation including air, road, rail, subway and light rail.

7 *General conditions, logistics and experience*: This section requires information on population expectations at the time of the event, meteorology conditions, environmental conditions and impact, security responsibility, resources and issues. It also requires information on the experience the city has in hosting international sports events and multi-sports events in particular. Specifically it asks for the last 10 major events over the previous 10 years.

Each of these themes consists of several questions. Each question is requested in French and English and is limited to one page, making a maximum of 25 pages in each language. The IOC keenly looks for brevity in this document and emphasizes the importance of fact versus presentation. Answers for certain sections use pro-forma charts, venues for example, and request fine detail on elements such as spectator capacity, construction and upgrade dates, costs of upgrades and sources of finance specifically. Fifty copies of the questionnaire are to be submitted to the IOC.

Candidature phase

Accepted Candidate Cities are required to submit a Candidature File to the IOC and have between 18 May and 15 November 2004 to complete it. This is then evaluated by a Commission that is comprised of members of International Federations, NOCs, IOC members, representatives of the Athletes Commission and the International Paralympic Committee, as well as IOC experts. The Commission analyzes the files received, and then from the end of January 2005 undergoes a visit programme, taking in all of the Candidate Cities. An evaluation report is then compiled and presented to the IOC Executive Board in May 2005 and at the latter's discretion, a formal announcement is made of the Candidate Cities that will be submitted to the IOC Session (the election).

Candidate Cities can, upon submission of their files and acceptance by the IOC, undertake international promotion of their candidature during this stage.

The Candidature File provides each city with an opportunity to embellish on the information provided by their earlier questionnaires and the IOC provides a comprehensive guideline for its completion via its *Manual for Candidate Cities*. The manual supplied to the Candidate Cities for the 2008 election consisted of a model to follow and included general information on layout, illustration and format, together with clear instruction for the completion of three volumes in order to cover 18 prescribed themes (IOC, 2002):

- Volume One
    1 National, regional and Candidate City characteristics
    2 Legal aspects
    3 Customs and immigration formalities
    4 Environmental protection and meteorology
    5 Finance
    6 Marketing

- Volume Two
    7 General sports concept
    8 Sports
    9 Paralympic Games
    10 Olympic Village

- Volume Three
    11 Medical/Health Services
    12 Security
    13 Accommodation
    14 Transport
    15 Technology
    16 Communication and media services
    17 Olympism and culture
    18 Guarantees.

Election

The IOC Session takes place in Singapore on 6 July 2005 and the Candidate Cities will each make a presentation of their bid. After all the presentations from each bidding city have been received there are various rounds of voting by IOC members and a winning city will be declared.

For New York and London this will have taken up to 6 years of planning in reaching this stage and this all prior to the decision to go ahead with the event. For one of the nine bidding cities there is then a further 7 years of implementation planning before the implementation of the event in 2012.

The IOC process here is highly sophisticated, and in this comprehensive display of detail and scrutiny there is the basis for a useful model for bidding requirements for other sports events. Some event rights owning bodies do offer much simpler processes. FINA offers little guideline other than deadlines for receipt of bids, for example for the 13th FINA World Championships in 2009 (swimming, diving, water polo, synchronized swimming and open water events), interested host cities must put in their bids by 31 October 2004, under 5 years out from the event. For their FINA Junior Diving World Championships the lead-time is under 3 years (FINA, 2003). In contrast, the guideline offered by USA Track & Field (USATF) to bidders for their National Championships is more informative and highlights the key areas that are to be covered in any bid. It also covers similar criteria to the IOC model as Case study 7.1 illustrates. Both FINA and USATF display their available events over the long term on their web sites.

Case study 7.1

USA Track & Field: Bidding Guideline

The 2005–2007 USATF Championships

USATF, the US NGB for athletics, provides those cities that want to bid for its events with handbooks. The Request for Proposal and Bidding Handbook provided to those that wish to bid for the USATF Outdoor Championships is a 43-page document with details on what amounts to a 3-year process. The handbook is designed to guide interested host cities and advises on how the document can be used to compile a bid.

Timetable for the Award of the 2005 Championships:

25 August 2003: Cities/Communities register interest
10 October 2003: Submit 10 Bid documents to USATF

A $25 000 deposit is required at this stage. This is one-third of the rights fee that is required from the winning host. $3000 is retained from all deposits by USATF for administrative purposes.

3 December 2003: Final presentations by bidders if required
7 December 2003: Awarding of the 2005 championships

The bid document itself is required to cover the following criteria:

1 Local Organizing Committee
2 Management Committee and Staffing
3 Bidding Host City/Community Characteristics
4 Facilities
5 Housing and Meals
6 Logistics: Transportation, Security, Medical
7 Climate
8 Business Arrangements: Budgets and Sponsorship

Source: USATF (2003).

Key bid components and criteria

There are a number of key factors that may be critical in the winning of bids. They include the gaining of stakeholder support (in particular the local population), political risk analysis, knowledge of the bidding and evaluation process, the recruitment of key management, communications and a thorough bid book.

Bid book and presentation

The bid book, sometimes referred to as a bid document, is the hardcopy of the proposal prepared and delivered by each bidding city. The IOC requires 20 copies of what it refers to as a Candidature File, in English and French, and controls the release of the contents into the public domain. In addition copies of the file are to be distributed to a number of other recipients including IOC members, the International Sports Federations affected and the library at the Olympic Study Centre, based at the Olympic Museum in Lausanne. This distribution is important for future Candidate Cities and their capacity to learn from past bids.

The preparation required needs to be thorough and the list of considerations in the previous section provide only the headers for the level of detail necessary. There is an opportunity to make a presentation and for the Olympics this is limited to 1 hour.

These two essential elements of the bid process are the critical tools by which a bid city can seek to differentiate itself from other bids. The 18 themes of information required by the IOC, as listed above, are the key elements by which a city is evaluated and so it is in these areas where the differential is required. For example, Sydney in its bid for the 2000 Olympics is famed for its 'Green' approach. The Australian Government claims that it was the first true Green Games and was the force behind the introduction of environmental criteria for Olympic hosts (Department of the

Environment and Heritage, 2003). The Sydney bid made much of this approach and is now seen as a key factor in its election, but the bid also focused on the care of athletes in its attempt to set itself aside from the competition (Meisegeier, 1995). The competition included a bid from Beijing that was clouded by human rights issues. Beijing bid again and won the 2008 Olympics under similar clouds but used Weber Shandwick as its communications agency, as Sydney had done previously. The importance of bid communications is highlighted here. Weber Shandwick focused the communications efforts for the 2008 bid on de-linking the city with political issues, emphasizing social changes within China and making the case for a country with the world's largest population as deserving the games (Weber Shandwick, 2003). These themes were considered to be key content in the Candidature File.

For other events there are other opportunities to gain a differential advantage. The team owners vote for the host city for an NFL Super Bowl and for the winners for 2008, Phoenix, Arizona, the key factor was their newly planned stadium. The stadium is to be completed in 2006 and will have a 75 000 seat capacity and a retractable roof. Prior to the secret ballot, several team owners were freely exalting the attraction of Phoenix's bid. It was recognized as early as during the recruitment for funding that the new facilities would provide the differential needed to win (Harris and Bagnato, 2003; Sports Tricker, 2003). The other bids from Washington and Tampa (New York had previously pulled out) did not involve new facilities.

Hockey Canada has a reputation in the world of ice hockey for excellent event management. The country has staged the World Junior Championships six times and most recently in Halifax in 2003. The International Ice Hockey Federation president, Rene Fasel, stated that no country does a better job than Canada in putting on these championships due to their unparalleled fan attendances. A record attendance of 242 173 was set in Halifax and as a result the 2006 event will again return to a Canadian city in what is the quickest return to a country in the events bidding history (Spencer, 2003). Hockey Canada has recognized where its strengths lie and is maximizing their use.

Stakeholders

Commitment from all the events stakeholders is a necessary element in order to win the bid. Clearly funding and organizing partners from both the public and private sectors are key stakeholders as is the evaluation committee representing the awarding body.

A principal stakeholder group is also the local community. It is essential for the community to be behind the bid and most events recognize this importance by researching their interest and involving them in consultation. A contemporary tool for this process is a web site and early in the planning process both London and

New York developed sites with information on the benefits of hosting the 2012 Olympics.

The name of the game at this stage is to convince stakeholders that there are more benefits than costs in hosting an event. Other media are also key vehicles and the use of public forums, launches and press liaison are all key communications activities. Web sites form suitable anchors for the distribution of event strategies, impact reports and feasibility studies, spokespeople comments and progress to date (London 2012, 2003; NYC2012, 2003a).

New York has recruited volunteers with the help of its web site and has then used them in turn to spread the word. Their 'Go Team' was utilized at other sports events, such as the 2003 New York City Triathlon and the USA National Weightlifting Championships. They are also being used to distribute promotional materials at stadiums, subways, at festivals and in telesales campaigns to recruit further volunteers (NYC2012, 2003b).

The Toronto bid for the 1996 Olympics was marred by public protests and anti-Olympic demonstrations against spending on sports events when poverty and homelessness was a city challenge. Toronto was thought to have the early lead with its bid at the time (Thoma and Chalip, 1996), but did lose out to Atlanta. The costs of getting to that stage and still not understanding the needs and feelings of the public were clearly very high. It is important to programme the campaign so that when the bid is launched there is a tide of public welcome. Late in 2002 Britain was expressing some interest in staging the 2012 Olympics. The media followed the story as London Mayor Ken Livingstone pushed the claims of the city, supported by the BOC, but against the seemingly cautious national Government. The previously completed impact study by Arup was used as evidence of short- and long-term impacts. Later, a public meeting and a Government fact-finding trip to Lausanne were reported widely in most media. The Government's decision of whether it would support a bid was further delayed by an invasion of Iraq. The media and public speculation increased as a result to a point where it appeared unlikely that the Government would provide a sanction. That in turn appeared to inspire a feeling of support for a bid. The media were used to enhance that and on 15 May 2003, the Government announced that it had set aside £2.375 billion to pay for the staging of the 2012 Games in London (London 2012, 2003). The delay, possibly delaying tactics, appeared to have driven public support.

Research plays a key part in this public education exercise. Measures for levels of perception are necessary before a communications plan can be devised. In polls conducted in November and December 2002, New York city and state residents were surveyed about their perception of potential games in 2012. About 84 per cent of city residents and 74 per cent of state residents were in favour, and 90 and 89 per cent respectively believed that games would have a positive impact on the city (NYC2012, 2003b). Research of this kind serves two purposes. Firstly, it provides a benchmark and secondly, it provides good content for communications activities.

Political risk analysis

Thoma and Chalip (1996) stress the importance of assessing the risk of political issues. Whilst strife of any kind is likely to influence the decision to award an event to a bidder, there are other considerations for the bidders themselves. For example, changes in government in stance or personnel may alter bid support. The Millennium Dome in London was initiated by a Tory government and was hampered by problems when in 1997 a Labour government was elected. The new Prime Minister, Tony Blair, came very close to ending the project despite considerable already sunk costs. Economic changes, whether taxation or importation related, can also have affect. For example, Manchester City Council's Candidature File for the 2000 Olympics was submitted to the IOC with a question over the amount of value added tax (VAT). The file was submitted when it was not clear whether the event would be liable for VAT or not and so the financial implications at the time were unknown (Department of Environment, 1993).

Knowledge

Knowledge of the bidding process and how candidates are evaluated is essential but is perhaps only attainable through experience. Patterns exist to substantiate this. Consider those cities that continue to bid after failure, as discussed later in this chapter. There are also those events that have recognized the importance of key personnel and prior knowledge. Vancouver used the expertise of Calgary to support its winning bid for the 2010 Winter Olympics, and the 25 Sydney 2000 executives who worked on the 2002 Commonwealth Games were clearly considered to be experts in their field.

Emery (2001) conducted research with 400 major sport events organizers and identified key elements for the improving chances for future successful bidding. They were all concerned with superior knowledge. He identified that a portfolio of events and evidence of successful event management was an advantage for any bidding candidate and if that was not possible at least the recruitment of carefully selected personnel was required. In this way a bid can gain professional credibility. An understanding of the formal decision-making process and those that are to evaluate it was also considered key. One point was that it should not always be assumed that those that evaluate a bid are in fact experts, and thus bids should reflect that in the way that they are presented. The formal processes, and in particular the protocols, were identified as essential knowledge and for those that are new to bidding this can be a steep learning curve. Individual response from the research demonstrated that not knowing the voting panel members well enough and not being able to politically compete with others on that basis were fundamental barriers to success. Relationship building is clearly important here and knowledge of the needs of the decision-makers is critical.

In addition to knowledge of the processes involved, is knowledge of the owning body and its existing corporate partners. More sophisticated organizations like the IOC have various levels of sponsors and suppliers and there are certain rights that they exercise at Olympic events as well as on a year round basis. For other events the owners may have existing partners and so it becomes important to recognize how these will relate to the plans for any commercial activities for the event (Graham et al., 2001). Inclusion of competing partners may well weaken the bid for example.

Knowledge of other past bids and scrutiny of games reports is also necessary (Allen et al., 2002). Where bids went wrong is just as important as where they went right. The transfer of Olympic knowledge (TOK) service should be of help to future Olympic bidding cities. This service currently has useful knowledge on the 2000 Sydney and 2002 Salt Lake Olympics.

The nature of the bidding process is competition and as with all competitions knowing the other competitors is paramount. This is sport after all. One further key factor identified by Emery (2001) was that bidding teams should acquire knowledge not only of rival bid content but also of those individuals that will be presenting it. The capacity to highlight where one bid is better at meeting the required criteria can only be achieved once information on other bids is understood.

Management

In addition to experienced executives, bid teams also need leaders and figureheads. At all levels of bids it is personnel that make it winnable. Olympic bids commonly use key figures with national and international influence in their teams. The English F.A. employed Bobby Charlton and Geoff Hurst, members of the 1966 World Cup winning England football team in its bid for the 2006 World Cup. Germany utilized Frank Beckenbaur, a member of the West German team that lost the 1966 World Cup Final, and won that bid. David Beckham, Tony Blair and Matthew Pinsent are currently being used by the London 2012 bid team and give comments of support. These are examples of the use of spokespersons but what is of more importance perhaps is the appointment of the senior executive that drives the bid through. Emery's research identified that a known key figurehead for inside knowledge of the decision-makers in the bid process was key (Emery, 2001). As far as the New York and London bids for the 2012 Olympics are concerned, it looks like being a battle between two Americans, Daniel Doctoroff and Barbara Cassani respectively.

Communications

The importance of the use of strategic communications in the winning of bids has already been made but a key aspect of this is the need to create a strong brand. The larger the event the more agencies, partners and organizations are involved and so the importance of having one message becomes even greater. Whatever the scale of the event, a brand will help integrate communications. Of course, neither a brand nor communications alone will win a bid and if a bid does not meet all the specified requirements, as discussed above in the IOC model, then it will be technically flawed.

Key components of the branding process are the creation of themes and logos, and London and New York were both active with designs launched in late 2003. However, it will be the ability to overcome any key issues as a part of the content of the bid and how that is incorporated into that brand that will determine whether they are successful or not. For example, the issues that Beijing overcame to win the Olympics for 2008 involved the building of a brand that required the repositioning of a city and changes in international perception. Aside from the controversy that still remains, this re-imaging was at least achieved as far as was required to win the bid; the objective in hand.

Losing bids/winning strategies

Bidding can be an expensive and risky exercise but it can be used as a means to an end in itself.

For both large and small scale events there are lessons to be learned from the bidding exercise. The lessons learned as discussed above can become invaluable in winning next time or at least putting in a bid document that is better prepared.

Several cities have continued to bid for Olympic Games and then used that experience to win. Table 7.1 shows that since 2000, three out of the six past and known future games hosts, Winter and Summer, have had previous bids and finished in second

Table 7.1

Recent successful Olympic bidding cities: indicating previous bidding history by each city or cities from the same country

Host		Previous bidding history
Vancouver	2010	Nil (Toronto 2008, 1996)
Beijing	2008	2000 (2nd)
Turin	2006	Nil (Rome 2nd 2004, Aosta 5th 1998, Cortina 5th 1992)
Athens	2004	1996 (2nd)
Salt Lake	2002	1998 (2nd)
Sydney	2000	Nil (Melbourne 4th 1996, Brisbane 4th 1992)

Adapted from GamesBids.com (2003).

place in those elections. In addition, whilst the other three cities had not bid in recent history, there were previous bids from neighbouring cities from each of the countries concerned. However, Sweden has made five consecutive bids and not yet hosted an Olympics (Ostersund in 2002, 1998 and 1994, Falun in 1992 and 1988). England too has had three recent successive failures, in 1992 with Birmingham, and 1996 and 2000 with Manchester. There is therefore no conclusive relationship between bidding and eventually winning. However, the use of previous experience has probably been of use in improving and developing bids and it is worth noting that of the cities that are bidding for the 2012 Olympics as shown in Table 7.2, Paris and Istanbul, have each had two recently previous failed bids and will no doubt be calling on their previous experience in an attempt to be more successful in 2005 when the winning city is declared.

If there are objectives that can be achieved via the submission of a bid, whether that bid wins or not, then stakeholder support may be that much more forthcoming. If the local population can see that there are benefits both in the short term even from a failed bid then they may be more supportive. It is important not to lose sight of the overall goal however, and so there must also be a strong case for the benefits that will be gained during and post the event in the longer term. Torino did not expect to win its bid to stage the 2006 Winter Olympics and the IOC needed to spend time with the city in order for it to more fully consider constructing facilities that would be of long-term sporting benefit in the city (Felli, 2002). Torino's objectives would appear to have changed since the bid was won.

Though difficult to evaluate, there is also political impact and benefit that may be gained from bidding for the right event. This can also be used to develop business links and demonstrate a commitment to staging sports events that may bear well for future political and trade profile. There have no doubt been other Olympic candidates that have prepared their bids and not thought

	Previous bidding history
Havana	2008 1st round elimination
Istanbul	4th 2008, 5th 2000
Leipzig	Nil
London	Hosted 1908 and 1948 Games
Madrid	2nd 1972
Moscow	Hosted 1980 Games, 2nd 1976
New York	Nil
Paris	Hosted 1900 and 1924 Games, 3rd 2008, 2nd 1992
Rio de Janeiro	Nil

Adapted from GamesBids.com (2003).

Table 7.2

2012 Olympics bidding cities: indicating previous Olympic hosting and bidding history

that they would ever be successful. A bid for 2012 by Havana can at least be part of a wider strategy for the development of tourism in particular and possibly the lobbying for the lifting of US embargos (they also bid for 2008).

Summary

The bidding process is becoming increasingly more important as sports events become catalysts for wider strategies. Whilst this is a relatively recent phenomena, it is nevertheless one that has also become quite sophisticated for some events. The comprehensive model provided by the IOC and the bidding for Olympic Games is one that can provide important guidelines for those parties that want to bid for other sports events. There are many event owners that do not require such a sophisticated bid and yet with competition becoming more intense, bid teams could do worse than follow such a detailed approach.

Key factors in the winning of bids include the management of and communication with stakeholders, in particular with the local community. There are cases and research to propose that without the support of a local community a bid will not win. For the IOC it is a required measurement via survey methods and is also a key factor for the recruitment of volunteers, sponsors and media interest, all of which are important if the bid is to be won. An analysis of the political risk, the recruitment of key management including leadership, and knowledge of the competition and the bidding process are also all considered vital factors.

Bidding can be an expensive strategy, even if the objectives are wider set and involve tourism and facility development over the long term. The cost implications need careful consideration at this stage of the event planning process. One strategy is to write-off any costs for a failed bid. Alternatively, and from a strategic standpoint it is also possible to identify positive outcomes from failed bids. There may be long-term legacies that can be gained. If costs are high and yet it is still possible to achieve benefits, then it is more likely that the bid will receive support from stakeholders. The longer-term benefit of stadia, tourism or social benefits may exceed the costs. Additionally, it seems likely that previous experience of bidding for an event is a key factor in formulating a better bid next time, and so a long-term strategy, of possibly several bids, can also be cost effective if the event is eventually won.

Questions

Visit the London and New York 2012 Olympic bid web sites at www.london2012.com and www.nyc2012.com:

1 Compare and contrast their efforts in attempting to win local support for their respective bids.

2 What key elements would you consider as important considerations for each city in their preparation of their respective bids?

3 What might either city gain in the longer term from their bid
despite failing to win the right to host the 2012 Olympics?

References

Allen, J., O'Toole, W., McDonnell, I. and Harris, R. (2002). *Festival and Special Event Management*, 2nd edition. Queensland, Australia, John Wiley & Sons, Chapter 5.

Arup (2002). *London Olympics 2012 Costs and Benefits: Summary.* In association with Insignia Richard Ellis, 21 May 2002. www.olympics.org/library/boa (accessed 11 November 2002).

Department of Environment (1993). *The Stadium Legacy, in The British Olympic Bid: Manchester 2000.* Manchester, Department of Environment, Section 12, Vol. 2.

Department of the Environment and Heritage (2003). *Why the Green Games?* 19 September. Australian Government. www.deh.gov.au/events/greengames/whygreen (accessed 15 December 2003).

Emery, P. (2001). Bidding to host a major sports event: strategic investment or complete lottery. In Gratton, C. and Henry, I. (Eds), *Sport in the City: The Role of Sport in Economic and Social Regeneration.* London, Routledge, Chapter 7.

Felli, G. (2002). Transfer of Knowledge (TOK): A games manage-ment tool. A paper delivered at the *IOC-UIA Conference: Architecture and International Sporting Events*, Olympic Museum, Lausanne. June 2002, IOC.

FINA (2003). www.fina.org/feds_bids (accessed 14 December 2003).

GamesBids.com (2003). www.gamesbids.com/english/past (accessed 12 December).

Getz, D. (1997). *Event Management and Event Tourism.* New York, Cognizant, Chapter 4.

Graham, S., Neirotti, L. and Goldblatt, J. (2001). *The Ultimate Guide to Sports Marketing*, 2nd edition. New York, McGraw-Hill, Chapter 12.

Gratton, C. and Taylor, P. (2000). *Economics of Sport and Recreation.* London, Spon Press, Chapter 10.

Harris, C. and Bagnato, A. (2003). *Valley is Super Bowl Favorite.* The Arizona Republic, 30 October. www.azcentral.com (accessed 14 December 2003).

IOC (2002). *Manual for Candidate Cities for the Games of the XXIX Olympiad 2008. Part 2.2 Model Candidature File.* 13 February. www.olympic.org/uk/utilities/reports/level_2uk (accessed 15 December 2003).

IOC (2003). *Candidature Acceptance Procedure: Games of the XXX Olympiad 2012.* 20 February 2003. Lausanne, IOC.

Kronos (1997). *The Economic Impact of Sports Events Staged in Sheffield 1990–1997.* A report produced by Kronos for Destination

Sheffield, Sheffield City Council and Sheffield International Venues Ltd. Final report, December 1997.

London 2012 (2003). www.london2012.com/ London/Timeline_of_the_Bid (accessed 9 December).

Meisegeier, D. (1995). *Sydney Olympics and the Environment. Case No. 184, The TED Case Studies Online Journal.* www.american.edu/TED/SYDNEY (accessed 15 December 2003).

NYC2012 (2003a). www.nyc2012.com/team.sec6.sub1 (accessed 9 December).

NYC2012 (2003b). www.nyc2012.com/news.20021028.1 (accessed 12 December).

SOCOG (2001). www.gamesinfo.com.au/postgames/en/pg000329 (accessed 12 September 2003).

Spencer, D. (2003). *Canada Awarded 2006 World Junior Championship.* 18 September. Canoe.com www.slamsports.com (accessed 14 December 2003).

Sports Tricker (2003). *Arizona to Host 2008 Super Bowl.* 30 October. Sports Tricker Enterprises. www.clari.net/qs.se/webnews (accessed 14 December 2003).

Thoma, J. and Chalip, L. (1996). *Sport Governance in the Global Community.* Morgantown, WV., Fitness Information Technology, Chapter 6.

USA Track & Field (2003). www.usatf.org/groups/event Directors/bids/openBids (accessed 14 December 2003).

Weber Shandwick (2003). www.webershandwick.co.uk/imia/content.cfm (accessed 14 December 2003).

Event implementation

After studying this chapter, you should be able to:

- identify the implementation planning and execution requirements for sports events.

- understand the requirement to align implementation planning and the execution of the event to long-term objectives.

- understand the importance of preparing for a successful event closedown, handover, after-use and long-term event evaluation.

Introduction

The next two stages in the event planning process occur after the decision to go ahead with the event. Collectively these two stages involve the implementation of the event. The first involves the pre-planning of all that is required to produce the event where the aim is clearly to deliver an event at the time and on the day required. The second stage is the execution of the event itself, that being the management of all that has been planned. Both of these stages are discussed in detail in this chapter with the intention of highlighting the processes that are required rather than being a definitive production list.

Whilst it is the period that lasts from the decision to go ahead and the closing of an event that is the theme of this chapter, the focus will be on how important it is to strategically identify these areas at an earlier stage in the planning process. The processes to be discussed are required whatever the scale of the event. Whilst the level of complexity and quantity may differ, the same kind of organization, planning, division of responsibility and careful attention to detail is required as much for the local sports event as it is for the major event (Hall, 1997). This chapter is therefore concerned with the processes that are applicable for all scales of event rather than with a detailed checklist approach. The chapter will conclude by identifying all that needs to be implemented during this period for the achievement of long-term requirements, principally by discussing the needs for after-use and of after-users during implementation planning and the implementation of the event itself.

Event implementation

Having made the decision to go ahead with the event, the planning that is required becomes very specific and complex. Initially there is the planning of all that is required for the production of the event and then there is the execution of the event itself. The focus here is not just to identify how these two stages are managed in real time, but also how and why it is strategically important to have considered the areas at the concept formulation and feasibility stages of the event planning process.

Implementation planning

The duration of this stage of the planning process can vary greatly. An Olympic host city gets to know it has won its bid 7 years ahead whilst fixture lists for major professional sports leagues can be available up to 3 months before kick-off. Annual events of all sizes are often scheduled more than 12 months ahead and yet there are those that have shorter lead-times particularly those that are rescheduled or relocated. The nature of the planning of an event, whatever the lead-time and whether there are existing models from previous events to follow or not, can become extremely complex.

The process here is concerned with everything that is required to successfully execute the event. This requires special management skills. The event, whatever its timescale, is transient, with a start and finish. It is a project and it requires project management.

At this stage an event manager needs to be able to draw on organizational skills, manage personnel, negotiate (sometimes barter), relate to different publics, read a balance sheet, be a role model and often get his or her hands dirty. Above all it is the ability to multi-task effectively and efficiently that is prevalent here. It is a complicated requirement that becomes more sophisticated as the event gets larger and therefore requires systems and methodology to ensure effective management. Project management methodology is wholly appropriate for the task (Allen et al., 2002; Emery, 2001). Emery suggests that sports event management is a subset of project management and is bounded by three key factors: external pressures, organizational politics and personal objectives. The complexity of the task may be explained by further evaluating the relationships that have to be managed. For example, as the numbers of people and resources grow so does the requirement for new relationships. The event management project can be further complicated by the requirement for long planning periods.

The successful management of an event project therefore requires a system that will manage the assessment of what has to be done, by whom and when, and plan it in sufficient time so that the execution of the project is as a result of the planning that has gone before. The event management process proposed by Allen et al. (2002) forms the basis for the six-step process below.

Step 1: Scope of work • • •

An assessment of the amount of work that is required. This is not such an easy first step, as it will be modified at each of the next five steps. The process must therefore be iterative.

Step 2: Work breakdown • • •

The categories and sub-categories involved in an event need to be identified and broken down into manageable units. The following serve as a general list of typical areas and provide a guideline on the time lines involved in their planning. Key issues for long-term planning are discussed where appropriate.

Personnel

Staffing

Managers, crew, stewards and security staff are required for event management teams and depending upon the scale of the event there will be different points at which they will be recruited. In bidding for the Olympics the New York 2012 Olympic Bid Organization (NYC2012) and London 2012 bid teams started recruiting in 2003. The latter appointed Barbara Cassani, the former chief executive of budget airline, go on the 20 June 2003 as Chairperson. She is an American by birth but is an example of an organization appointing who they believe is the best person for the job.

The appointment of managers is key for all the decisions concerning the implementation of the event and most events start with the appointment of the leadership. Barbara Cassani was appointed prior to any other members of the current team but she was quickly involved in the selection of a Chief Executive, Chief Operations and Marketing Officers.

In creating an event the creator can remain in control and appoint key personnel as and when required once the decision to go ahead has been made. In the case of New York's bid for the 2012 Olympics, the idea of bidding was first conceived and is still led by Daniel Doctoroff, who is the Deputy Mayor of the city. He first had the idea in the late 1990s and it was inspired out of his role in leading New York's Economic Development and Rebuilding efforts (NYC2012, 2003). He also oversees the city's physical and economic response to the events of 11 September 2001 including co-ordinating with other city agencies and the federal government. His appointment in strategically leading the New York bid secured the enthusiasm of a creator as well as harnessed the efforts of an event bid that has incorporated long-term redevelopment plans and legacies.

In a top-down process, managers are appointed into position. Which positions are filled is dependent upon the remainder of the breakdown of the work that follows. This process begins post the decision to go ahead with the event but if there is a bid involved then the process starts at the point after a decision has been made to bid.

Once a senior management structure is in place further decisions concerning the implementation planning of the event can take place and so there are two key components of this process:

1 Senior management needs to be appointed as soon as possible in order for planning to continue effectively.
2 An event leader has to be put in place first.

One further factor here is that it is essential that there is a clear line of management that has one and only one leader. Leadership is a discipline for discussion elsewhere but for the effective project management of sports events, one clearly identified leader is necessary. The management of an event needs to be integrated, flexible and dynamic (Hall, 1997) and whilst it requires clear management procedures, management decision-making needs to be responsive and effective and when decisions are required from the strategic apex they are better from one leader. Emery's (2001) research showed that this was an important factor for the bidding process and most major events have made the appointment of their figurehead their first task. This includes NYC2012 and London 2012.

Volunteers

Hall (1997) indicates that one of the key management problems to be addressed is the dependence of events on the support of both the local community and volunteers. The latter are in fact dependent on the former. Management sophistication may depend on the size of the community in which the event is hosted which will in turn affect the numbers of volunteers that are able to assist the event. It is clear that at major events the need for volunteers is large. The 2002 Commonwealth Games recruited approximately 13 000 local volunteers from the surrounds of Manchester. Salt Lake City provided up to 30 000 for the 2002 Winter Olympics and Sydney had up to 62 000 (47 000 for the Olympics and 15 000 for the Paralympics), which is claimed as the largest gathering of volunteers at one time, in one place, in Australia's history (Brettell, 2001). The implications are that this is an area that requires considerable planning and also costing. Whilst they are volunteers there are still costs for recruiting processes, uniforms, food, transport, etc. (Graham et al., 2001). The partnership with agencies in training is also an educational component that requires planning. The 2002 Commonwealth Games intended there to be educational benefits for those that volunteered and provided senior appointees to receive certificated training. The Pre-Volunteer Programme and Passport 2002 was set up by the North West 2002 Single Regeneration Board in order to engage people in local communities and was intended as being of social importance in the longer term (Manchester City Council, 2003).

Officials

Many sports officials that are recruited to work at sports events are also volunteers. During the summer there are numbers of just such people working at UK athletics track and field meetings as lane and pit judges. Whether they are paid or not, their recruitment can be made easier via association with the appropriate governing bodies and for that there may be long lead and planning times involved.

Stakeholders

Customers

Customers, whether they are purchasers of tickets, hospitality, sponsorship, advertising or merchandising, they have the potential to spend with the event again. With care and attention they may remain loyal for the long term. The key is customer relationship marketing (CRM) where the customer's lifetime asset value to the event is considered over the long term. This is dealt with in other appropriate chapters but this process continues throughout the planning and implementation of the event.

The entertainment of customers is part of this process because it is the meeting of these fundamental needs that will help with their adoption. Therefore, the show element of the sports event is critical. Not necessarily dancing and pom-poms, but customer orientated provision according to needs for presentation for example. A tight production that runs seamlessly, can show due respect for the customer and should impress them. So what is achieved here, at these stages in the short term, is key for the long-term retention of that customer.

Partners and associate partners

Whether they are funding partners, media partners, providers of key supply to the event or governing bodies, there are the same long-term relationships to be nurtured during these stages of planning and implementation.

Participants

The performers that form the focus for the spectacle are clearly an important element in the provision of customer value. As can be seen above, this is of critical importance over the long term too. Therefore the choice, if there is one, of who participates is key. If you are identifying potential key teams or individuals who will add value to your event then they need to be nurtured as key customers themselves. What is also critical is that participatory-based events rely on not only these customers re-entering or taking part next time, but also on them being intrinsically a part of everyone else's event experience. Their singular enjoyment will impact on the enjoyment of others and so on. The show in which they participate also needs to give value. As in all of these cases researching the customers needs provides a way of identifying what kind of show is required.

In the short term the following categories are important for the successful implementation of the event.

- Communication
  - Technology
  - Management communication
  - Audio visual

- Venues and equipment
  - Venue agreement and contract
  - Procurement and purchasing
  - Sponsors supplies

- Franchises
- Show effects
- Access and security

- Legal and licensing
  - Public entertainment
  - Alcohol
  - Governing body affiliation and sanction

- Financial control

- Marketing
  - Ticket sales
  - Corporate sales
  - Communications
  - Public relations
  - Design
  - Sponsorship
  - Merchandising
  - Space sales
  - Advertising sales
  - Print and publication

- Services
  - Transportation
  - Accommodation
  - Food and beverage
  - Merchandising and licensing
  - Environmental consultancy
  - Sanitation

- Health and safety
  - Risk assessment
  - Certification
  - Emergency procedure
  - Crisis management process

Step 3: Task analysis • • •

Each of these categories and sub-categories need to be resourced and so they are assessed for costs, time, staff and supplies. The total costs amount to the total cost of implementing the event. This is an area of planning that must be initiated at the feasibility stage of the event planning process, then continuously monitored and then finalized here. The total budget amounts should not change at this stage, only the allocations between cost centres, and within the budget, should be adapted.

Step 4: Scheduling • • •

Each of the tasks is then put on a time line and deadlines in particular are identified. See Figure 8.1.

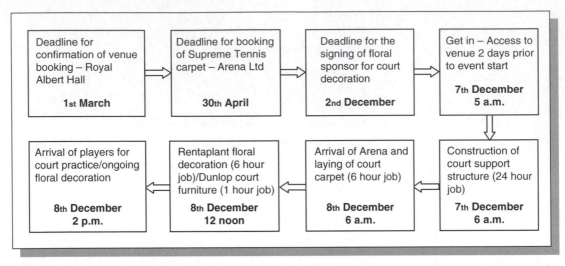

Figure 8.1 A critical path – Nabisco Masters Doubles. A network depicting one sets of tasks – the construction of the tennis court for the event at the Royal Albert Hall. The critical path is represented by the arrow and shows that the failure of one task impacts on those that follow

Step 5: Critical path • • •

The timelines for each task are then combined into a Gantt chart. This then provides a backbone for production planning and a calendar with deadlines for all tasks.

This chart can become overcrowded and so in order to identify clashing schedules tasks need to be prioritized. Network analysis can be applied to determine a critical path; the determination of deadlines by which tasks have to be achieved in order for each to be achieved sequentially. The analysis graphically portrays how many tasks the non-arrival of equipment or the late delivery of merchandise will impact on. This enables the event manager to identify the consequences of not achieving each task. All aspects involved in the production of the event are integrated into the critical path.

Allen et al. (2002) note that the use of Gantt charts and critical paths can become very complex and as a result difficult to use for major international sports events. Even the use of software packages have their limitations as the event increases in size.

Step 6: Responsibility allocation • • •

Each task becomes an area of responsibility and depending on the event there need to be organizational structures created with appropriate lines of communication so that these areas can be managed in harmony rather than in isolation. Each manager may run their own micro critical path but if they do it must feed directly into an event master copy. It is essential that the event director controls and maintains the event master copy and that all subsequent and micro paths derive out of it in order to avoid misinformation and dysfunctional operations. Graham et al. (2001) cite Frank Supovitz, of the National Hockey League (NHL), and his use of individual production schedules that are incorporated into a master plan document in order to create synergy.

This event project management process is further developed in Event management 8.1. World Championship Tennis Inc in its management of the Nabisco Masters Doubles in the 1980s operated with task sheets that were manually derived from a master time lined plan on a year round basis. No software was available for aiding this process at that time. O'Toole and Mikolaitis (2002) maintain that the fluid nature of events means that milestones, completions of key tasks, are changeable and therefore recalculations of all linked tasks are constantly necessary. This is still unfortunately not achievable with most current project management software. O'Toole and Mikolaitis (2002) recommend the use of Gantt chart and other software for unlinked task approaches.

Event management 8.1

Event project management

Successful sports events require an effective project management approach. This applies to all scales of event but the more complex an event the more critical this becomes. The scope of the task is determined with the early identification of the work that is involved, whom it will be done by and when. The project management process should include:

Work breakdown structures (WBS)

Segmentation: A breakdown of the event and the areas of operational work required, first of all by category, such as finance, marketing and human resources (HR).

Task analysis: A further breakdown of these categories into smaller work units that can be managed as tasks.

Assignment

Any tasks that have predecessors (tasks which have to be completed first) have to be identified and placed in the appropriate sequence.

Each task can then be allocated a timeline or an estimated completion time (ECT). The most commonly used types of ECT for events are latest start and latest finish times because they are absolute deadlines.

The tasks are then allocated for implementation in work packages either internally or externally to the organization, to appropriate personnel/teams.

For larger events increased delegation will be required. More discretion can then be applied by individuals for the completion of the schedules in their own task areas.

Schedules

These consist of a calendar covering the whole of the event life cycle.

All key tasks are entered into the calendar at the appropriate times and dates that they are to be completed by. This necessitates the consideration of all tasks in relation to each other, including the sequences involved, so that they can be moved forward or backward for action accordingly.

This can also be put into a graphical display (Gantt chart). By prioritizing the tasks and applying network analysis, the necessity for punctuality can be highlighted. This analysis identifies the critical path for the event by also highlighting all those tasks that absolutely have to be completed on time for the event to be a success.

143

Implementation of the event

The next stage in the event planning process is the implementation of the event itself. This is the execution of an event that has been effectively planned so that it is delivered as intended, at the time, and on the day required; the effective management of the project. The above categories covered in the implementation planning now become the areas for execution and so the process of breaking down the work and allocating responsibility also come into play.

Long-term planning

There are two long-term requirements that require consideration both in the implementation planning and the implementation of the event. These concern the after-use of any facilities and equipment, and any ongoing projects and strategies that are intended as legacies and long-term benefits of the event.

After-use and after-users

The continued involvement of after-users in these two stages is important if there is to be a smooth event closedown, handover of facilities, legacies and any long-term evaluation.

The organizations that will own and/or manage any physical facilities after the event has closed need to be involved with their design. It is the organization that have to make the long-term objectives work and so their' contribution to architectural design, systems for conservation and choice of sports equipment may be key for that process. There may be contention in agendas, for example, a design for changing facilities for the event that does not work for after-use. The determination of the specific objectives and decisions at the feasibility stage are critical if this is to be avoided.

A professional sports organization such as Manchester City Football Club needed to satisfy itself that it was going to be able to use the facilities at the new City of Manchester Stadium before signing the contract for their long-term use after the Commonwealth Games was over. The consultation that transpired included discussions on the removal of a temporary stand and the year-long preparation of seating; seating capacity being key to the economic proposal that was put to them by Manchester City Council in the first place.

After-users include tourism agencies, local authority leisure departments, commercial sports management organizations, educational institutions, sports clubs and societies, as well as professional sports organizations.

The handover of facilities, either back to original users or to new after-users, needs to be a smooth transition and in a form that presents as few problems as possible. This requires the planning of time and resources in order to return or turn a facility into the amenity that was originally agreed. This might be a stadium or an open field and might involve various time spans to be achieved. For example, returning a farmers field from the orienteering course, it temporarily was, will involve the removal of overlay, litter and possibly regeneration of some kind. The preparation of the City of Manchester Stadium took 1 year to get right. There is one unwritten rule here. Provide what was agreed should be provided. Clearly there needs to be after or previous users put in place and this is a requirement that needs to be implemented prior to the decision to go ahead with the event if risks are not to be taken.

Long-term evaluation

The objectives form the benchmarks for all evaluation and so the question might arise why is there a need for the handing over of this task at all. Up until now there has been little long-term evaluation done of sports events. The International Olympic Committee (IOC) has only established Transfer of Olympic Knowledge (TOK) in the last 12 months and only just as recently claimed that it was considering evaluation systems that would consider the legacies and benefits of events 10 years after they have closed (Felli, 2002). Sydney has maintained that it will evaluate the success, or not, of Sydney Olympic Park, in the long term (Adby, 2002).

As these processes start to develop there are the following key considerations:

1 At what stages does evaluation need to be implemented and in what form so objectives can be measured?

2 Who is responsible for ensuring that the evaluation is implemented? Who is the evaluation for?

3 How will the evaluation be used to contribute to the success of the facility, benefit, etc?

However, these questions are not for this stage of the planning process. They need to asked and answered and incorporated into the objectives and in that way they can become intrinsic to the event and a part of the alignment process that is ongoing throughout the event.

The important task during implementation is to ensure that those that are to carry out evaluation are supplied with all the necessary information they require when it is available and easy to pass on. When the event ends, this information increasingly becomes obscure as the IOC identified in realizing the need for TOK.

Summary

The implementation planning stage of the event planning process provides the time for the preparation of everything that needs to be implemented for the execution of the event. The short-term focus, for the delivery of an event on time, can become a preoccupation and at the expense of long-term objectives. In particular the after-use and the after-users need to be considered as well as the process by which evaluation can be conducted in order to assess long-term objectives. A longer-term perspective in the management of key relationships, such as those with stakeholders in particular, is a more strategic route to long-term success. Depending upon the scale of the event this process can become sophisticated.

A project management approach is required in order to make a success of this managerial challenge. The use of a process that assesses the scope of the work involved and then breaks it down so that responsibility can be allocated is useful provided that it is implemented correctly and at the right timing. Some of the task needs to be undertaken earlier, at the feasibility stage, so that budgets can be set. Provided there is flexibility and the managerial system can respond to forces of change, this process should enable the implementation planning and then the implementation of the event to be undertaken.

Questions

1 Select a sports event and draw up a list of categories and subcategories that cover the extent of the short-term implementation planning required. What potential issues do you see in the planning for the implementation of this event?

2 Select a sports event. Research, identify and evaluate the timing necessary for the recruitment of key personnel.

3 Select a sports event where sports facilities have been built and were intended as long-term legacies. Research, identify and evaluate the use of consultation with after-users during the planning process.

References

Adby, R. (2002). *Email Questionnaire: Director General*, Olympic Co-Ordination Authority 2000 Olympics. 9 July.

Allen, J., O'Toole, W., McDonnell, I. and Harris, R. (2002). *Festival and Special Event Management*, 2nd edition. Queensland, Australia, John Wiley & Sons, Chapter 13.

Brettell, D. (2001). *The Sydney Olympic and Paralympic Games Volunteer Program*, a Keynote Presentation by the Manager for Venue Staffing and Volunteers for the Sydney Organizing

Committee for the Olympic Games. Singapore, July 2001. www. e-volunteerism.com/quarterly/01fall/brettell2a (accessed 9 December 2003).

Emery, P. (2001). Bidding to Host a Major Sports Event: Strategic Investment or Complete Lottery. In: Gratton, C. and Henry, P. (Eds), *Sport in the city: The role of sport in Economic and Social Regeneration*. London, Routledge, Chapter 7.

Felli, G. (2002). Transfer of Knowledge (TOK): A games management tool. A paper delivered at the *IOC-UIA Conference: Architecture & International Sporting Events*. Olympic Museum, Lausanne. June 2002. IOC.

Graham, S., Neirotti, L. and Goldblatt, J. (2001). *The Ultimate Guide to Sports Marketing*, 2nd edition. New York, McGraw-Hill, Chapter 3.

Hall, C. (1997). *Hallmark Tourist Events: Impacts, Management And Planning*. Chichester, Wiley, Chapter 6.

Manchester City Council (2003). *The Impact of the Manchester 2002 Commonwealth Games*. www.manchester.gov.uk/corporate/ games/impact (accessed 25 February 2003).

NYC2012 (2003). www.nyc2012.com/team.sec6.sub1 (accessed 9 December).

O'Toole, W. and Mikolaitis, P. (2002). *Corporate Events Project Management*. New York, John Wiley & Sons, Chapter 2.

Marketing planning and implementation

After studying this chapter, you should be able to:

- understand the role of marketing planning and its importance in the sports events industry.

- identify the marketing planning process and explain its logical progression.

- understand the importance of internal and external analyses and their contribution to the formulation of marketing objectives and strategies.

- identify the strategic choices and the role of the marketing mix in achieving a market position.

- understand the importance of organization, implementation and control in marketing planning.

Introduction

In an industry that consists of many substitutable products, it is becoming increasingly difficult to provide a product that is of better value. The common practice of marketing to mass audiences is not an approach that will bear rewards in such operating domains and so the need for marketing planning in the industry, where customers can be more finely targeted, is becoming more critical. The focus of this chapter is on the marketing planning process and how an event can be systematically positioned into a carefully targeted market for better results.

Marketing planning

The marketing planning process can be implemented in a step-by-step progression that consists of seven stages.

The marketing planning process

1 *Organizational goals*

2 *Internal and external analyses*: Including an internal marketing audit, situational analysis using strengths, weaknesses, external opportunities and threats (SWOT) technique to identify internal SWOT, customer and competition analyses.

3 *Marketing goals*: The setting of objectives for the marketing plan.

4 *Market selection*: Segmentation of potential markets and selection of target markets.

5 *Marketing strategy*: The identification of strategic thrust and the specific marketing mix required for each target market in order to achieve competitive advantage.

6 *Organization and implementation*: The scheduling, co-ordination and execution of the marketing plan.

7 *Control*: The creation of controls and performance indicators to enable correction throughout the implementation of the marketing plan, post-event measurement and comparison of results against the objectives set with feedback for future performance.

This traditional approach to marketing planning (Boone and Kurtz, 2002; Jobber, 1998; Kotler, 2000) involves a process that begins with a strategic approach and the consideration of organizational goals. As with every business activity, there needs to be an alignment with the mission statement and corporate objectives. The next step is also from a strategic perspective whereby an analysis of the organization as a whole is required in order to assess internal and external environments. The perspective then becomes more specifically market driven with the tactical planning required for the marketing plan. This consists of devising market and product strategies, and the tactics and tools by which these strategies will succeed. The outcome is a marketing plan that then needs to be implemented, controlled and evaluated. Each step of this process will now be considered in more detail.

Organizational and event goals

The plan needs to be aligned with the overall goals for the organization, specifically its mission statement and corporate objectives. If an organization is involved in a range of business activities then it will set objectives for each of these. Therefore, if it is running an event it will set specific event objectives that will be aligned with its overall goals. For example, a municipal authority that puts on a sports event has objectives that cover wide issues and the event will be used to try and achieve some of those in part. In some cases an organization is created just to implement the event and so the organizational goals and event goals can become one and the same. For example, a host city organizing body for a major event, Manchester 2002 Ltd for the Commonwealth Games, Beijing Organising Committee for the 2008 Olympic Games (BOCOG) and New York 2012 Olympic Bid Organization (NYC2012), the team putting the bid together for New York and the 2012 Olympic Games. Before the more specific marketing goals can be identified and the event marketing plan created however, important information is needed in order to progress.

Internal and external analyses

The life blood of all planning is information and therefore the marketing plan requires the collection, storage and analysis of information, and from a variety of sources. This can become a complex and sophisticated activity and the more this is the case the more an organization needs to consider how this information can be managed. Firstly, there are both external and internal sources of information. Secondly, various levels of research can be required in order that a comprehensive understanding of the current organizational situation, competitor activity and customer groups is attained. A Marketing Information System (MkIS) needs to be developed however simple the collection and storage of the information is.

An MkIS consists of four elements of data (Jobber, 1998). The first is internal data that is continuously available, such as meetings' minutes, ticket sales data and transactions. The second is internal ad hoc data such as from a one-off analysis of the success of particular sales promotions, such as ticket discount schemes. The third and fourth elements are derived externally, via environmental scanning and market research. The former consists of an analysis of the political, economical, sociological and technological (PEST) forces that may bear influence on the organization. A continuous scanning or monitoring of the environment is required so that a response to change in these key areas can be more effectively implemented. How will new laws for employment, licensing or local bye laws on the use of pyrotechnics affect the event? How will an unstable market with increasing inflation affect the take-up of tickets? Will sponsorship revenue become scarce? Will the non-take-up of the latest telesales technology leave the event at a disadvantage? Will the hosting of a multi-cultural event positively or negatively affect local issues? These are all key questions to consider for the event. Market research is also an essential element so that there is not a total reliance upon inward looking internal analysis on performance (Jobber, 1998). Conducting customer's surveys and interviews can reveal insightful data that if at odds with internal analysis will serve to enlighten managers.

The beauty of events is that there is a captive audience and on-site surveys become a relatively easy tool to use. The use of the mystery shopper method can also be useful at events where there are opportunities to interact with customers and employees to get more depth in information (Mullin et al., 2000). Research of non-attendees is also an important resource in order to determine why potential audience do not attend and possibly change the product accordingly.

Research will also aid competitor analysis with intelligence on the competition and their marketing activities.

The two key factors in MkIS are that the data needs to be collected and stored in such a way that it can be efficiently analysed and then distributed to those that can then use it effectively. It is a management tool that at the end of the day aids managers in taking decisions. Wood (2004) has developed a model for events organizations that highlights the wide range of sources an organization can tap for information (see Event management 9.1).

It can be seen from the model that information needs to be stored in order for it to be usefully analysed. It revolves around stakeholders and the storage of information pertaining to each so that a greater understanding of them can be achieved. An MkIS provides an effective tool for the collection, storage and dissemination of three key areas that event managers need to gain a full understanding of.

The first key area of information involves the organization looking further into its operating domain for knowledge about its competitors. A competitor analysis will reveal further opportunities and threats in the market. A market-driven approach, such as that of Porter (1980), looks at a number of areas of where competition derives. For an event his five forces model of market competition would involve an analysis of the extent of the rivalry with other events, the strength of the market to withstand and repel new events, the extent to which substitute entertainment may offer opportunities for purchase switching, and the bargaining power

Event management 9.1

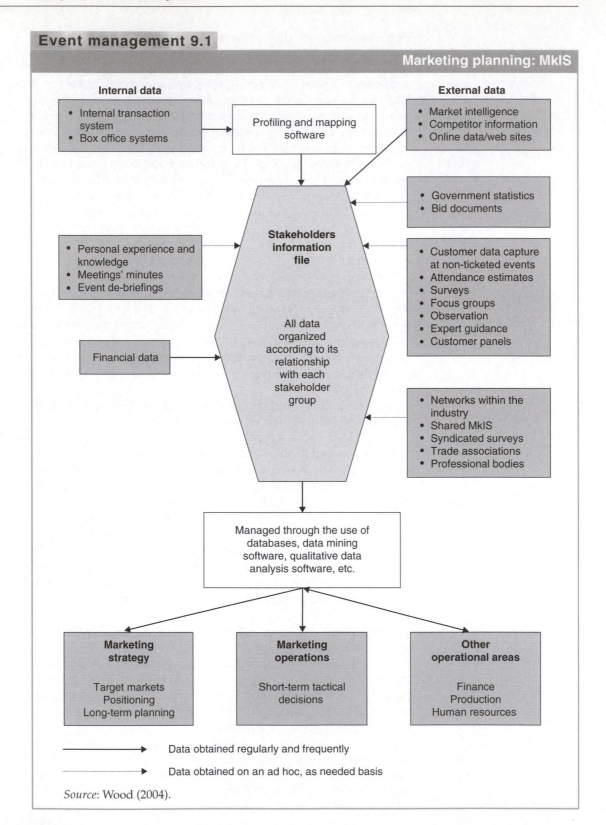

Source: Wood (2004).

held with suppliers and buyers because they can affect the events costs and prices and its ability to compete. Direct competition from other sports events is not often an issue due to the creation of non-competing sporting calendars produced by co-operating sports bodies. For many events it is the threat that is imposed by substitutes that causes the most concern. When, an event is broadcast by the media, an important consideration is clearly to what extent that coverage is having an impact on attendance at the event. Indirect competition from the likes of other forms of entertainment, such as cinema, theatre, family unit leisure, including quality and vacation time, is also an important competitive aspect. For example, the whole fixture list in football in the UK is adjusted when the pre-holidays weekend falls just prior to 25 December. Losing the fan to Christmas shopping is a major concern for clubs.

Research into the competitions' current marketing activity is key knowledge. Information on market share and profit are important, but it is their market position and the marketing mix that achieved them that share that are perhaps most important. The research needs to focus on the strategies that have been used and critically what strategies are to be used by the competition. This may require personal enquiry but can also be available via the regular storing of market reports, media and web site activity.

The second key area of information required by the organization concerns an understanding of its existing and potential customers. This provides data that can be used to help the segmentation process and select target markets in the fourth stage.

The third area is a gaining of an understanding of the current situation of an organization: an internal analysis. There are two ways in which this can be achieved. Firstly, via an internal audit of marketing activities that produces information on marketing strategies, resources used and an evaluation of the results produced. The aim is to assess what is required to be changed, this therefore necessitates a review of current activity but may also require a historical perspective in order that an understanding of how current activities are evolved.

Secondly, an assessment of the events SWOT that exist in its operating environment is required. This can serve to summarize all the areas that are assessed. An SWOT analysis can be a dynamic tool for the event manager but in practice is not used to its full potential. Piercy (2000) suggests that it is commonly used to look at issues that are too wide, for example considering the organization or the event as a whole, and that organizations also conduct the analysis with an inward look at themselves using their own opinion. As a result an analysis can produce a set of criteria that are unfocused and lack sufficient depth to be of use. In conducting the analysis it is important to avoid the ambiguous and unqualified values and statements that are often made when identifying the four SWOT criteria. For example, it is insufficient to list the 'strong image' of the event as a strength and equally too vague to describe the event as one with a weakness if it remains in its present venue. For these criteria to be of use in the analysis, each one needs to be broken down until the analysis produces criteria that can underpin management decision-making.

Piercy (2000) maintains that in order for an SWOT analysis to be most productive there are three key factors. The first is that there needs to be a focus on a particular issue, product or service. For an event this may mean focusing on one particular marketing strategy, one product line or an aspect of the sales process. In this way the analysis can highlight the need to gain further knowledge and can thus achieve a greater level of detail than analysing the wider picture. A series of analyses can then be pieced together to form a comprehensive and more global picture. The second concerns the perspective from which the criteria are viewed. What an organization thinks about its own strengths has no bearing if its customers think otherwise and so the analysis also needs to be conducted from the customers' perspective in order for it to be customer focused. The analysis must consider the way in which customers view a particular phenomenon and how and why they consider strengths to be strengths and weaknesses to be weaknesses. A comprehensive analysis in this case might further breakdown the strength of the events image and identify that a high percentage of customers are loyal and have had repeat ticket purchase for each of the last four events. Meanwhile, remaining in the existing venue may be a weakness because customer accessibility is difficult due to a lack of local transport provision and there being insufficient car parking facilities. Whilst Piercy (2000) proposes that the external factors of opportunity and threat in the environment should be viewed from the manager's perspective and thus focus on what is attractive or unattractive for the event, it is maintained here that it should also be a consideration that is also conducted with customer perspective. In order to attain competitive advantage any analysis of the external opportunities and threats will always need to be conducted with customer focus.

Another common failing is not using the analysis as a management tool. The third key factor for SWOT analysis is that it has the capacity to aid managers in deciding on strategy and is a means to an end if used correctly. Piercy (2000) proposes a matching process and the use of conversion strategies as the next stage of the analysis. Having brainstormed and analysed a full set of SWOT criteria, each criteria can be given an arbitrary score and ranked according to their importance. In this way strengths may be later matched with opportunities but only if there is a suitable fit. Those opportunities that have no match are those that provide event managers with future challenges. The idea then is to convert the higher scoring weaknesses and threats into strengths and opportunities, respectively. This is not always an easy task and therefore many may remain unmatched, they then act as important limitations and considerations for future business practice.

Marketing goals

The next step is to provide a focus for the plan. It is important to consider corporate goals so that the marketing objectives can be aligned with them. Marketing goals can differ from event to event in the way they are evaluated and measured, but will usually involve the maximization of one or more of the following: market share, the building of the event brand equity, target market awareness for the event, target market awareness for event sponsors and partners, and their association with the event, event product sales, sponsor and partner product sales, and leads and sales for other and repeat events. The key factor here is specifying the extent, level and quality that is to be attained and within what time frame. By how much does market share and awareness have to grow, for example? Brand equity could be measured via increased repeat sales as loyalty to the product is considered to be a sign of developing the brand (Jobber, 1998).

Once the goals have been identified the selection of target markets can be implemented.

Market selection

Segmentation

The business of sports events marketing involves two types of target market. For all events there are participants and for many events there are audiences, spectators and fans too. One of the unique factors of the sports events industry is that both participants and audience are an intrinsic part of the event product. Your fellow runner or the person next to you in the bleachers is contributing to your event experience. With this in mind the marketer now needs to address the most efficient and effective methods of reaching these customers.

Knowledge of customer behaviour allows an organization to identify groups of customers with similar and generic attributes that make it possible for the organization to then be more efficient and effective in reaching them with its communications. This part of the planning process is called segmentation. A method of dividing large mass markets into smaller identifiable segments where the constituents have similar profiles of needs that may be attractive to the organization.

Knowledge sought can include psychographics as well as geographic and demographic information of customers. The aim of segmentation is to identify customer's needs that can be better met by the organization than by its competitors. Jobber (1998) maintains that there are three criteria for achieving this differential.

The basis of segmentation • • •

- *Behavioural segmentation*: What benefits do they seek, how and where do they buy, are they brand switchers, are they heavy or light users and do they view the product favourably?

- *Psychographic segmentation*: What kind of lifestyle do they lead? For instance, are they trendsetters, followers, conservative or sophisticated? What kinds of personalities do they have? Are they extrovert or introvert, aggressive or submissive?

- *Profile segmentation*: Age, gender, stage of life cycle, social class, level of education, income level and residential location.

Often a combination of these forms of segmentation can provide a comprehensive approach to reveal a level of knowledge that will enable event managers to ascertain a number of segments of larger markets that are attractive propositions for its products. For example, the sales of daytime off-peak tickets to appropriate target markets would require demographic information on jobs and personal addresses, and psychographic information on interests and availability at those times. The filling of off-peak seats for the Nabisco Masters Doubles at the Royal Albert Hall in London has included the targeting of teachers from schools for blind children based in the home counties of England that were perhaps available for school trips. The offering was made all the more attractive with the help of a partner that provided commentary via personal headphones.

Whilst segments are a division of the mass, niches are an even smaller part of the whole. Segments in definition are still quite large and prone to competition whereas niches can offer single corporate opportunities to provide a small part of a market with a product that will not realize great profits, but can offer market share domination and be more than sufficient for a smaller organization. The identification of a niche follows the same segmentation process. Within the sports events industry there have been examples of organizations creating niches for themselves. In the 1980s, the development of a version of racquetball for the UK was led by two separate manufacturers, Dunlop and Slazenger (they merged at a later date). The game was called racketball (name differentiation) and a slower ball was produced so that it could be used for longer rallies on a squash court. There were very few racquetball courts in the UK other than on US Air Force Bases and they had restricted access. There were no sales of racquetball equipment in the UK at the time and in order to create a market this niche was therefore organization led. The British Racketball Association was formed and is still organizing events and thriving today.

Going through a process of segmentation however, does not guarantee success. There are four key criteria that must be met according to Boone and Kurtz (2002):

1 The market segment needs to offer measurable buying power and size.

2 The market segment needs to be able to offer an appropriate level of profit.

3 The organization needs to be capable of providing the segment with a suitable offering and distributing it at an appropriate price.

4 The organization's marketing must be capable of effectively promoting and serving that segment.

Mullin et al. (2000) encapsulates these four criteria into three measures of identification, accessibility and responsiveness. Dunlop and Slazenger, with their stocks of rackets (acquired from the US), were ready to extend into a UK market but they still had to identify a group of customers that they could access and serve effectively. They identified a mainly female focus on those that could or already did access squash clubs during off-peak hours. The clubs welcomed the idea and worked with the companies to market a game that was easier to learn than squash and utilized courts that were easier and cheaper to book. The clubs developed the offering with the introduction of crèche facilities and the result was that an attractive, and sizeable market, were successfully accessed by two co-operating manufacturers.

The process for segmentation below has been adapted from Boone and Kurtz's (2002) model.

The segmentation process • • •

1 *Identify the basis of segmentation*: This consists of the choice of the basis for segmentation basis and the selection of promising segments. Having predefined a segment, a selection can then be made based purely on observation or via market-driven research.

2 *Develop a segment profile*: Further understanding of the customers in each segment, so that similarities and differences can be identified between segments. The aim is to arrive at typical customers for each segment.

3 *Forecast the potential*: Identify market potential for each segment.

4 *Forecast market share*: Forecasting a probable market share by considering the competitions' market positions and by designing marketing strategies to reach each segment. The latter will identify necessary resources and weigh up the costs versus benefits.

Target market selection

There are several approaches for target market selection. A mass-market approach entails selecting large numbers where the appeal can still be successful with little wastage of marketing effort. An event that has appeal to people of all ages, either single or part of family units might successfully select a mass market.

However, many events will require differentiated target markets that are more finely selected via the segmentation process. An example here would be an extreme sports event where the appeal is not so widespread. Further differentiation again can be provided via a niche approach. For example, an event that runs during off-peak hours will be required to be more focused still, perhaps in the form of local schools or women's groups.

Following segmentation an organization can make an informed decision about which segments it wants to target.

The marketing strategy

The marketing planning process has so far identified options for a choice of markets. The internal and external analyses offers strategic options and the segmentation process identifies which markets are target options. Having selected target markets and marketing goals, the task then is to determine which strategies will achieve these objectives.

There are four generic approaches for market strategic thrust but two of these are options that are mainly applicable for an organization and its long-term direction. A short-term strategy will consist of penetrating the market in order to increase event sales or more realistically improve it each time in order to increase sales via a product development strategy. Over the longer term an organization might adopt a strategy of developing new products for either the same target markets with new sports events or indeed move into other sports or entertainment sectors and offer events to those new markets.

The process of segmentation, identification of the events target markets, followed by the selection of market strategies, enables the organization to position the offering in the market so that it meets the target customers' needs by differentiating the offering from that of the competition. The differentiation is achieved via a carefully selected marketing mix. The mix consists of the four Ps: Product, Price, Place and Promotion. The determination of the marketing mix for an event involves creating a product that satisfies customers needs, at an acceptable price, in appropriate places so that it can be promoted in such a way that the whole offering becomes known, attractive and bought by target customers. It is described as a mix because the components of four Ps cannot be considered in isolation. The event concept may be undesirable at a certain ticket price but more accessible at a certain venue for example, and so the identification of the options for each component and selecting the right mix is the task here.

Events are services and are therefore subject to the consideration of a separate service sector marketing mix. In addition to the four Ps, three further components should be considered, those of people, physical nature and processes (Jobber, 1998). Events are run, participated in and attended by people and it is therefore important to consider the personal interactions that take place in the nature of the product. For example, how the audience themselves play a big part in the entertainment at the event or how the stewards and ticket sales staff also play a part in the customer experience. The physical nature of the event and its ambience, in particular, has a large bearing on customer enjoyment and is therefore a consideration in the design of the product and the choice of venue. The processes involved in servicing the customer, such as those of getting tickets and accessing the venue, are critical aspects of the determination of the mix of four Ps. It can be seen that there is not necessarily any need to add these components to the four Ps when they can be seen as key components of the product.

Product

The questions asked here are who, what, why and when? Sports event products include the event as a whole and also all the various components that it can consist of. These include goods, services, information and media, places, people and also ideas (Mullin et al., 2000; Pitts and Stotlar, 2002). Prior to the first modern Olympics in Athens in 1896 for example, Baron Pierre de Coubertin pursued and championed an idea that was to become an outstanding sports product. He realized this concept with the formation of the International Olympic Committee (IOC) in Paris in 1894 (BOC, 2003).

The venue and the facilities are an important choice for event organizers. They have to match budget requirements in numbers of seats, suites and commercial opportunities in order to provide and project revenues. From a customers perspective they have to be accessible, suitably aesthetic and properly equipped. As customer expectation increases the quality and number of facilities may also need to increase. For example, more bars, car parking and plasma screens that add to customer value, but are of course all at an extra cost to the event. The weather too is an important consideration when selecting a venue. Whilst it is not controllable, contingency plans for unsuitable weather are.

The timing of the event is also an inherent part of the product. Consider the ways in which seasons are a considerable part of the offering in UK sport. For instance, a Cricket Test at Lords, rowing at Henley, or strawberries and cream at Wimbledon. Winter sports depend on their time of year too.

The product also encapsulates the service that is received via ticket sales processes, purchasing food and merchandise, and at the turnstile. The participants also play a key role. One thousand runners or two guest star players are an intrinsic part of the offering. The audience too are providers of entertainment as well as the ones who are entertained. The atmosphere they create is as important as the game on the court, pitch, wicket or ballpark. Empty seats are not just poor for financial reasons.

Price

Pricing strategies are determined in relation to other parts of the marketing mix. A simple meeting of costs and then profit is probably required for example, and a cost-plus strategy might appeal. However, a customer focus is required and so the identification of the customer's idea of what good value is needed in order to determine if a profitable event is achievable. Other considerations include competitive position and if low prices are necessary or whether differentiation is an option. In order to get customers to adopt and become loyal for example, a discount or free entry strategy may be required. The customer adoption process involves making potential customers aware of the product, giving them information, letting them evaluate the product, then getting them to trial and finally commit to it and therefore become loyal. Empty seats are a concern and so a seat-filling contingency plan may be a required practice just prior to the event. Attracting groups that have been previously identified as target segments can serve several purposes. One is to sell tickets at discounted prices. The second is to fill the seats even without potential revenue so that the atmosphere at the event is not diminished. The third is that these customers do get to trial the product and may adopt it in the future.

Prices have to be determined according to target market requirements. There are those events that can apply a high market price due to having a highly valued product, customers that have the ability to pay, low competition and high demand. This is skimming strategy and the major events around the world are testament to this, for example the Football Association (FA) Cup Final, the Ryder Cup, the Six Nations Rugby, the Stanley Cup, the Super Bowl and the World Series of Baseball where there is more demand than supply. It is not only the end of season finales that attract such demand. Regular season match sell-outs at the majority of National Football League (NFL) games are currently a feature throughout the season. Events that are not in this position are constrained by different conditions. Where the only alternative is to offer low prices, there is little differential from those offerings of the competition and therefore competition is high. New events to the market may also apply low prices as part of a penetration strategy and in order to launch the event and get a foothold in the market. In this case they may also have strategies to make revenue elsewhere through merchandising or catering for example. An organization with a number of events in its portfolio may even launch one event as a loss leader, with low prices, with the objective of making more revenue in the future.

Ticket pricing strategies are determined and balanced in relation to what commercial assets the event has available. For example, there are three levels of corporate hospitality at London's Royal Albert Hall in its Grand Tier, Loggia and Upper Tier levels of corporate boxes and prices can be set accordingly. Most venues have similar differentiations.

Season tickets and corporate box tickets are traditional ways of packaging tickets and achieving revenue in advance. These can be ways of also offering cheaper tickets in advance. Shank (1999) suggests that in the late 1990s Personal Seat Licences (PSLs) were a new way of getting similar revenue, whereby a fan could buy a seat(s) for a number of years. With such schemes sports clubs can achieve large amounts of revenue to contribute to the building of new facilities. In fact, debenture schemes have been around for some time. The All England Lawn Tennis Club (AELTC) first used them at the Wimbledon Lawn Tennis Championships in 1920 to raise revenue in order to develop its grounds (AELTC, 2003).

Place

The question here is where is the product best marketed in order to successfully reach target markets? This would not only include distribution channels that might include the venue, but also include the use of web sites and ticket agencies.

Promotions

The promotions component of the marketing mix is also commonly referred to as the communications mix. This consists of the use of tools, such as advertising, personal selling, direct marketing, sales promotion and public relations, to promote and communicate to the events target customers. This element of the marketing mix is no more important than the other three elements (product, place and price) but for event communications to be effective there is a need for constant innovation and an effective use of a greater range of techniques. The next chapter is therefore devoted to the production of effective communications.

It can be seen that the building of the marketing strategy so far has resulted in an offering that is customer focused. Now it may be necessary to consider what is best strategically for the organization and how it should manage the event over the long term. Whilst this text is ostensibly concerned with the management of events and not the management of organizations it is worth considering the organizational decisions that affect events. The event organization has four generic options if it has an event product that it manages over a number of times. It can (a) build the market for more sales, market share or profit, (b) hold the market position and maintain current sales, (c) harvest the event by allowing sales to decrease but maximize profits via a decreasing of costs or (d) divest the event by dropping it or selling it off to others. Adoption of any one of these strategies clearly has an effect on the way in which any one event is managed.

Not all event organizations seek the same strategic objectives of course. Many soccer clubs, in divisions one, two and three of the Football League in England are sufficiently financially challenged to have no desires to have more success on the field of play. They are content to remain in their division. The prospect of promotion to the division above might entail expensive improvements to facilities and would almost certainly lead to greater payments to players and a less stable financial position. This raises the question of events that are focused on playing sport for sports sake. Even in amateur sports the need for events to financially break even is usually a necessity and so the management of sports events in a business fashion becomes a requirement too. The dilemma that currently exists in European professional football is that the business requirements of football clubs are often in stark contrast to the requirements of fans. This is also an issue in US professional sports. Shareholders demand a return on their investment and when that requires the sale of a player it becomes point of resentment for the fan. The appeasing of disgruntled fans alongside the selling of players is developing into a required art for many clubs.

The development of loyal fans is a particular concern in the sports industry and a common focus for sports marketers in the management of the same event over a number of years or on a regular basis. Kelley et al. (1999) produced a case study for the fan adoption plan that was implemented by the Carolina Hurricanes. In a major relocation of the franchise from its home in Hartford, Connecticut (where they were the Hartford Whalers) to Raleigh in Carolina the marketing planning required in order to make the transition as effective as possible involved a customer adoption strategy. Raleigh had previously never seen ice hockey in any of its stadia and so the adoption process not only involved making potential fans aware of the club but also had to educate them in to how entertaining the NFL and the game could be. The planning focused on the long-term adoption of a brand new fan base. The Hurricanes used several tactics to grow their relationship with new fans. This included taking their players out into the community and building on the history and tradition of the Whalers at first and on the exciting experience of ice hockey. Milne and McDonald (1999) maintain that in order to increase fan identification with the team and grow loyalty, there are four key factors. Fans need to be able to access the team and players, community relations need to be developed, team history needs to be a part of communications and there needs to be creation of opportunities for fans to affiliate with the club so that they can feel a part of it. Mark Cuban, in taking over at the Dallas Mavericks, focused on making the fans a part of the club to great effect. The National Basketball Association (NBA) team managed to create loyalty in its fans, despite its losing seasons, by listening to what the fans thought about how they should be entertained. This is used as case study in the next chapter.

Despite there being growth in the use of market research by event organizations, research as a management tool is still much under utilized. The NBA in the US is active in supporting its member teams and regularly works with the Mavericks and all other teams in supplying research support. Some of their support research is extensive and in 2002 they presented findings to the league teams on research into what motivates season ticket holders to renew. The location and cost of the tickets were found to be the first two most important factors for customers when deciding on whether to renew. Good customer service was ranked third but the fourth placed reason was the attitude and behaviour of neighbouring fans, in other words their effect on the event experience (Cann, 2003). Team performance was only considered to be the fifth most important factor and arena cleanliness and in-game entertainment were sixth and seventh, respectively. It was important for NBA teams to note that only one of these factors was effectively out of their control (team results) and that they could act on the others in order to improve customer relations. It is worth noting that the NBA's research team consists of four staff members and yet it is the largest such team in US major leagues. Whilst the results of their work would appear to be important, the use of research generally is not so widespread in the sports event industry.

Organization and implementation

If an event is fully committed to its marketing strategy the organizational structure will reflect that. There will be people and roles that are organized in order to get the strategy done. Unfortunately, it is far too common that event managers, particularly in smaller organizations, are required to wear several hats and adopt a number of different roles.

If the marketing planning process is to be followed at all then it needs to be a reflection of the customer's needs and that the offering is produced and positioned so that it satisfies both those and the organizations own needs. The aim is to provide an offering that is customer driven and for it to be an offering that is better than that offered by the competition. A critical part then is how this is organized and whether the organization structures itself to facilitate the plan it has devised. The problems with the distribution of tickets for the 2000 Olympics in Sydney demonstrate this. Thamnopoulos and Gargalianos (2002) produced a case study on the problems that arose at the Sydney 2000 Olympics Games over ticketing arrangements. The problems revolved around the failure to sell and distribute tickets early enough. Following the research, the recommendations included proposals for organizational structure that would assist in providing better services. These included a structure that could manage operational and customer handling processes effectively when sales activity is at its greatest. Whilst the marketing of tickets for the event was effective in creating the demand, the processing of the sales was not. This was a case of not anticipating the structure required for the handling of the whole of the operation and the treating of one element of the planning in isolation from the other. The research indicated the need for more effective communication between ticket operations and ticket marketing divisions and in particular for necessary reports of work in progress to all parties.

There are many events that do not have marketing departments and may only have one titled role even remotely concerned with marketing. This is not necessarily a hardship. The marketing effort needs to be organization wide with all members playing a part. For example, the creation of a marketing mix requires those from financial, sales, distribution and operations areas of the organization to be involved in order to be effective. However, it is critical that there are people, systems and processes in place that reflect the requirements of such integrated marketing strategies.

Another critical factor is the need for a macro- as well as a micro-perspective. The strategic thrust is a key element of the marketing plan and for that to be implemented the organizational structure needs to be flexible enough to allow managers to get above the nitty-gritty of the operational tactics of the event and have time to focus on the longer term. This has ramifications for control as well. In order to keep control a manager needs to have the time in order to be able to perform that role.

The employment of key figures and professionals into instrumental roles is also a key factor. For example, the Los Angeles hosting of the 1984 Olympics was better off for the abilities of Peter Ueberroth and a $225 million financial surplus (Toohey and Veal, 2000). The appointment of ex-player and general sports icon Wayne Gretzky as Executive Director of Team Canada was a move by Hockey Canada that the organizers of the 2004 World Cup of Hockey (ice hockey) will hope to use to their advantage (*Sports Business Daily*, 2003).

Control

This is the stage where alignment with objectives is evaluated and maintained. As the plan is implemented it may be possible to correct and realign if objectives are not being met. The only way this will be possible however is if the objectives are measurable. Improving ticket revenue on last year can only become measurable if there are targets, either with an absolute figure or percentage growth. It can be seen now why the planning process, with its logical development of assessing markets and customer needs prior to the setting of objectives, is an effective approach.

Evaluation needs to be undertaken at the end of the process as well as continually throughout it. The success and failure of future marketing activities determined via post-event evaluation and reporting, documentation and archiving are of paramount importance in the event industry. Many sports events are an annual occurrence and whether the event management team is the same the following year or not, there is a need for accurate detailed feedback the next time the event is being managed.

Summary

Successful marketing planning requires a methodical process that addresses the needs of customers whilst satisfying corporate objectives. In order to do that target markets need to be identified and an appropriate event delivered; an event that provides those markets with an offering that makes them choose and stay loyal. To be successful the event needs to position itself so that it is not only attractive to the customer but it is more attractive than any alternatives. The marketing planning process featured in this chapter is a logical progression through the stages that will achieve that objective.

Recommended by generic and sports marketing theory, the process begins strategically with corporate goals and an assessment of the organizations internal and external environments so that one, the process is aligned to the organizations mission and objectives, and two, that the process begins with an assessment of resources and opportunities in order to provide a relevant base for marketing. The process then becomes more specific with the development of marketing goals and a tactical plan consisting of the marketing mix that will achieve the desired market position. As with most management mechanisms the plan has to be implemented and so the process leads into the development of suitable organizational structures and systems that can effectively achieve that so that it can be controlled and evaluated against the objectives set.

Questions

1 Evaluate the importance of the marketing planning undertaken by the Carolina Hurricanes, identifying where possible the progression of the marketing planning process.

2 Select an event and identify the types of internal and external information that is critical for marketing planning.

3 Select two similar events and evaluate how they position themselves in the market by identifying, comparing and contrasting the key features of their marketing mixes.

4 Identify one event manager who in your opinion has played a critical role at a specific event. Evaluate that role and the contribution made.

References

AELTC (2003). www.wimbledon.org/en_GB/about/debentures/debentures_history (accessed 4 November 2003).

BOC (2003). www.olympics.org.uk/olympicmovement/modern-history.asp (accessed 4 November 2003).

Boone, L. and Kurtz, D. (2002). *Contemporary Marketing*. London, Thomson Learning.

Cann, J. (2003). *NBA Season Ticket Holder Research*. Presentation by Senior manager, NBA Research and Analysis. NBA Store, 5th Avenue, New York. 2 December 2003.

Jobber, D. (1998). *Principals and Practice of Marketing*, 2nd edition. London, McGraw-Hill, Chapter 8.

Kelley, S., Hoffman, K. and Carter, S. (1999). Franchise relocation and sport introduction: a sports marketing case study of the Carolina Hurricanes fan adoption plan. *Journal of Services Marketing*. **13**(6), 469–480. MCB University Press.

Kotler, P. (2000). *Marketing Management; The Millennium Edition*. London, Prentice-Hall.

Milne, G. and McDonald, M. (1999). *Sport Marketing: Managing the Exchange Process*. London, Jones and Bartlett Publishers, Chapter 2.

Mullin, B., Hardy, S. and Sutton, W. (2000). Human kinetics. In *Sport Marketing*, 2nd edition. Champaign, Il, Chapter 6.

Piercy, N. (2000). *Market-led Strategic Change: Transforming the Process of Going to Market*. Oxford, Butterworth-Heinemann.

Pitts, G. and Stotlar, D. (2002). *Fundamentals of Sport Marketing*, 2nd edition. Morgantown, Fitness Information Technology Inc., Chapter 8.

Porter, M. (1980). *Competitive Strategy: Techniques for Analysing Industries and Competitors*. New York, The Free Press.

Shank, M. (1999). *Sports Marketing: A Strategic Perspective*. London, Prentice-Hall International (UK).

Sports Business Daily (2003). *Hockey Canada Set to Bring Wayne Gretzky Back into the Fold for World Cup*. 4 November. Morning Buzz. Street and Smith. www.sportsbusinessdaily.com (accessed 4 November 2003).

Thamnopoulos, Y. and Gargalianos, D. (2002). Ticketing of large scales events: the case of Sydney 2000 Olympic Games. *Facilities*, Vol. 20, No. 1/2. MCB University Press. pp. 22–33.

Toohey, K. and Veal, A. (2000). *The Olympic Games: A Social Science Perspective*. Sydney, CABI, Chapter 10.

Wood, E. (2004). A strategic approach for the use of sponsorship in the events industry: In search of a return on investment. In Yeoman, I., Robertson, M., Ali-Knight, J., McMahon-Beattie, U. and Drummond, S. (Eds). *Festival and Events Management: An International Arts and Cultural Perspective*. Oxford, Butterworth-Heinemann.

Innovative communications

After studying this chapter, you should be able to:

- understand the role and value of innovative marketing communications in sports events marketing planning.

- understand the process required for achieving successful Integrated Marketing Communications.

- identify the marketing communications tools that are available for sports events.

Introduction

In an increasingly competitive industry where traditional media and methods are no longer as effective, sports event managers need to be using innovative marketing communication methods. This chapter aims to build up a conceptual framework for the development, planning and implementation of the methods that are now required for successful communication. The focus will be on the importance of effectively integrating a range of tools and techniques to communicate the event.

The chapter is in two sections. The first provides an approach for Integrated Marketing Communications (IMC) planning and its application for the sports events industry. The second provides the event manager with a communications toolbox and considers how personal, interactive and mass media methods are incorporated into an overall strategy for a sports event.

Section 1: Integrated Marketing Communications

In a highly creative industry it is disappointing to see so many events. Consider their customers as a mass market not use segmentation techniques to determine more focused target markets. It is also disappointing to see them use such a limited range of tools. The approach has too often been one of managing promotional choices in isolation from the management of the event.

How many events are undertaking research in an analysis of stakeholders and using that research in decisions about the product, its prices and the choice of venue, and how it is then promoted? For major events the importance of communications is generally acknowledged. In the bidding process for example, it is clear that recent host cities have used extensive communications techniques to win local stakeholder support. Take the Sydney 2000 Olympics and the Manchester 2002 Commonwealth Games and their use of web sites and volunteer programmes for instance. The London and New York 2012 bids are following suit. The London site encourages interaction by inviting messages of support. Outside of major events though the use of innovative communications is scarce. When it comes to communications decisions the aim is to reach as many people as possible with only a mass-market mentality. However, due to limited budgets, the selection of mass media advertising for communication purposes is not even an option when the high costs make it an inefficient solution for a return on a promotional investment. A more effective approach should consider the use of focused and highly targeted communications methods.

An IMC approach considers the customer first and then co-ordinates all communications for a unified organization wide message. This necessitates agreement and ownership of consistent communications by the organization as a whole. The traditional approach to marketing has been to create separate functions for sales, mass media activity, public relations (PR) and promotions. An IMC approach integrates all aspects of the communications mix into one effort by devising a customer-focused programme that provides synergy between all activities.

The choice of which media to use, mass, personal or interactive, must effectively meet the communications objectives set but must also be an efficient use of resources and so it is a costs versus benefits exercise. During the implementation of the strategy the results need to be monitored so that an alignment with objectives can be maintained.

This approach has developed as a consequence of less confidence in mass media advertising and an increasing reliance on targeted communications. As a result there is more effort in measuring the success of communications and return on investment. Schultz et al. (1996) maintain that the reason for the development of IMC is that marketing communications will be the only way organizations will be able to sustain competitive advantage in increasingly undifferentiated product markets.

The purpose of communication is to create a message that inspires positive action from stakeholders. According to Lavidge and Steiner (1961) this response process moves through a number of effects, a hierarchy of effects. Their model was based on the earlier AIDA (attention, interest, desire and action) theory (Strong, 1925) (see Figure 10.1).

Other models follow a similar process although not all conclude with purchase. Engel et al. (1994) move through five stages of exposure, attention, comprehension, acceptance and then retention as the final action allowing for the fact that the communications process is a tool for reaching all stakeholders of an organization not just its customers.

The psychology behind communication is to create as clear a message as possible, one that can avoid the noise and clutter of the market and become memorable. If it is memorable it may therefore become persuasive and change or enhance opinion (Wells et al., 1995). Vaughn (1980) proposes a useful four-stage view of how communication works. The information feed has to aid learning, appeal with a sense of value and may require relatively long copy such as through the use of e-mail, advertisements,

Figure 10.1
Hierarchy of effects
Adapted from Lavidge
and Steiner (1961).

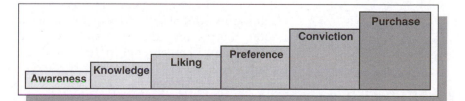

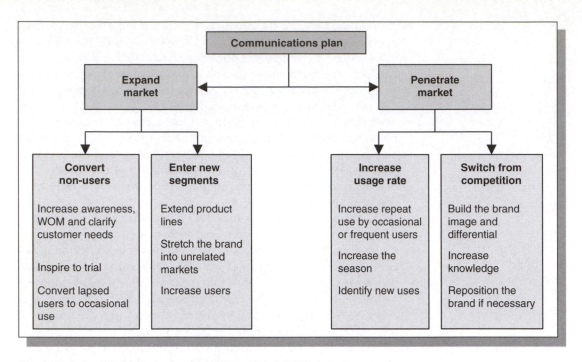

Figure 10.2 Communications plan. Adapted from Michell (1988).

brochures and leaflets. To be affective at stage two there needs to be a reinforcement of the message that inspires a desire to trial and sample which may be best achieved by image building through the use of large space media, such as billboards and posters. For it to become habit forming in stage three the aim is to increase use by further reinforcement via such small space media such as sound bites and point of sale (POS). Finally, self-satisfaction is achieved when the appeal is socially pleasing and communications reflect that life-style possible through large space media, print and POS. The task is to identify which target stakeholder should receive which message by what communication method.

There are two choices of focus for this task, to expand or penetrate a market and for each focus there are criteria that can guide an event manager in determining the communications plan. This is represented in Figure 10.2.

Once a focus has been identified the integrated message can be designed. The key is to manage this across the whole of the marketing mix so that whilst there are communications to be made about the product, the price and the place, they are not made in isolation. They are considered together and then the appropriate methods are used to impart these communications. This is represented in Figure 10.3. Other models are proposed by Fill (2002), and Pickton and Broderick (2001).

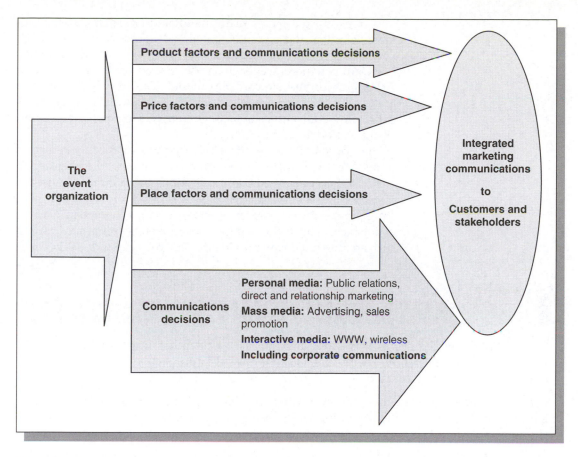

Figure 10.3 The IMC process.

There are barriers to the successful implementation of an IMC approach not least the issue of how it is managed. If external agencies are contracted to supply any part of the process then their integration becomes an issue when their objectives are different from those of the organization. An advertising agency with creative design at the top of its agenda might well be at odds with the client that requires measurable increased awareness or sales not an industry award. The involvement of staff and them buying into the organizations objectives is critical where face-to-face customer relations are concerned but is not always an easy managerial task. It is also an internal task to manage the transition of those that lean towards the traditional segregation of the communications components, in particular those that manage PR in isolation.

For the current events market there are new and exciting targets. The emergence of the extreme sports market has allowed marketers to reach the teenagers and 20-somethings that are active in skateboarding, surfing, windsurfing, parascending and more.

This has attracted mainstream manufacturers such as Nike and Mars as well as those brands that already produce for these markets, opening up new opportunities for event communications. The Ogilvy marketing agency has developed what it refers to as a 360 degrees brand stewardship model. The idea is that it integrates all forms of communications for clients and has had success in reaching these anti-establishment markets for such mainstream clients as Kodak (Ogilvy, 2003).

The approach can be effectively applied in the marketing of teams. Mark Cuban, the owner of the Dallas Mavericks basketball club, used an integrated communications programme to turn the franchise into a very successful NBA outfit. From a position of a struggling team and poor fan attendance it took more than just a lot of dollars to achieve the change. The innovatory techniques used in such an integrated way provide the case in Case study 10.1.

Case study 10.1

Innovative communications: The Dallas Mavericks

Since taking over the Dallas Mavericks in 2000, Mark Cuban has transformed the fortunes of this NBA franchise. The results, via an innovative approach, include taking half empty home match nights to sell-outs in every game in the 2002–2003 season.

Cuban set out to change the relationship the club had with its fans to enhance their experience. The focus in the beginning was to sell a brand that may or may not win on the court but would provide great entertainment.

He started with the organizations culture. He himself got involved at the front end of sales, tripled the number of sales staff and trained them to focus on the entertainment not the on-court results. At one point there was a target of 100 telesales calls per member of staff per day and those staff that could not buy into this culture were asked to leave. Bar codes were put onto tickets so that they could be tracked and when corporate customers did not attend for a number of games they received a phone call to ask if there was any dissatisfaction. The intention was to ensure that every seat was occupied, not just for revenue, but because full stadiums can provide a great atmosphere.

Cuban himself still sits in the stands with the fans as opposed to in a corporate area. He socializes with them after the games. His personal e-mail address is also still advertised all around the arena and he consistently responds to his e-mail. He encourages suggestions for improvement and importantly is seen to act on them. In 2001 a fan corresponded that the 24-second shot clock was difficult to see. At that time such clocks were intended for player information but the Mavericks installed a three-sided clock only weeks after that e-mail. Since then most NBA teams have equipped themselves with similar equipment.

The rebuilding of the brand clearly involved the fans. Cuban made the fans, the night, and the experience into the brand itself. The adding of a now extremely successful team on court has only enhanced that. When Cuban took over their record was nine wins and 23 losses. In 2003 the team reach its third play-offs in a row and added the Western Conference title.

Cuban also hired key personnel who embraced this 'have-a-go' approach to marketing. The investment has been there to support errors along the way but ideas are tried and fans are made a part of that progress.

Maverick by name, maverick by nature!

Sources: Caplan (2003); McConnell and Huba (2003).

Section 2: Communications toolkit

The basic media forms of personal media, interactive media and mass media will be discussed in this section. PR can be both personal and mass media and is therefore discussed first.

Public relations

Whilst the use of PR techniques for successful communications is not without cost, they are nevertheless often a less expensive alternative to many of the others that exist in the event manager's armoury. They also carry the highest level of credibility. Consequently, they are arguably some of the most important.

PR has two roles. On the one hand it supports marketing activity in the form of promotions. On the other hand it is also the tool that disseminates non-promotional information to other target publics that are important to the organization. PR has a much wider role to play than to support the marketing push, it extends to managing communications with all those organizations, groups and individuals that are considered an important factor in the successful implementation of the event, otherwise known as target publics. These might involve communications concerned with the changing of opinion or provision of information that are targeted at local pressure groups, community leaders, financial institutions and event participants (see Figure 10.4). A target public is an

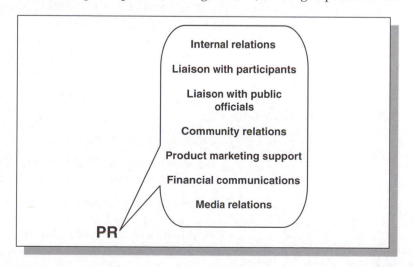

Figure 10.4
The role of PR

Internal relations

Liaison with participants

Liaison with public officials

Community relations

Product marketing support

Financial communications

Media relations

PR

individual or group that has sufficient influence to have bearing upon the success of an organization.

Whatever the nature of the communication, the targets need to be identified. This is achieved via a process of target analysis, the first stage of the process of PR communications. The analysis extends to the identification of all of the event's stakeholders and publics and the form of communication they should receive. At this point it is critical that these messages are an intrinsic part of the overall communications plan and certainly not in conflict with it. The result is a list of who should receive what communication. An event's publics could consist of any of the following:

- *Customers*: Ticket and corporate buyers.

- *Participants*: Competitors, celebrities, performers and acts.

- *Sponsors*: Fee paying and supply-in-kind.

- *Partners*: In organization, promotion and funding.

- *Financial providers*: Shareholders, investors and lenders.

- *Suppliers*: Event equipment, merchandise and service providers.

- *Staff*: Permanent, temporary, sub-contracted and voluntary.

- *Community*: Local operating environments and pressure groups.

For economic and efficiency reasons it may not be possible to reach all of these targets and so this analysis also requires scheduling, costing and then prioritizing. The result is a PR plan that is integrated into the event communications plan. Jefkins and Yadin (1998) follow a six-point process consisting of, appreciating the situation, defining objectives, defining publics, selection of media and techniques, budget planning and evaluation. They emphasize the importance of identifying corporate objectives and aligning PR accordingly. The following proposed seven-point process highlights this still further and acknowledges the need for corporate objectives to be identified at the beginning of the process so that the situational analysis can be aligned too.

The PR planning process

1 *Corporate mission and objectives*

2 *Situational analysis*: SWOT (Strengths, Weaknesses, Opportunities, Threats) analysis and an audit of current communications.

3 *PR objectives*: Alignment with the corporate mission and objectives and devised in accordance with the strengths and weaknesses of the event, and the external opportunities and threats.

4 *Strategy*: Identification of publics and choice of appropriate mass, personal or interactive media with prescribed measurement criteria.

5 *Implementation of plan*: Schedule the choices of media and specific mediums to be used with copy deadlines.

6 *Budget*: Cost out the schedule so that all communication activities have line costs.

7 *Evaluation*: Assess the effectiveness of the plan for costs versus benefits prior to execution and iteratively realign where necessary.

PR encompasses the task of creating media opportunities and so it is important to consider the relationship events have with the media. On the one hand there is the value of recruiting all-important media partners for the attraction of sponsors that is discussed in Chapter 11, and there is the creation of positive media exposure that is the focus here in this chapter.

Sports events are reported in or commented on by many media but the event has no control over that content. Whether the comment is negative or positive the media will air or write what they feel is appropriate for them, to meet their objectives and not the objectives of the event. Conversely, an event's overriding aim is to achieve positive coverage for the event without paying for the space or air-time it occupies. Ultimately it would be desirable for the media to take whatever the event gives it and then disseminate it as it was delivered, but that is seldom the practice. Editors will have the final decision and so the importance of forming positive relationships in media relations is critical. There may be any number of PR objectives to achieve. On the one hand there are the marketing objectives of supporting sales, possibly prior to the event, and also the wider communications that are needed internally with employees, with the community, and other target publics before, during or post the event, all of which are not necessarily attractive enough for the media. Consequently, strong relationships with key media and a range of innovative techniques and tools in order to evoke an attraction are important when trying to create the desired media exposure.

Media relationship building

The cliché of whom you know and not necessarily what you know might easily be applied to the area of media relations whereby having a strong relationship with media can be a key factor. The difficulty of course is getting started, particularly for those events that do not have sufficient power to attract almost any media attention. For new events the challenge is in creating newsworthy items as well as build up key relationships.

Maintaining the relationship once it is forged is easier but needs to be an ongoing task. As with most relationships it often takes giving something you do not want to give on one occasion so that you can have the favour returned on another. The feeding of the media, and the tabloid press in particular, is commonplace in football in the UK. Agents and clubs are prone to supplying reporters with stories that can often start the stories that in effect instigate the transfers of players and other business. The process needs to be handled with care. In 1996 Mars agreed a sponsorship with Team Scotland and its participation in Union European Football Association's (UEFA's) Euro '96. The story was leaked to the press before Mars had given an approval for communications but in an attempt to try and attract further sponsors. Mars took objection to the leak and the action, and relations became strained between team and the sponsor.

The recruiting of media partners is a method of forming a strong bond with particular media. Having an agreement with newspapers, local television and radio stations can provide the event with a package of promotional traffic pre-event. The media can also contribute to the event with free entertainment by broadcasting live and distributing products or merchandise. The event can gain more control over the media output in this way by agreeing activities in a contract, but there are dangers. For the smaller event guaranteed exposure is only to the events advantage but for larger events with greater profile there is the risk of alienating the media with whom there are no agreements.

Event PR techniques

The techniques that are at the event manager's disposal can be broadly categorized as follows:

- *Advertorials*: Paid for space but designed to read like editorial.
- *Feature articles*: One-off contributions or regular columns that can be by-lined by a representative of the event or by a journalist briefed by event management.
- *Advance articles*: An advance notification of the event using pictures, information and competitions.
- *Spokespeople and expertise*: Event managers creating a reputation for always having something to say and a strong opinion so that media will readily call when they want a reaction to a story. The key is to be available at any time and ensure key media know how to contact you quickly.
- *Results servicing*: For major events results there are mechanisms in place that will distribute scores, reports and league standings. For new events and events with a lesser profile there is more work to be done but results are of general interest to media particularly local media.

- *Reader offers and competitions*: One of the mechanics that has commonly been used in the events industry is the use of event tickets and hospitality, given to all range of media, printed publications, Internet, television and radio, for use in reader offers and/or competitions. The competition feature will include details of the event and ticket hotlines thus aiding pre-event sales. The exchange of tickets for editorial coverage is mutually agreeable as the media are seen to be providing a service if not extra value to their own customers.

Event PR tools

The tools that are available include leaflets, direct mail, newsletters both internally and externally to the organization, special events, sponsorship and the various methods of making personal contact. The hooks or mechanics highlighted above form the focus for the content and these tools are the means by which the target publics are physically contacted. As with most tools there are advantages and disadvantages depending on their point of use.

- *Leaflets*: The positives are that they are relatively low cost and may be distributed by hand, door to door or by dispenser. The negatives are that there is low retention of the information by readers and high wastage.

- *Direct mail*: They offer opportunities to personalize the communication and send it directly to homes and businesses. Events can send them when they want and by associating with organizations and using their database the event gains a friendly conduit for the transmitting of the communication. There is however a high cost attached to direct mail in that databases can be expensive as can mailing to large numbers. The mail may also be perceived as intrusive and wastage occurs as a result.

- *Newsletters*: This medium can provide an informal and credible communication and can involve and engage the reader. If they are not totally uncritical however they may not be perceived that credibly. They need to be carefully targeted for them to have effect.

- *Special events*: Events are tools in themselves of course and media launches are a common form of communication. They require targeted invitees and provide opportunities for social interaction that can be useful in reinforcing the communication. The downside is that they can be expensive and time consuming to organize. Events can also include exhibitions, conferences, seminars and public consultations. Major events use organized public debates as part of their communications activities in the lead up to bidding. In January 2003 the Greater London Authority organized a debate in conjunction with the Observer Newspaper, part of the Guardian Newspaper Group, at the Royal Institute of Architecture building in London to discuss the prospect of London bidding for the 2012 Olympics. Anyone was welcome to apply for a ticket and both supporters and non-supporters attended together with a full complement of all media.

- *Sponsorship*: Event managers might also select sponsorship as a means of communicating their event. The 2002 Commonwealth Games attached its image to a number of sports and cultural events in the 2 years prior to the event. The negatives are that there may be fees attached and further investment is required in order to make the sponsorship work.

- *Personal contact*: Such contact can take the form of face-to-face, by telephone or electronically. It can attain a very personal communication where there are opportunities to argue the case and overcome objections. It can offer opportunities for relationship building but can equally be seen as intrusive with costs that can be as high as they are time consuming.

PR innovation

The above generic PR techniques and tools are commonly used by sports events so where does the innovation come in? The key stage of the PR planning process above is the situational analysis. It is there that the events assets are evaluated and as each event is unique it is there where an advantage may be achieved in the attracting of media attention.

The categories of assets that are to be considered for the PR plan together form what is uniquely newsworthy for the event, the PR equity in the event. Figure 10.5 identifies the categories of participants, products, programme and partners. They form another set of invaluable 'P's. The equity lies in the interest attracted from the media and how they can become newsworthy entities. The innovation lies with the skills of event managers in maximizing the opportunity.

Product placement is not a new tool. However, the 2002 Commonwealth Games was used in a particularly innovative way on ITV television during the run-up and the games themselves. Coronation Street was at the time, and remains one of the UK's highest watched television programmes. The programme is set and filmed in Manchester. An adapted script saw one particular character develop a role as a game's volunteer and wearing an Asda provided and sponsored event volunteer tracksuit. Filming was also conducted at the City of Manchester Stadium.

Evaluation of PR

Traditional evaluation methods of PR for sports events typically include measuring frequency and size. Specific approaches will

---

PR equity

Participants

The teams and players, either individually or collectively, are unique to any one event at that particular time. Their celebrity, sporting prowess, sporting or other achievements and personality.

Examples
Taking one or numbers of players and using them as figure head(s) or spokespersons in the marketing communications plan. Specific activities might include interview features in the media, appearances at special events.

Products

The numbers, nature and availability of tickets, corporate hospitality, merchandise, whether free or priced.

Examples
Use of sold out, sold in record time, record number of sales, exclusive merchandise, limited free merchandise on purchase or attendance/participation.

Programme

Current perspective: The nature and prospect of the competition and entertainment on offer, player and team matches, its duration, rules used, technology used, calendar position, prices, competition with other offerings (direct and indirect competition), dignitaries and celebrity attending.

Examples
Sports records under threat, intriguing matches of key participants in prospect. Latest technology and new rules on trial, new dates, timings and ticket prices, head-to-head competition and reasons for competitive advantage.

Historical perspective: Previous programmes, competition and entertainment provided, records and achievements accomplished, data, facts and figures concerned with competition and event operations.

Examples
Sports records broken, great archive sporting performances, record numbers of champagne and strawberries served, largest number of stewards to ensure safety.

Partners

The sponsors, funding and supporting shareholders and stakeholders.

Examples
Credible sponsors make news when they are recruited and in their activities. Supporting partners may include local dignitaries, officials or celebrity. Responding to local pressure groups or the competition with comment.

Figure 10.5
PR equity

count up the numbers of opportunities to see, increasing or decreasing complaints and enquiries. There are also unfortunate uses of gains/losses in market share that can only be linked to PR campaigns, at the most indirectly. Assessing impact value is of use but the allocation of an arbitrary level of importance to each media is very subjective and a delicate decision.

One of the most common evaluation methods is by quantifying the value of the space/time achieved as if it were advertising. This involves counting up the column inches/centimetres and minutes of PR and calculating how much it would cost to purchase the same as bought space. There are two problems with this method. One is that only rate card cost may be applied as there are no actual negotiations going on and rate card prices are seldom paid in the industry. Secondly, the advertising is a paid for medium and PR is gained via third parties acceptance and so it is simply not possible to compare the two together. However, the use of Equivalent Advertising Costs (EAC) can be used to evaluate the frequency and quantity of PR over time. By tracking EAC it is at least possible to see by how much PR activity has increased or not.

In an industry that is increasingly looking for return on investment the surest methods of evaluation are by market research. The use of survey and interview methods is required in order to get usable evaluation of PR success. The issues are that it is expensive and as a result is not a common occurrence.

Personal media

Personal media marketing methods include the use of PR and direct marketing such as by mail, face-to-face or personal selling, catalogues, kiosks and telemarketing. Other methods that have direct response mechanisms can also be categorized here too and these would include advertising in all media, and home shopping television channels. Neither of which are currently that common in the sports events industry. Use of interactive methods such as web sites and wireless communications are dealt with separately but can also considered to be personal media.

The value of personal media is in the development of customer relationships to a point where they are loyal fans and will consistently return to an event. The Dallas Mavericks provide an example of a sports team attempting to build relationships with its customers where the stages of adoption are to progress non-fans to casual fans and then on to season ticket holders. There are two separate focuses for the management of customer relationships. The first is the corporate business-to-business relationship that is predominantly led by relationships between individuals and face-to-face marketing methods. The other involves the events target markets where the mass audiences are more difficult to get close to. Personal media marketing methods can be used to try and alleviate these difficulties.

Much is made of the differences between traditional transaction marketing and the new marketing approach of relationship-based marketing. Piercy (2000) highlights the key differences. He sees Customer Relationship Marketing (CRM) taking the perspective that total sales to a customer are viewed over the long term. The communication with a customer should be interactive to enable this to happen as opposed to focusing on a single transaction. Technological innovation and the development of new tools for communicating is making this approach much more achievable.

Direct marketing

Methods for marketing directly with the customer include by mail, e-mail, personal selling, catalogues, kiosks and telemarketing. The common thread with most of these methods is that they require the building of databases. This information comes directly from the Marketing Information System (MkIS) as discussed in Chapter 9.

Each method has advantages and disadvantages in marketing events as discussed here.

Direct and e-mail • • •

This involves the sending of highly targeted offers, announcements, reminders, in printed or electronic mode, to a specific address (Kotler, 2000). This is a common event marketing tool that clearly depends for its success on the quality of the database of addresses. Letters, leaflets, flyers, foldouts, audio tapes, videotapes, CDs and computer disks can all be sent out to a named recipient. This targeting capability is clearly an advantage and the capacity to test small numbers also offers efficiency. The ability for events to send out direct mail that is signed by a key figure is another advantage. In the US a letter from a major league owner is of value but in sending out e-mails the San Francisco 49ers have more success with players names on a recipients alert screen (Berridge, 2003). Mullin et al. (2000) maintains that direct mail can be more than just an offer and proposes the use of previous event success data, photos and thank-you quotes as ways of making the vehicle an attractive one.

There are two main disadvantages. Customer response can be as low as 2 per cent and therefore cost per thousand people reached can be high compared with advertising (Jobber, 1998). There can also be a lot of wastage if the database is of poor quality and clearly the collection of useful data is also a cost and time consideration. One way to collect address and personal data is to run promotions and offers. The Dallas Stars offered free seats at four games in 2003 with the purpose of collecting data. The result was a database of 50 000 and that was achieved in only 2 weeks. The Stars did run the danger of decreasing the customer value in adopting this approach. It is critical not to devalue the product to existing customers and those that take up such an offer may only be interested in free products. Combinations of discreet and targeted promotions such as sweepstakes or the distribution of very important person (VIP) passes may take longer but may be more productive.

Personal selling • • •

There are two types of selling that are applicable in the sports industry, order taking for in-store operations and order getting by salespeople (Jobber, 1998). In the main the latter involves the prospecting for new business with key accounts and new organizations such as sponsors, advertisers, etc. These relationships are discussed in greater detail in Chapter 11.

Catalogues • • •

Mail order catalogues are of particular use in event merchandising operations where they can be in printed or in electronic form via a web site. They can be expensive to produce and variations in image reproduction can mean the delivery of items that are not exactly as seen. The use of web site online stores is now a popular way to sell merchandise in the industry and if they are affordable they can offer year round visibility for less frequent events. Sports teams continue to use both mail and e-mail order and in the UK their use can be seasonal too with Christmas and Season Kick-Off editions a common occurrence. Leeds United Football Club has used mail order catalogues the past three seasons for dual-purpose merchandise and season ticket sales.

Telemarketing • • •

There can be both one-dimensional telemarketing and the managing of incoming enquiries and the more pro-active two-dimensional approach used to prospect for new customers (Mullin et al., 2000). This direct marketing method is a growing and is a major tool in the event communications toolbox. When Mark Cuban first took over the Dallas Mavericks he took on more sales staff and targeted them each with 100 calls per day and the communication was never mind the results, come to our arena for a great sports experience (Caplan, 2003). They also make calls to those seat holders that do not turn up for games and so for them it was not just about selling, it was also about the building of a relationship. The advantages of telemarketing are that the caller can overcome objections if given the chance. The downside is clearly that a cold call into the home can be seen as an intrusion of privacy and so the key is to ensure that the database is targeted and consists of event friendly people.

Kiosks • • •

Ticket and merchandising booths of various kinds are ways of personally selling event products. They can be located on or away from the event site, prior to or during an event. Whilst they do not require database construction they can be a means for gathering data. Their implementation on-site during the event is of importance when advance tickets can still be purchased. They are of great importance too for the sales of other tickets for other future events. For major events high street medium-term locations can be worthy of consideration. In 1999 for example, an Amsterdam shop lease was acquired for the 2000 UEFA Euro Championships that were staged in Holland and Belgium. Kiosk operations can also be achieved with partners for a less expensive solution. In the 2 years preceding the 2002 Commonwealth Games a ticket operation was implemented out of the City Hall Information Outlet in Manchester. There are also advantages in getting ticket agents to cross-sell from their outlets. However, whilst more outlets is normally a good thing the downside is that there is a lack of control over the sales process and in how much emphasis is placed on the sales of one event over another when in the hands of agents.

Interactive media

The use of web sites is still a relatively new phenomenon and yet there are examples of innovative applications in supply of information and in generating incremental revenue. Those events that are utilizing their sites with interactive communications are exercising advanced customer adoption techniques. In addition there is the emergence of wireless technology that is so much in its infancy that managers are unsure as to how it will manifest itself and be an aid. The early signs though are sufficient for this author to want to highlight some innovatory potential.

World Wide Web

The development of event led web sites is now widespread and their use as a marketing media is being advanced everyday. Self-managed sites are more controllable but agreements with ticket agencies can also provide supplementary and primary sources. Ticketmaster.com (2003) on the 19 November was selling tickets for 393 sports events in the New York/Tri-State area alone.

In the main it is the desire for information that drives customers to such sites and so if merchandise and tickets sales are to be achieved, site sponsors are to be satisfied with site traffic, the content has to be attractive. Sometimes this is best achieved in-house but is not always an operation an event can afford. The National Hockey League (NHL) operates all year round with numbers of hockey events and it can afford to operate its web site content in-house. Doug Perlman (2003), Senior Vice-President for Television and Media Ventures at the NHL, maintains that no one will give their site the care and attention that they will.

49ers.com is a site that has previously run the dangerous game of editing out key team information when it is contentious, as discussed in Chapter 6. However, it has identified that this is a slow deterrent for fans and needs to be revised (Berridge, 2003). They have been able to build a very commercially driven site that is able to transcend both corporate as well as consumer communications. The promotions such as 'Dynamic Rotator' on its homepage is a corporate online sales brochure that cost $4000.00 to build and now reaps $100 000.00 per year and acts as data collector via registration compliance (Berridge, 2003). My49ers News offers consumers preferential e-mail notifications of game information, merchandise and special events such as auctions, promotions and competitions, all of which give the organization ample opportunity to interact with their fans whilst gaining $150 000.00 in sponsorship revenue from 12 companies including Budweiser, Nextel, Visa and Miller Lite. Its 49ers Fan Travel product, in collaboration with Prime Sport Travel, is another revenue earner from a much valued fan service. One of the big opportunities for sports teams and their web sites is their capacity to offer dynamic action and colour. All web sites are unique in that every organization is different but it is critical that all opportunity to create a unique selling point (USP) is achieved. The web site needs to create differential therefore and even if the products are similar, one organization needs to look to how it can gain competitive advantage (Bergman, 2002). Sports organizations and events have USP via their logos, action, first hand breaking news and official merchandise. The aesthetics of the site are critical in order to retain visitors. The 49ers use only four primary colours (gold, black, red and white) to recreate the look of their official team uniform and do not sell intrusive banner or pop-up spots.

A final key factor for the use of web sites concerns the development of customer relationships via word of mouth (WOM). WOM is considered an important tool for business-to-business relationships. Good suppliers are commonly recommended within business sectors and this can be the case amongst individual customers too. This also applies for negative as well as positive recommendation and when in the past it perhaps took a lot longer for such WOM to have an impact, the emergence of the Internet where bad news can travel faster, has now made this a critical consideration (Strauss et al., 2003).

Wireless communications

The opportunity for communications takes on new meaning with the advent of the wireless age. Mobile or cell phones are commonplace now and technology for playing games, receiving text, organizing diaries as well as managing telecommunications is advanced. What broadband technology has brought is the capacity for telecommunication carriers to send high quality still and moving graphics to mobile wireless devices such as mobiles. This potential is already being realized in worldwide with sports teams and events sending customers downloadable logos, pictures, ringtones and message alerts. Depending on the deal with the carrier, the sports organization can generate revenue via traffic spend as well as sponsorship. The NHL receives a percentage on traffic that they pass on to teams on an incremental basis.

In Europe, broadband technology has also made it possible to send video clips to mobile devices and so football action is receivable anywhere a signal can be achieved. As mentioned earlier, this technology is forecast to not be available in North America for some time (Hughes, 2003).

On the one hand wireless technology is giving sports organizations opportunities new ways of reaching customers, keeping them informed and selling to them. On the other the fact that this is wireless communications means that there are now more opportunities to reach these customers potentially in all places and at all times. This is not achievable with any of the traditional methods available. It is not these two factors that make this technology so much of an exciting opportunity however. It is the fact that with the right communications wireless technology can get customers to interact with organizations anywhere at any time. For example, with balloting, NHL fans can vote for their favourite players by responding to prompts sent to their mobiles and results can be accumulated for league wide as well as team outcomes (Hughes, 2003). Teams can then post results on their jumbotron screens during games. All kinds of information via alerts get the customer closer to their team and with instant response to last-minute ticket alerts they can be at the game that night. According to Hughes (2003), the NHL's Director of New Media Business Development, wireless communication is the evolution of the NHL's web site. They predict that there will be 456 million mobile owners by 2007 and with a target market of hockey fans that are more technologically savvy than others, the market would appear to be very attractive. Informa Media Group forecast that revenue from game playing on mobiles will rise by $1 billion a year between 2005 and 2010 to $9 billion. The NHL is ahead of the game and currently sells a monthly download of NHL Power Shot Hockey to subscribers (Hughes, 2003). Its thoughts for the future include video clips and gamecasts, game time photos, live game audio and merchandising offerings.

Mass media

In addition to media coverage resulting from PR, mass media marketing methods include the design and placement of advertisements and the use of sales promotions. Event budgets do not always extend to the use of methods that cannot be targeted as well as others but for some events mass media are essential. Large scales one-off events with large audiences often require the use of heavy mass media exposure in order to be successful but there are ways in which this can be innovative. For those that can agree media partnerships there are opportunities for advertising packages that can also provide less expensive campaigns.

Advertising

The media available for event advertising includes television, radio, printed press and publication, street media in the form of transportation, billboards and street furniture. The latter can include the placing of advertising on bus stops, community information notice boards, and in the UK advertisers are known to 'sponsor' roundabouts (road network junction points). Also in this area is the use of fly-posting which in many places is either illegal or a licensed opportunity at identified locations.

The budgets required for television are often beyond the scope of many events and even major events avoid these high costs. The 2002 Commonwealth Games utilized a number of media but steered clear of paying for television advertising. In particular it took advantage of several key partnerships not least the building and venue owners and the use of large signage, posters and billboards. One side of one multi-storey building in central Manchester was adorned with a jumbo sized picture of Jonah Lomu, the New Zealand All-Black, throughout 2002 prior to the games.

A sports sector that is currently growing is extreme sports print advertising. Oxbow is an example of a manufacturer that has placed advertising in collaboration with their partner events. The Oxbow sponsored Longboard surfing event, in Raglan, New Zealand, November 2003, was promoted via Oxbow paid for and derived advertising (The Surfer's Path, 2003). It also featured in editorial form on the magazines web site (surferspath.com, 2003). The access to this attractive and discerning group that is non-main stream is also attracting mainstream advertisers. Alongside extreme industry brands such as Billabong, Ripcurl, Vans, Quicksilver and O'Neil in industry magazines are Snickers in an attempt to reach different segments from the traditional football fans they have been targeting. For extreme events this may have possibilities for the attraction of new spenders and perhaps new communications partners for joint media promotions.

The NBA also produced an advertisement in association with partners. Its NBA All Star Game, 15 February 2004 in Los Angeles was the event and in collaboration with Foot Locker, Champs Sports, Circuit City, Loews Cineplex Cinemas and Verizon, they ran advertisements that incorporated a public vote promotion (NBA Inside Stuff, 2004). By visiting any of the stores or using a Verizon wireless cell phone fans could vote for NBA basketball players they thought should play in the All Star Game, the end of season play-off between the best players from each of the two NBA conferences.

The London 2012 Bid team launched its first advertisements in January 2004. The theme was 'Leap for London' and the series of adverts featured famous landmarks as athletes hurdled and leaped over them. The need to use mass media is obviously important to the team even during the bidding process. The target markets were the UK population and the effort was to convince the nation that the games would be of great benefit for local communities, the regeneration of the Lower Lee Valley (site of the proposed Olympic Park), UK sport, and increased job opportunities, business investment and tourism (London 2012, 2004).

One further example of event advertising is unusual in that it is recruiting its participants via a combination of techniques including mass media. The Clipper 05–06 Round the World Yacht Race advertised for crew via a national Sunday newspaper in January 2004, 21 months ahead of the event. The organizers were recruiting crew for its 10 month, 35 000 mile race for amateur sailors in its ten 68 foot yachts. Applicants could come from any background and did not have to be experienced at sea and so a mass media approach was appropriate. The full-page colour advertisement included a phone number and a web site address. It also promoted its stand at the London International Boat Show.

Sales promotion

Two types of sales promotion apply to the sports events industry, trade and consumer offerings. Attracting ticket and corporate hospitality agents can be achieved by offering discounts for bulk and/or early purchase. Commonplace consumer sales promotions include any discount schemes for tickets with vehicles such as season tickets where the offering has savings over a season/series of events, etc. Other promotions include free giveaways or discounts with early purchase. The following types of promotion, adapted from Jobber (1998), may be used by events.

1 *Prices discounts*: Ticket agencies may be offered or they may have sufficient bargaining power to demand discounts on prices.

2 *Money off*: A short-term consumer option is to offer money off but a key factor is not discrediting and cheapening the brand by under-selling.

3 *Premiums*: Any merchandise may be offered directly or by mail-in vouchers. A package of goods consisting of tickets, car parking, and programmes may be offered at full price but a value added incentive might be the supply of event goody bags for each member of the party. These may be more cheaply obtained by bringing in event sponsors as suppliers.

4 *Coupons*: Coupons as part of PR and direct mail operations may be used so that consumers may access cheaper tickets.

5 *Competitions and prize promotions*: Prizes can be offered as inducements to partner sales agencies employees for the highest sales. These may also include offering sponsors the same rights. There are two methods. A competition involves skill whereas a prize promotion does not and both offer an attractive solution, as the costs for either may be determined at the outset.

6 *Loyalty cards*: Depending on the frequency of events a loyalty card scheme is a relatively recent retail offering. For event organizing bodies of all kinds the capacity to offer incentives over a portfolio of events is an easy way to reward key customers and build customer relationships.

The problem with most sales promotion tools is that the costs can rise with the success of the vehicle in place. The intention for sales promotion is to achieve any one of five objectives (Jobber, 1998). A fast sales boost, encourage trial, incite repeat purchase, stimulate purchase of larger amounts and gain more effective distribution.

Summary

An innovative approach towards event communications is essential for today's sports events manager. Traditional methods of mass or personal media communications are not obsolete but require new and creative ways of being used in order to adopt and retain customers. The key is an integrated effort that consists of communications that work in harmony together and communicate consistent event messages.

The tools that are available include traditional approaches again but alongside the vehicles of print, television and radio for mass media communications, and direct mail, PR and face-to-face selling for personal media communications, sit the bright new applications that are offered by developing technology. The Internet and the opportunities it affords events with web sites and the future promise of wireless communications for the development of interactive communications are exciting prospects for the industry.

Questions

1 Select an event and critically evaluate its communications activities from an IMC perspective.

2 Using the same event, develop a new plan in an attempt to improve communications to each of the events identified target markets.

3 What were the key elements of Mark Cuban's marketing mix for the Dallas Mavericks? Evaluate whether and how differential advantage was achieved?

References

Bergman, T. (2002). *The Essential Guide to the Web Strategy for Entrepreneurs*. Upper Saddle River, NJ, Prentice Hall.

Berridge, K. (2003). Marketing and enabling technology: beyond content, turning a team website into a profit center, paper delivered by Senior Manager of Corporate Partnerships, San Francisco 49ers, at *Sport Media and Technology 2003*. November 13–14, New York Marriott Eastside, New York. *Street and Smith's Sports Business Journal*.

Caplan, J. (2003). Business insider: Cuban has the ticket to selling news. *Star Telegram*. www.star-telegram.com (accessed 12 October 2003).

Engel, J., Warshaw, M. and Kinnear, T. (1994). *Promotional Strategy*. Chicago, IL, Irwin.

Fill, C. (2002). *Integrated Marketing Communications*. Oxford, Butterworth-Heinemann.

Hughes, R. (2003). Expanding the fan experience with wireless applications. A paper delivered by the NHL Director of New Media Business Development, at *Sport Media & Technology 2003*. November 13–14, New York Marriott Eastside, New York. *Street and Smith's Sports Business Journal*.

Jefkins, F. and Yadin, D. (1998). *Public Relations*, 5th edition. Harlow, FT/Prentice Hall, Chapter 5.

Jobber, D. (1998). *Principals and Practice of Marketing*, 2nd edition. London, McGraw-Hill.

Kotler, P. (2000). *Marketing Management: The Millennium Edition*, 10th edition. London, Prentice Hall.

Lavidge, R. and Steiner, G. (1961). A model for the predictive measurements of advertising effectiveness. *Journal of Advertising Marketing*. American Marketing Association, October, pp. 59–62.

London 2012 (2004). Leap for London. www.london2012.org/en/news/archive/2004/january/2004-01-16-10-27 (accessed 22 January 2004).

McConnell, B. and Huba, J. (2003). Case: Dallas Mavericks. www.marketingProfs.com (accessed 24 June 2003).

Michell, P. (1988). Where advertising decisions are really made. *European Journal of Marketing, Bradford*. 22(7), 5.

Mullin, B., Hardy, S. and Sutton, W. (2000). *Sport Marketing*, 2nd edition. Champaign, IL, Human Kinetics.

Ogilvy (2003). www.ogilvy.com/360 (accessed 7 January 2004).

Perlman, D. (2003). Expanding the fan experience with wireless applications. A paper delivered by the NHL Senior Vice-President of Television and Media Ventures, at *Sport Media & Technology 2003*. November 13–14, New York Marriott Eastside, New York. *Street and Smith's Sports Business Journal*.

Pickton, D. and Broderick, A. (2001). Integrated marketing communications. *Corporate Communications: An International Journal*. 6(1), 97–106.

Piercy, N. (2000). *Market-led Strategic Change: Transforming the Process of Going to Market*. Oxford, Butterworth-Heinemann.

NBA Inside Stuff (2004). December–January edition. New York, Professional Sports Publications.

Schultz, D., Tannenbaum, S. and Lauterborn, R. (1996). *The New Marketing Paradigm: Integrated Marketing Communications*. Chicago, IL, NTC Business Books.

Strauss, J., El-Ansary, A. and Frost, R. (2003). *E-Marketing*, 3rd edition. Upper saddle River, NJ, Prentice Hall.

Strong, E. (1925). *The Psychology of Selling*. New York, McGraw-Hill.

Surferspath.com (2003). www.surferspath.com (accessed 16 November 2003).

The Surfer's Path (2003). Issue 29, November/December. Oxon, Permanent Publishing.

Ticketmaster.com (2003). www.ticketmaster.com/browse (accessed 19 November 2003).

Vaughn, R. (1980). How advertising works: a planning model. *Journal of Advertising Research*. New York. October, 20(5), 27.

Wells, W., Burnett, J. and Moriarty, S. (1995). *Advertising Principles and Practice*. Englewood Cliffs, NJ, Prentice Hall.

Sports event sponsorship

After studying this chapter, you should be able to:

- understand the importance of the role that sponsorship plays in the sports events industry.

- identify the objectives that sponsorship can achieve for sponsors.

- identify the critical success factors in the production of sponsorship programmes.

Introduction

In 2000, DVAG, a German asset management company, paid Michael Schumacher £5 million for a 10-cm wide space on the front of his cap. A cap that he wore whenever he was in the eyes of the media after winning a Formula 1 championship race, which was and still is often. Such is his pulling power that his Ferrari team were able to attract an estimated £60 million of sponsorship that included branding space on the rest of his racing attire (Henry, 1999). This revenue is clearly important to the running of the team but you do not have to look too far to realize that to some teams sponsorship income is critical for survival. In recent times both the Prost and Arrows teams have departed the Formula 1 motor racing scene with financial problems. Such problems in Formula 1 motor race events are ongoing and a constant source of concern about the re-shaping of an events industry that is worth £1.7 billion in the UK alone (Motorsport Industry Association, 2003).

Sports sponsorship is now a highly developed communications tool with much of the spending being focused on sports events. The market is in growth but the signs are that it is maturing with on the one hand increased revenue and on the other fewer new deals (Mintel, 2000). Indeed whilst the sports sponsorship sector is the most sophisticated and developed, other sectors are also in growth. The arts, music, broadcast, cause and community related, and education sectors are all developing and with more communication choices like these available there are key implications for the sports events industry.

With increased spending the expectations of sponsors are increasing and with fewer new deals there are fewer sponsors to go around. In order to achieve competitive advantage therefore it is critically important that event managers focus on what those expectations are. There are essentially five key areas that sponsors' aims fit into. These are: to increase product or corporate awareness, to develop product or corporate image, to drive sales, to develop market position, or to achieve competitive advantage. What sponsors are looking for, therefore, is a return on their investment, clearly showing that sponsorship has moved on from the times when sponsorship decision-making was more philanthropic than it was strategic.

This chapter will first of all set the scene by putting the sponsorship industry into an historical perspective in demonstrating how sports event sponsorship has grown. The direction of this growth is then considered by looking at the types and levels of sponsorship and how sports event sponsorship programmes are structured.

A strategic approach to the process of achieving successful sports event sponsorship is introduced. This consists of four key areas: targeting, building relationships, rights exploitation and evaluation. Finally the chapter will discuss two important issues: ambush marketing and the question of ethics, and how they affect the perception of sponsorship.

A historical perspective

Sports sponsorship continues to experience growth. On a global scale the market was worth $30.7 billion in 2002 showing a year-on-year increase of 10 per cent and in 2003 it is expected to rise another 14 per cent (Sponsorclick, 2003). The largest contributor to the market is the US at 38.5 per cent but Europe is close behind and is expected to provide an equal contribution by 2008. Its importance can be clearly seen where once the origination of corporate involvement with sport was more philanthropic than strategic and is now seen to be addressing a number of corporate communication objectives including the driving of sales. The Sanitarium sponsorship of the Weet-Bix Kiwi Kids Triathlon in New Zealand has two main objectives for example, brand building and sales with increases of 50 per cent (Sponsorshipinfo, 2003). The importance of sponsorship to events has also grown and in many cases is critical to the realization of the event.

It is not entirely good news. In the UK new sports sponsorship deals are slowing. Whilst sports sponsorship continues to be the largest sector in the market it is fees that are increasing rather than new deals. Of concern too is that 90 per cent of all money spent on sports sponsorship is on the top 10 sports (Mintel, 2000). Meanwhile other sectors are on the increase including broadcast, arts and community related sponsorships. Other research has revealed that this shift away from the sports industry is prevalent in the US too again showing that the numbers of quality non-sports options are on the increase and the numbers of new deals less (Lachowetz et al., 2003). The implications are that in order to retain or gain competitive advantage, sports events must improve their sponsorship recruitment processes.

Sports event sponsorship programmes

There are two fundamental approaches when it comes to recruiting sponsors. Firstly, there is what can be described as 'off-the-shelf.' This approach is common within the industry and is the selling of a fixed package that consists of a prescribed bundle of benefits that has been determined prior to any approach to a potential buyer. This clearly entails little involvement of the potential sponsor in the process until negotiations start, and gives no credence to the importance of meeting mutual needs. This is a common practice and evidence can be found at any number of event web sites. For example, pro-forma agreements that require the sponsor to tick a box to identify the benefits they require. Secondly, there is a tailored or bespoke approach whereby potential sponsors' requirements are considered first and a series of benefits then proposed. The advantages of following something nearer to the second approach are discussed later in this chapter. Prior to that it is important to identify the types and levels of sponsorship that are available via sports events.

Different terminology is used from sector to sector and event to event, to a point where onlookers might be confused as to the nature of the agreement. This need not cause a problem as long as the terminology is understood and agreed by the parties that are involved. There are no rules.

The term sponsorship is becoming unfashionable with a development that sees more use of the word 'partnership' in an attempt to depict a greater relationship and perhaps even increased competitive advantage. This can be seen in the way events construct their sponsorship programmes. There are various levels of status available at an event and these relate to the rights that they receive as a result of their association with the event. These rights consist of a bundle of benefits that can offer the use of certain titles and more often than not these titles are an acknowledgement not only of the status that the sponsor has with the event but they are also indicative of the relationship they have with other sponsors at the event. Here are the levels of status that are available.

- *Title rights*: A status that involves the sponsor in the title of the event that more often than not will include rights for inclusion in the event logo graphics. Corporate, product or brand names can be used. Examples include: Flora London Marathon, Samsung Nations Cup (showjumping), Heineken Open (tennis championships in Auckland, New Zealand) and the TNK Cup (a Russian schools volleyball competition). Bayer, the German multi-national pharmaceutical organization, supports a number of sports teams in its homeland and the name Bayer is fully utilized. Bayer 04 Leverkusen (the soccer club) and TSV Bayer 04 Leverkusen (the basketball club) are two examples. They were also the first to sponsor an Association of Tennis Professionals (ATP) tennis tournament in Russia, the Bayer Kremlin Cup.

- *Presentership rights*: This is a status that allows acknowledgement of the sponsor alongside the title of the event (as opposed to being a part of it) and also possible inclusion with the event logo graphics. Corporate, product or brand names can be used. An example is the Bank of Ireland who is the 'premier sponsor' of the 2003 Special Olympics World Summer Games in Ireland and who paid €2.86 million for those rights (Special Olympics, 2003). A 2003 International Big Air snowboarding event in Bulgaria is sponsored by O'Neill, the sportswear manufacturers, and their involvement entitles them to presenting rights where the event is referred to as the 'Todorca Cup by O'Neill.' A final example is the University of Massachusetts (UMass) whose athletics department is sponsored by Mass Mutual, a financial services company that uses the same state abbreviation in its name.

- *Naming rights*: These rights are associated with physical structures and more commonly in long-term agreements whereby a building such as a stadium can be renamed so that it is referred to using the sponsor in that name. Corporate, product or brand names can be used. Examples are common within the US and include Edison Field in Anaheim, American Airlines Arena in Miami and the Pepsi Center and Coors Field in Colorado. The McCain Stadium in Scarborough, UK was one of the first stadium naming deals in Europe.

- *Category rights*: Sponsors with category rights enjoy uncompetitive status with the event in that they are the sole representation from the sector/market in which they operate. These rights offer sector, market or category exclusivity for the sponsor. Title or presenting sponsors may also have these rights. MasterCard was an official sponsor of the 2002 Federation Internationale de Football Association (FIFA) World Cup in Korea and Japan, and Bank of America, Pacific Life and State Farm Insurance have different sector rights, also in the general area of financial services, as corporate partners at the Pac-10 Conference college sports championships in the US. A prize for the longest acknowledgement might go to Canon and their association with the Professional Golf Association (PGA) as 'Official Camera, Binocular, Facsimile and Copier of the PGA Tour and Senior PGA Tour.'

- *Supplier rights*: Supplier rights allow acknowledgement to the suppliers of event services, equipment and products they provide. They may also enjoy sole category rights. An event may have one or more such sponsors and there is nothing to preclude title or presenting sponsors also having these rights. Returning to the 2003 Special Olympics World Summer Games as an example, Aer Lingus provided flights as Official Carrier, Toyota supplied fleet cars as Official Vehicle Sponsor and Kodak provided accreditation technology and badges for more than 70 000 staff (Special Olympics, 2003).

These levels of status are important considerations for event sponsorship programmes. They have to be strategically deployed in order to maximize the opportunities for the recruitment of the right sponsors. The considerations include the numbers of sponsors, the benefits offered to them and the way in which they pay.

There are three basic structural approaches to take in the building of sponsorship programmes:

- *Solus structures*: Where only one sponsor is involved with the event and no matter what the extent of the rights offered (Figure 11.1).

- *Tiered structures*: A pyramid effect where there are levels of incremental status that are determined by the amount of payment received and types of benefits offered. Typically a title sponsorship receives more benefits and pays more than the next level of status. It is not unreasonable for an event to have several levels to the pyramid and for there to be one or more sponsors at each of those levels including those with title rights, presenter rights and category rights (Figure 11.2). In the case

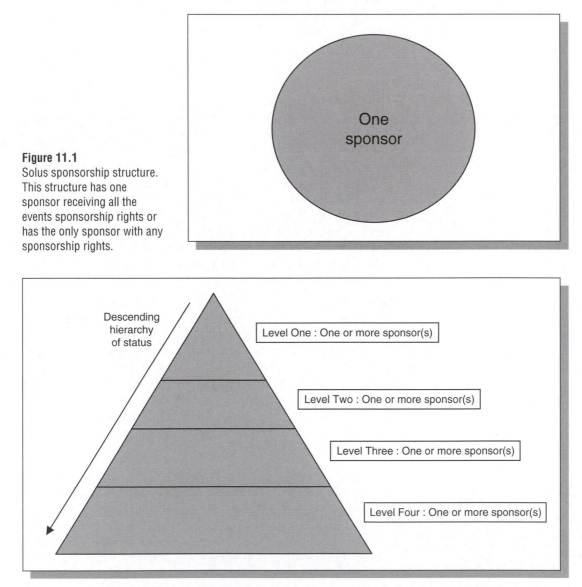

Figure 11.1
Solus sponsorship structure. This structure has one sponsor receiving all the events sponsorship rights or has the only sponsor with any sponsorship rights.

Figure 11.2 Tiered sponsorship structure. This structure, which consists of a hierarchy of sponsors, can be represented by a pyramid. The structure has a minimum of two but no maximum number of levels. There may be any number of sponsors at any level and their benefits may be identical or differentiated. Each level of sponsorship has a different status with the event.

of the Nabisco Masters Doubles, see Case study 11.1, there are even two levels of category rights, namely those that include television coverage exposure and those that do not.

- *Flat structures*: This is where all sponsors enjoy the same status though not necessarily the same types of rights or benefits and do not always pay the same (Figure 11.3). The key is that there is no differentiation in the way that they are acknowledged as in the case of the Football Association (FA) Partners in Case study 11.2.

Case study 11.1

Event sponsorship programme: Nabisco Masters Doubles

The World Championship Tennis (WCT) Inc owned Nabisco Masters Doubles ran throughout the 1980s in association with the ATP Tour as the Mens Doubles tennis world championship. Set in the Royal Albert Hall, London, 20 per cent of the audience were seated in corporate hospitality. At its height in 1988 the event was broadcast on television in 20 countries. Star players included Noah, Wilander, Edberg, Forget, McNamara and Fleming. The 1988 sponsorship programme and rights were was as follows.

Title sponsors

Nabisco International
Title sponsorship status and image rights. The objective was for increased corporate awareness as opposed to any brand awareness for Nabisco divisions such as Huntley & Palmer and Shredded Wheat.

Presenting sponsors

Nabisco UK
Nabisco UK bought the presenting sponsorship rights in order to prevent them being sold on elsewhere. The use of any titling was not required because of the Nabisco International title sponsorship. The package involved significant corporate hospitality consisting of two 12-seat boxes and ticketing.

Courtside sponsors

Boss: Official Clothing
Courtside platform boxes for courtside line judge officials with Boss decals. Officials wore Boss blazers and slacks in the day-time sessions, and black tie and dinner suits in the evening sessions.

Ebel: Official Timing
Courtside platform boxes for courtside line judge officials with Ebel decals. One courtside clock and scoreboard with Ebel decals.

Schweppes: Official Drink
Use of Schweppes drinks on court. Provision of all sponsor brands to corporate hospitality. Two 12-seat corporate hospitality boxes for all tennis sessions.

Dunlop Slazenger: Official Ball
Use of Dunlop tennis balls for all tennis. Ball tubes displayed on the umpire chair. Dunlop Slazenger decals on the ball tubes and legs of the umpire chair.

Cundell
No official titling. Cundell, a cardboard packaging company, were converted from corporate box buyers to courtside sponsors of the towels used by the players. They provided cardboard dining structures for each corporate box and Harrods (their client) Christmas puddings in Nabisco Masters Doubles cartons for Gold Star corporate boxes.

Sponsors

Lanson
Official champagne and receptions sponsors.

Lufthansa
Official airline for player transportation. Previously an American Airlines contra-deal.

Mazda
Official transport for players and very important persons (VIPs) around London. Cars with Mazda decals. Contra-deal.

Interplant
Floral decoration suppliers courtside but with no corporate television exposure. Corporate boxes were given floral decoration and business introduction promotions. A contra-deal that was important for event aesthetics and the covering of the large elliptical voids either side of the court.

Minolta
Official photocopiers and business centre sponsors providing secretarial services and business facilities for corporate box holders and their guests.

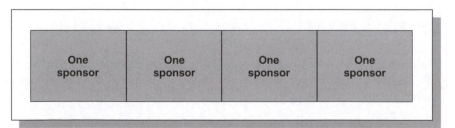

Figure 11.3 Flat sponsorship structure. All sponsors in this structure have the same status. Each sponsor may receive the same or differentiated benefits and may pay the same or different fees or in kind.

Case study 11.2

Event sponsorship programme: the FA partners

The English FA launched a new sponsorship programme in 2002. The programme consists of five partners each of which is directly linked by benefits related to what the FA refers to as its 'pillars:' Men's football, Women's football, Youth football, Community football and Elite football. Each partner also has access to the FA's top two brands, The FA Cup and the England football team.

Umbro

Umbro are sportswear manufacturers and are the partners for the 'Elite Pillar.' As part of that association they supply team kit to England teams at all levels. They are also associated with the new National Football Centre by using it to research and support the production of new football products. The partnership began in 2002 and lasts until 2010.

Nationwide

Nationwide provide financial services in the UK and are the partners for the 'Women's Football Pillar.' They have direct association with the development of the women's game with title rights to the Nationwide Women's Premier League, the FA Premier League Cup and the FA Women's Community Shield. They also have joint sponsorship of the FA Cup. The deal is for 4 years, finishing in 2006, and is at a time when football has become the number one women's sport in the UK.

McDonald's

McDonald's are the partner for the 'Community Pillar' and are thus associated with the development of football volunteering through the Football Workforce. They are also involved in the launch of such initiatives as the FA Club Coach qualification and are presenting partner of the FA Community Shield, sponsors of the FA's Effective Football Club Administrative Programme, the FA's Disability programmes and the International Disability Teams. The deal began in 2002 and they will be helping to try achieve an increase in the numbers of qualified coaches by 57 per cent to 22 000 by the end of their deal in 2006.

Carlsberg

The contract with Carlsberg, the brewers, began in 2002 and will continue until 2006. It sees them as the partner for the 'Men's Football Pillar.' As that partner they have sponsorship of the England Team and the FA Cup. They also have title rights to the FA Trophy, FA Vase and Sunday Cup which are key tournaments involving non-league football clubs, and access to the England Fans Scheme and the two million strong database of UK football players.

Pepsi

Pepsi were the last partners to sign up to the programme and their deal began in 2003 and lasts until 2006. It involves them as the partners for the 'Youth Pillar.' As the partner they enjoy title sponsorship of the FA Youth Cup and FA County Youth Cup. They are also involved with the development of the National Football Centre.

Source: www.thefa.com

It can be seen from these basic structures that it is possible to have various numbers of sponsors fitting together in one sponsorship programme and all having a productive association with the event. There is a balance to be achieved between what each sponsor receives and what each pays in order for a sponsorship programme to work productively and harmoniously. This can be particularly important when it comes to payment because not all sponsorships have to be paid for in cash.

The use of sponsorship-in-kind is growing. Sometimes referred to as trade-outs or contra-deals, sponsorship-in-kind has no mystery to it and is not any different from any other form of sponsorship. It is just another way of exchanging mutual benefits and in this case one that does not involve any rights fee or payment to the event by the sponsor. Instead they will agree a value of services, resources, goods or products that are clearly useful to the event and receive an agreed level of sponsorship status and benefits in return. Whilst Mintel (2000) reports that it is a growing area it is not a new practice. Sports events have for some time saved on expenditure by acquiring sponsors that can deliver important event requirements such as human resources, equipment, supplies, support services and the like. Case Study 11.1 features the contra-deals the Nabisco Masters Doubles negotiated with Mazda, Interplant and American Airlines in the 1980s.

There are two important guidelines to adhere to when negotiating sponsorship-in-kind. Often borne out of the development of relationships with existing suppliers and/or the identification of key aspects of the event that incur expense, it is of benefit to the event to get services or products that are required without having to pay for them. The key point here is how much of a requirement they are. Only when they are a budgeted item, and an expense that would necessarily occur, can a saving be made. The amount saved can also only be up to the amount that was budgeted. For example, the provision of £10 000 worth of IT hardware to an event will only save the event £5000 if the latter figure is all that was written down in the budget. Secondly, the £5000 may be a saving in expenditure but the bottom line may not benefit to the same amount. If the event rights and benefits (tickets, corporate hospitality or advertising), that are given in exchange to the sponsor are also targeted as sales and therefore expected revenue, then that will have an impact on the bottom line. For example, £3000 worth of event benefits given over to the sponsor means there is an actual benefit of £2000 on the deal.

It is important though to balance this with the impact the deal will have elsewhere even though it may not be as objectively measured as in the impact on the budget. The provision of services and products might enable the event to be that much more effective and safe. For example, Qwest provided the 2002 Salt Lake City Olympics with communications equipment including 700 hand-held radios and 16 000 public safety radios (Wilcox, 2002). Other provision may enhance the customer experience, participant or spectator, and mean the event surpasses customer expectations and may ultimately lead to increased revenue elsewhere. Gateway paid the 2002 Salt Lake Olympics nothing in dollars but did provide 5700 personal computers and 400 servers. Their CyberSpot at the Olympic Village provided information about athletes and the games to spectators and another such facility in downtown Salt Lake City provided the same for the media. Over 1000 messages of goodwill were e-mailed by spectators to specific athletes.

The negotiation for sponsorship-in-kind, begins with the agreement of the value of the exchange to be made. The aim is parity but the practice of course is one of trying to get the upper hand in the trade. There can therefore be an exaggeration of the values of provision on both sides. For example using rate card or retail prices as opposed to costs.

Many sponsorship agreements have a mixture of both sponsorship-in-kind and paid fees and it is unlikely that successful title sponsorship will not have some form of provision of products or services to the event. Asda, the UK supermarket chain, paid 10 per cent of the total value of its sponsorship deal with the 2002 Commonwealth Games in cash and the remainder in a provision of uniforms and human resource services.

In determining sponsorship price generally, there is no standard practice. There are various theoretical guidelines offered including Grey and Skildum-Reid (1999) who recommend a price that is at least 100 per cent over costs. There are two considerations here. Firstly, how much the event wants to sell for and secondly, how much the sponsor is willing to pay. The latter consideration is made entirely by the sponsor having firstly determined the value of the offering. It is therefore essential that the event is also mindful of how much the offering is worth to that particular sponsor especially if it may be worth more to another. Whilst this can clearly be a difficult task an awareness of prices in the market will be critical. It is therefore inappropriate to put any standard mark-up on the sale but it is essential to know the exact extent of costs involved in offering it. This should include all overheads apportioned appropriately. Equivalent opportunity cost is a guideline that can be used because sponsors will look to the cost of using other communications tools to achieve the same outcomes. Careful research into how much exposure will be achieved via the sponsorship compared to the equivalent costs for achieving the same through advertising will assist the process.

The event needs to consider the sponsorship programme as a whole and the potential revenue it can bring in as a whole as it may be possible to bring in a sponsor at less than expected but achieve the budgeted sponsorship target revenue. A loss leader approach and the acceptance of a lesser price in year, one could also have the potential for future realization of improved prices.

The Nabisco Master Doubles (see Case study 11.1) devised a sponsorship programme where the sponsorship revenue as a whole amounted to 50 per cent of the overall event revenue. The fee-paying sponsors paid the following percentage of the overall sponsorship target budget:

Nabisco International	52%
Nabisco UK	21%
Boss	7.5%
Ebel	7.5%
Schweppes	4%
Minolta	4%
Dunlop Slazenger	2%
Cundell	2%

A final consideration for the production of sponsorship programmes is the danger of over-commercialization. A cluttered programme not only detracts from the perception of the event in the eyes of its audience but may also interfere with target market retention of brand messages.

There are several more examples of events that have used various structures to produce their sponsorship programmes in Case studies 11.3 and 11.4. Both the Alamo Bowl and the Credit Suisse First Boston Hong Kong Sevens implement a several levels of sponsorship. Note the universal use of category rights and sector exclusivity in these examples.

Case study 11.3

Event sponsorship programme: the Alamo Bowl

The Alamo Bowl, San Antonio, US is the play-off game for the Big 10 and Big 12 Football Conferences, but it is more than an important college championship, it is also a month-long festival of related events. Played at the Alamodome the average crowd since 1997 is 61 035. By researching its target audiences' demographics the event has been able to target appropriate sponsors. It has increased its sponsorship revenue by auditing its assets and creating new rights.

Audience research has identified these demographics:

Gender: 67% male/33% female
Income: 20% earn $50 000/20% earn $50 000–75 000/23% earn $76 000–100 000/
                  21% earn $101 000–150 000
Age: 18% under 18 years/10% 18–24 years/69% 25–54 years/14% 55 years plus
Education: 6% high school/16% some college/46% college graduates/32% masters
                  and higher
Marital status: 71% married

The 2002 Sponsorship Programme

Presenting sponsor
MasterCard

Partners
ESPN   Television partner 10th year
SBC Southwestern Bell   Telecommunications partner
Includes title rights for the Alamo Bowl Pigskin Preview, Alamo Bowl Golf Classic, Alamo Bowl Fan Zone

Sponsors
American Airlines   Official airline
TicketSports   Ticketing partner
San Antonio Express   Media partner
Wells Fargo   Sponsors of the Alamo Bowl Kickoff Luncheon
Corporate Express   Sponsors of the Alamo Bowl Pre-Game Party and the Corporate Hospitality Village

Source: www.alamobowl.com

Case study 11.4

Event sponsorship programme: Credit Suisse First Boston Hong Kong Sevens

Such has been the success of this event since its inception in 1975 that there is now a World Sevens Series (since 2000) run by the International Rugby Board. This rugby union seven a'side tournament is the most popular sports event in Asia and is staged in front of 40 000 people over 3 days in the Hong Kong Stadium, a stadium that was rebuilt in 1994 as a result of the success of the event. Twenty-three teams from all over the world take part.

Sponsorship programme

Title sponsors
Credit Suisse First Boston

Associate sponsors
Canterbury   Sportswear
Heineken   Beer
Mercedes Benz   Motor manufacturer
Coca-Cola   Soft drink
AOL Time Warner   Internet

Media partners
CNN
Fortune
Time

Official suppliers
The Marco Polo Hong Kong Hotel   Official hotel
Gilbert   Official match ball

Road show venues
Swire Properties

Source: www.hksevens.com.hk

Strategic process

In terms of the event planning process sponsorship can be an important factor in ensuring that the event is feasible and so consideration of potential sponsors can begin as early as stage 2, the creation of the concept. For many events the lack of sponsors is the one factor that leads to the decision to not go ahead and so the early identification of sponsors and indeed early contracted agreement with sponsors can be critical.

There are a number of stages in the development of an event sponsorship programme. Having identified the events objectives and possibly set optimum revenue targets it can become clear that sponsorship is an effective tool for the achievement of those objectives. What follows is a situational analysis. This provides an audit of the event assets that can be used effectively in delivering the communications requirements of sponsors. Having identified these assets they can be bundled together to form packages that can then be sold off-the-shelf to interested sponsors. The bundling up of corporate hospitality, programme advertising and use of logo flash opportunities has been much utilized in the past. Whilst this has been the common practice in the industry it is not a customer-focused approach in that it is selling what the event wants to sell and not necessarily what the sponsor wants to buy, sometimes referred to as marketing myopia (Levitt, 1960). This is where it is important to use research to produce more effective sponsorships that can develop over time. The key for event managers is that they recognize that sponsorship is a mutual relationship and that objectives have to be met by all parties.

The process consists of four key areas: targeting, building the relationship, rights exploitation and evaluation.

Targeting

Successful events are managed by those that have researched and identified their target markets. Such research leads to better marketing decisions for the event and is therefore also a key first step in the development of an event sponsorship programme. Potential sponsors are also looking for effective ways of reaching their target markets and an event that can reach the same target market, in sufficient quantity, becomes a potential communication vehicle. The second step is therefore to identify which those organizations are.

Step one • • •

The determination of the event's target markets is arrived at via a process of segmentation. As there is no set way that a market should be segmented (Jobber, 1998) there is an opportunity for innovation. By being creative with the criteria by which the market segments are identified, it is possible to further identify innovative ways in which the events audience will be of use to sponsors, therefore enhancing the prospects of achieving increased sponsorship revenue (Masterman, 2004). See Case studies 11.1–11.4 and the ways in which those events have been creative in helping their sponsors to reach their target markets.

Research data is required in order to determine the event's target markets. This research needs to determine the nature and characteristics of the various attendees of the event. This could include gaining information about their demographical, socio-economic and geographical profile. More in-depth information would be behavioural or psychographical in nature and would provide information on their lifestyle. For example, information on the types of products or services they buy would be of use. Information at different times in the event life cycle can be of use as well as they may be able to track changes over time. This can be achieved via audience surveys of various types, before, during and after the event. Focus groups can also be used and can achieve a greater quality of information. Simple observation of audience flow and purchases can also provide useful information. The more comprehensive the information the more clearly defined the target markets will be. Case study 11.3 shows how the Alamo Bowl has used its research of its target markets in the recruitment of its sponsors.

The data itself should be recorded so that it can be used in the identification of the target markets. In addition, the same data is required for the sponsorship sales process and due to its importance to the potential sponsor it should feature in any sponsorship proposals.

Step two ● ● ●

The next step is to research the potential organizations that have the same target markets. Sponsorship agencies and consultants can be used to find whether such sponsors or events can do the job in-house. The process requires time and effort in order to gain an awareness of the market. There is much information that is readily available in the public domain that can be used to more accurately target potential sponsors. This includes company accounts, trading figures, market trends and forecasts, government budgets, trade press, marketing media and of course, activity at other events and current sponsorship activities. A continuous awareness of the competition is clearly required but the activity of sponsors at other events can also feed the imaginative event manager. In New Zealand, Vodaphone entered the market in 1988 with an awareness level of 2 per cent. The company was a target for a number of sports properties clearly with the opportunity for increasing their market status. Vodafone involved themselves with soccer, extreme sports and netball, including the

Netball World Cup, and by 2000, increased awareness to 98 per cent (Sponsorshipinfo, 2003).

Building relationships

Having identified appropriate organizations that have the same target markets the work begins to establish a relationship. An off-the-shelf, or predetermined sponsorship package that has not been designed with any specific sponsor in mind is unlikely to meet the unique requirements that organization has. Moreover, the key to the achievement of successful relationships is in the provision of a tailored service and the production of a bespoke arrangement that meets the individual objectives and requirements of a potential sponsor. It is important that this approach is not just applied when recruiting new sponsors, as this is also an ongoing requirement for the development of an existing event sponsorship programme. The building of the relationship for the acquisition of a new sponsor needs to continue throughout the relationship in order that it might grow and that future changes in requirements on both sides may be met.

The objectives that sponsors seek via sponsorship fall into a number of categories:

- *Development of sales and market share*: The development of new sales opportunities at the event itself, where sales figures can be driven by event audience take-up, and/or via sales promotions in association with the event.

- *Customer loyalty*: The enhancement of relationships with existing customers.

- *Market penetration*: Increasing recognition of the brand in existing markets.

- *Market development*: The establishment of brand awareness in new markets.

- *New product*: The launch of new products into appropriate target markets.

- *Product knowledge*: Increasing the markets depth of awareness with more specific knowledge perhaps related to specification, capacity and capability.

- *Brand image reinforcement/revitalization*: The use of sponsorship to bolster the personality of brands.

- *Business to business*: The establishment and/or enhancement of key client and customer relationships in organizations markets.

- *Community relations*: The establishment and/or enhancement of the organization's relationship with the local community. This is an important concern, as a business has to be accepted locally in order to be successful not least because it supplies the majority of its employees.

- *Internal communications*: The enhancement of staff relations.

- *Financial sector confidence*: The use of sponsorship to increase confidence in the city and perhaps with investors through the declaration of corporate intentions and the well-being of the organization in order to depict a healthy perception of the organization.

- *Post-merger identity*: The use of sponsorship to establish and increase awareness of newly formed or merged organizations.

- *Competitive advantage*: Through the above areas but also through exclusion whereby an organization blocks the opportunity to its competitors by taking it themselves.

Any one or any combination of these objectives could be a sponsor requirement and there is therefore a need for careful consideration of the vehicle that will deliver these successfully. The process that is involved in ensuring this success consists of four clear steps.

Step one . . .

The mutual determination of the requirements of the sponsorship.

Step two . . .

The development of measures by which the requirements will be evaluated.

Step three . . .

The development of a series of event rights and benefits for the sponsor that satisfy and meet the requirements of both the sponsor and the event.

Step four . . .

The agreed payment and/or provision of services by the sponsor in return for the event rights and benefits.

Step Three has often included the offering of exclusivity as part of the sponsorship deal whereby a sponsor will enjoy association with the event as the sole representation from its own market sector. In such cases a sponsor can gain competitive advantage not only through the association but also by denying the opportunity to its market competitors. The Cola wars between Coca-Cola and Pepsi are testament to this. Mullin et al. (2000) suggest that offering sector exclusivity is a key benefit and cite that the International Olympic Committee (IOC) first designed its sponsorship programme with exclusivity benefits for the 1988 Seoul Olympics. Some 15 years later it is arguable that whilst sector exclusivity is not entirely 100 per cent used at all events it is nevertheless now a virtual necessity. The implications for event managers are that whereas previously this might have been the cutting edge in recruiting a sponsor the fact now is that sponsors expect such status as standard.

Exclusivity is not a rigid status however. Depending upon the negotiating power of the event it may be possible to very finely segment certain target markets and still achieve exclusivity. The power of Wimbledon and the All England Tennis Championships enabled the event in 2002 to recruit sponsors from the same broad market and sit Coca-Cola as official carbonated soft drink, Buxton as official mineral water and Robinsons as official still soft drink, all together in the same sponsorship programme.

This four-step process is a continual requirement. Even existing sponsorships that are successful can be developed into being more effective for both parties. An event manager needs to be aware of what it will take for a sponsor to renew their association too. The implications of fewer new sponsorship deals for sports events and the increase of quality options for sponsors is that sponsorship renewal becomes increasingly important (Lachowetz et al., 2003). By using this self-reflecting approach the changing needs of both sponsors and events can be adequately met and mutual benefits maximized.

For the acquisition of new sponsors there is an initial wooing which can take a long time, perhaps up to several years, and it is important that the relationship building starts from the first contact. Lachowetz et al. (2003) discuss both the concept of 'eduselling,' where an event engages with its sponsors early in the sales process, and the research that has shown that such relationships can lead to increased loyalty and as a consequence their retention as a sponsor. However, this must not stop at the point at which they first come on board. It needs to continue throughout the relationship and this may require going beyond the limits of the contract. Whilst contracts are an essential element of this mutual relationship there is often good reason to give more than has been agreed and signed off. If there are extra benefits that can be offered to sponsors they can be used to further enhance the relationship and this is applicable for both the event and the sponsor. If it is an effective arrangement then both sides will not only want to continue, but they will want to develop it further. For the event that means less time spent in seeking replacements and more benefits for the event in both revenue and exploitation.

A key element of relationship marketing is ensuring that it is sustainable and that customers (sponsors) can be retained over the long term (Piercy, 2000). A key customer relationship management (CRM) guideline for events is a development of a mutual trust via effective communication with sponsors (Varey, 2002). Communication is of particular importance considering the complexity and logistical nature of events. However, more than this is required if sponsorships are to be sustainable and this is where the innovation in meeting their objectives makes sponsorship the most creative communication tool. Whilst the continual evaluation of and feedback into a sponsorship will help to sustain it, the exceeding of expectations will go further and also grow it. It is therefore important that there is flexibility for change when and where it can enhance the relationship.

Whilst identifying appropriate sponsors that have mutual target market aspirations, an audit of the events assets is also required. The various categories of event assets can be seen in Event management 11.1. This is something that is commonly conducted by event managers and in many cases the results are the benefit

Event management 11.1

Event audits

Event audits consist of an evaluation of the assets of the event to create an inventory. The objective is to identify facets of the event that can be offered and/or developed into event rights.

The main categories for the audit are as follows:

Physical

A division of the event into physical facets such as site(s), zones, halls, venues, arenas, pitches, courts, concourses, rooms, levels and marquees.

Territory

A division of the event into its territories such as local, regional and national competition rounds or finals. Northern or southern areas for example.

Time

A division of the event into its timeframes such as by session of play, by day, or by qualifying and finals competition rounds.

Programme

A division of the event into its running order components such as pre-match entertainment, the awards ceremonies, a seminar series, associated charity programme or post-match party.

Supply

Identifying the areas of supply to the event such as kit, equipment, product, transport and accommodation where in particular sponsorship-in-kind is beneficial.

Identifying the areas of supply to the organization as opposed to just the event, such as print, travel, office equipment and even staffing.

Status

Identifying the potential for title rights, presenter rights, category rights and naming rights.

Communications

Identifying aspects of the event's communications that may be facets such as print requirements and Internet provision. In the provision, management and sponsorship of the event's web site for example.

Created

Laterally linking identified facets in new combinations to specifically meet sponsors requirements in bespoke tailored sponsorship recruitment.

bundles that meet only the requirements of the event. What is required is a mutual audit. The ultimate decision as to whether a sponsorship is of effective value is taken by the potential sponsor and so it is important that in presenting the assets that could be of use to them, they have the opportunity to identify how the event can best deliver their own objectives. This can and should be aided by the event with the considerable use of innovation.

The audit will reveal the commonly offered benefits of title and status acknowledgement, use of event insignia and imagery, media and print exposure, ticketing and hospitality. However, the innovation comes in the delivery of benefits that bond the event and sponsor in a way that they are seen to be inseparable. If the sponsor is intrinsically involved with the delivery of the event it will make more sense to the target market. This is more easily achieved with those sponsors that are suppliers of products or services to the event but less so for others and this is where the innovation and creativity is required. The use of fleets of cars as sports event courtesy vehicles is a common idea but nevertheless continues. Rover provided the courtesy fleet for the Manchester 2002 Commonwealth Games where a new model was launched and exposure achieved literally on the road and even away from event sites. At the same event Boddingtons were able to drive their beer sales with the provision of event site bars. SAP, one of the world's leading software manufacturers sponsored a New Zealand America's Cup boat and received rights to put its logos on the sales. The greater creativity was in its provision of ship to shore wireless technology to the team. Case study 11.3 considers how the Alamo Bowl has audited its assets. In order to maximize revenue it has identified sponsors for its associated events including a preview event, fan zone and golf tourney, all sponsored by SBC Southwestern Bell.

Sometimes the identification of where the bond can be achieved is more sophisticated. Case study 11.1 also gives examples of the ways in which innovation was used to enhance the bond between the Nabisco Masters Doubles and its sponsors. By getting the product in sight and used in the context of the event the sponsorship can possibly be perceived as a credible facet of the event and provide more leverage from the association in order to achieve the objectives. There is however, little research into customer reactions to sponsorship and how their perceptions are influenced. The research there is, is predominantly from the sports sector and is concerned with recall and recognition of brands (Lee et al., 1997) where typically the extent of the evaluation is on numbers of sightings and not the extent of the awareness.

Rights exploitation

It is extremely unlikely that the sponsor will achieve its objectives to the fullest capacity by relying solely on the event rights even with the use of innovation. Reaching the target markets to a measurable extent requires exploitation of the rights. This consists of communications activity by the sponsor in support of its purchase of the event rights and over and above what those rights alone achieve. Sometimes referred to as leverage or maximization, this involves more time and resources and the complete integration of the sponsorship into the sponsors overall communications programme. The greater the profile of the event, the more it would seem that this is the case. In 1996, Coca-Cola spent over 10 times the amount it gave for the rights it purchased for the Olympics in Atlanta (Kolah, 1999; Shank, 1999). There have been rules of thumb used in the industry whereby the ratio of outlay on exploitation has been 3:1 (Graham et al., 2001), but now the rule of thumb has to be that the outlay needs to be whatever it takes to achieve the objectives. This is good news for events. The sponsors that effectively support their rights are the types of sponsors that events want because whilst the event gains more exposure it gains it at its sponsors' expense. A sponsor that supports its rights effectively is also likely to be happier with the sponsorship and therefore more likely to renew the arrangement. This saves the event the resources it would need to implement in order to find a replacement.

Exploitation is strategically planned and can form the focus or a part of the overall communications strategy of an organization. If the sponsorship sits alongside other communications the key is that it is integrated. Hewlett Packard (HP) integrated its UK communications in March 2003 around one theme, '+HP = everything is possible' (HP Women's Challenge, 2003). Seemingly totally unrelated areas of activity were brought together by this campaign and their sponsorship of the BMW Williams Formula 1 racing team sat alongside associations with Amazon.com, Dreamworks animations, Fedex, birdlife conservation, and individual artists. The communications consisted of substantial newspaper and television advertising in addition to Internet spend in order to increase awareness for HP and their ability to help all kinds of organizations on an international basis. The sports sponsorship played its part in the overall campaign but also had dedicated communications activity that the organization implemented at their cost in order to make the most of its rights as principal team sponsor.

Flora, in its sponsorship of the 2000 London Marathon, had objectives for increasing its market and value share, awareness through television and employees involvement, all focused on the health of the family. Its UK public relations (PR) communications in support of this sponsorship consisted of schools competitions, charity and pub links, joint branding opportunities, the use of celebrity athletes and chefs, and press trips designed to target women's, children's and life-style media, and its staff internally.

Rover, mentioned earlier, used its sponsorship of the 2002 Commonwealth Games to launch two new cars, the Rover 25 and the 45 Spirit models. The cars were used extensively as a courtesy service for the event and were seen all over the UK with their event insignia. The sponsorship was supported by PR, television advertising and direct mail communications before, during and after the event.

Inmarsat, a satellite communications company, were looking for a sponsorship solution that would showcase the reliability, globality and mobility of its products. Following research undertaken by a sponsorship consultancy, Inmarsat became an exclusive partner of the World Rally Championship (WRC). By using Inmarsat satellite technology, rather than terrestrial transmitters, the WRC was able to facilitate rally teams so that they could send and receive an e-mail, and make calls from remote event locations such as deserts. In addition, Inmarsat was able to invite its distributors to entertain end-user customers with corporate hospitality and from 2003 provided the events television partners with satellite links that enable daily highlights, programming that was previously inaccessible (*Marketing Business*, 2004).

Evaluation

In order for the relationship to grow, there needs to be continuous evaluation of the relationship. This allows for feedback so that changes can be made for the better. This evaluation, like all evaluation, needs to be against objectives and if they are measurable objectives then decisions can be made in order to maximize the return on investment.

There are three questions that evaluation can answer:

- *Visibility*: How clear was the sponsorship?
- *Sightings*: Who took notice?
- *Objectivity*: Did it achieve what it was supposed to achieve?

There are various methods of evaluation. Media value methods are commonly used and quantify the amount of brand visibility at what it would cost to buy the equivalent in advertising space. This method is unfortunately unreliable firstly because there is no evidence that the brand has been seen and secondly that rate card prices are used in the calculation when they are seldom actually paid when buying media space. These methods can reveal that sponsorship provides logo or product sightings less expensively than advertising but another issue is that they are not interchangeable in terms of communication effectiveness (Lainson, 1997). Other methods include media audience measurements of circulation, viewing or listenership figures. A different approach is via the customer. By using focus groups, surveys and interview techniques, it is possible to identify the extent of the awareness of a sponsor and/or its products.

Media Related	Customer Related
• Media value and equivalent advertising costs	• Sales figures and enquiries figures
• Audience levels: printed media circulation, television viewing, radio listening or Internet hits	• Audience spectator numbers
	• Merchandise sales figures
• Impact value: quality values applied to media types and coverage	• Shifts in awareness assessments: of brands, image
	• Quality of awareness studies
• Frequency of media reports	• Tracking awareness over time
• Opportunities to see: coverage statistics	• Market share improvement and speed of improvement
	• Promotional response numbers: distribution of samples, redeemed coupons

Table 11.1

Event sponsorship evaluation methods
Source: Masterman (2004).

Awareness is difficult to evaluate accurately and for the evaluation to be effective it can also be expensive to either do internally or commission. It is as a result, an uncommon practice in the sponsorship sector.

A number of sponsorship evaluation methods are detailed in Table 11.1.

Increasingly, sales objectives are now being more commonly applied to sponsorships whereby sponsors seek to drive product sales (Mintel, 2000). Evaluation can also therefore use sales results (Lainson, 1997). A comparison of sales results pre- and post-event and then tracked over time can prove beneficial and provides tangible and measurable evaluation.

Ambushing

The increasingly used technique of ambushing is a relatively new phenomenon in the sports events industry but is being used to great effect. It is the exploitation of an association with an event via by an organization that has not purchased any rights from that event.

The protection of sponsorship rights is therefore a major issue in sport today. Despite considerable effort to police the activity of non-sponsors and their attempts to gain association with an event there appears to be no end to this type of communication tactic. This form of communication is planned and is designed to gain this association in order to achieve the sorts of benefits official sponsors pay a fee to the event to achieve. Consequently, sponsors are now expecting full protection from ambushing and they expect it from their agreements with their events.

Nike has built itself a reputation in using this type of communication and in reading sports marketing texts it is difficult not to find examples of their exploits. Shank (1999) maintains that the organization actually has its own ambush marketing director. One of its largest Nike sponsorships is of the Brazil National Football Team and it exploited this at the time of the 1998 FIFA World Cup in France. Adidas were the official sponsors of the sports manufacturer category of that event and yet the awareness figures showed that Nike had a great deal of success. According to a sport and market study, Adidas achieved a sponsor recognition rate of 35 per cent and yet Nike managed a rate of 32 per cent without the purchase of event rights (Hancock, 2003).

The policing of ambush marketing have taken on new proportions more recently. The Sydney Olympic Games Organizing Committee launched an AUS $2 million advertising campaign against the ambushing of the 2000 Olympic Games. In a rather more direct approach the 2003 Cricket World Cup in South Africa protected its sponsors by not allowing rival brands into its event grounds. In a controversially stringent control of potential ambushing, the event placed lawyers at each ground and warned that any spectator wearing a Coca-Cola T-shirt may be ejected and/or the shirt confiscated (Brown, 2003; Biz-Community, 2003).

The more sophisticated sports sponsorship becomes the more sponsors demand protection of the rights they buy. As sports events are prime communication vehicles they offer opportunities for more than just their sponsors. The implications are that this is an area that will become increasingly important and control will continue to be a key issue.

Ethical and moral issues

The dominant ethical issue in the sponsorship sector is the one of over-commodification and the selling of an event into the hands of product endorsement. The issue is concerned with how much control is being passed over. It is equally an issue in the sports industry as it is in the arts even though it might appear to have been and gone. On the one hand it is not only accepted as a financial necessity in order that events can be staged, on the other there are still examples of rights owners holding back on the 'selling of their soul.' The FA in England still refuses to sell a title sponsorship for its world renowned FA Cup. It is only in recent years that it allowed a sponsor to be associated with the competition but let AXA Insurance only use presenting rights as opposed to title rights. It was not therefore the AXA FA Cup it was the FA Cup sponsored by AXA. The FA no longer sells any title-associated rights for this competition. Whilst this is not quite as extensive as the rock musicians who resist product overtures for their endorsement over concerns about artist integrity and who controls artistic content, it is nevertheless an example of commercial power. The writing of course is already on the wall. In the UK there are few cases of the use of naming rights and stadia, and consequently the likes of the Reebok Stadium, Walkers Stadium and the former Fosters Oval stand-out. In the US however, 51 out of the 91 stadia used for major baseball, basketball, hockey and football events are sponsored by commercial organizations (McCarthy and Irwin, 2003).

There are also ethical implications in the sponsorships that involve products that are connected with poor health. Tobacco sponsorship is now coming to an end but alcohol sponsorship in sport remains. There are also issues with the sponsorship of educational institutions in the US by sports manufacturers. Of concern are schools that are able to attract the best basketball players as a result of them being able to give them sports gear via sponsorships and as a result create elite teams. Some believe the solution is to limit or even outlaw sponsorships of this nature.

The advertising of gambling in sport is another issue and the National Football League in the US rejected a Las Vegas Convention and Visitors Authority request for advertising space for the 2003 Super Bowl despite there being no gambling content in the proposed advert (Raissman, 2003). Gambling organizations are now very active in the UK in sports events and related sponsorships.

The issue of branding in sports is becoming increasingly imaginative and at the same time can raise ethical issues. The use of speed-skating suits that are transparent and the wearing of commercial advertising to the body or underwear are of concern to some and there are currently no regulations to restrict it. This has filtered through to boxing too where ESPN, the US sports broadcaster, wants temporary commercially related tattoos banned (Christie, 2002). Body billboards are currently legal in the state of Nevada as a result of a court hearing and boxers being declared the right to free speech in this way (Raissman, 2002).

Finally, the issue of spending money when times are hard and the messages that gives off came into play when the US Postal Service sponsored a Tour de France Cycling Team for $25 million. Whilst the choices of a communications vehicle in leading rider Lance Armstrong and the synergy of excellence in delivery are perhaps not at issue, the sponsorship is possibly at odds with the organization's $13 billion debt and downsizing at the time (Pugmire, 2002).

It is clear that there are no rules and that ethics are continually evolving especially in markets that are increasingly looking for new ways to achieve competitive advantage. The implications for event managers are that there will often have to be a fine balance between the competitive communication of an event and what will be ethically acceptable.

Summary

A successful sports event sponsorship is one that achieves the independent objectives of both the event and the sponsor but this is achieved via the building of a mutual relationship. For the event this relationship is first of all established as a result of targeting the right sponsor. Ultimately both event and sponsor want to know if the sponsorship has been an effective use of the budget spent and whilst evaluation will determine the extent to which this has been the case, it is important that the process starts with clearly defined, hopefully ethical objectives. After all it is the objectives that will ultimately be measured. The key issues are that a successful sponsorship is a relationship that has been nurtured to gain an ongoing mutual understanding of requirements, and that it is a provision of benefits that will require thorough exploitation in order that those requirements are met. Evaluation will reveal if there has indeed been a return on investment.

Questions

1 What key market forces are currently affecting the achievement of successful sponsorships?

2 How might the following events structure their sponsorship programmes? Evaluate all the options available:
   - A city school's athletics championship finals
   - A national amateur basketball championship
   - An international junior (under 15s) football tournament

3 By using your own researched examples, evaluate the importance of:
   - Researching and targeting the right sponsors and
   - Auditing event assets

4 Why is rights exploitation a necessary activity for sponsors and desired by event managers?

5 Discuss the role and importance of research and evaluation in the achievement of successful sponsorships.

References

Biz-Community (2003). *Ambush Marketing Bowled Out of World Cup*. www.biz-community.com/Article/196/48/1477, 24 January (accessed 28 March 2003).

Brown, A. (2003). *World Cup Chief Gets Shirty Over Ads*. www.theage.com.au/text/articles/2003/01/27/1043534003082 28 January (accessed 28 March 2003).

Christie, J. (2002). New meaning to bottom feeders. *The Globe and Mail*. 23 January. www.sportsethicsinstitute.org/sports_marketing_ethics (accessed 28 March 2003).

Graham, S., Neirotti, L and Goldblatt, J. (2001). *The Ultimate Guide to Sports Marketing*, 2nd edition. New York, McGraw-Hill, Chapter 8.

Grey, A. and Skildum-Reid, K. (1999). *The Sponsorship Seekers Toolkit*. Roseville, McGraw-Hill, Chapter 6.

HP Women's Challenge (2003). HP Women's Challenge sponsors. www.womenschallenge.com/sponsors.asp (accessed 19 March 2003).

Hancock, S. (2003). www.redmandarin.com/viewambush (accessed 28 March 2003).

Henry, A. (1999). Would you pay £5m for this space? *The Guardian*. 10 November. Guardian Newspapers.

Jobber, D. (1998). *Principals and Practice of Marketing*, 2nd edition. London, McGraw-Hill, p. 174.

Kolah, A. (1999). *Maximizing the Value of Sports Sponsorship*. London, Financial Times Media.

Lachowetz, T., McDonald, M., Sutton, W and Hedrick, D. (2003). Corporate sales activities and the retention of sponsors in the NBA. *Sport Marketing Quarterly*. **12**(1), 18–26. Fitness Information Technology Inc.

Lainson, S. (1997). www.onlinesports.com/sportstrust/sports13 (accessed 10 October 2002).

Lee, M., Sandler, D and Shani, D. (1997). *Attitudinal Constructs towards Sponsorship, in International Marketing Review*. Vol. 14. No. 3. MCB University Press, pp.159–169.

Levitt, T. (1960). Marketing myopia. *Harvard Business Review*. **38**(July/August), 45–56.

Marketing Business (2004). January, 2004. Chartered Institute of Marketing.

Masterman, G. (2004). A strategic approach for the use of sponsorship in the events industry: in search of a return on investment. In Yeoman, I., Robertson, M., Ali-Knight, J., McMahon-Beattie, U and Drummond, S. (Eds), *Festival and Events Management: An International Arts and Cultural Perspective*. Oxford, Butterworth-Heinemann.

McCarthy, L. and Irwin, R. (2003). Names in lights: corporate purchase of sport facility naming rights. *The Cyber-Journal of Sport Marketing*. www.cjsm.com/Vol2/mccarthyirwin23 (accessed 3 April 2002).

Mintel (2000). *Sponsorship Report*. Mintel.

Motorsport Industry Association (2003). www.the-mia.com/index.cfm?editID=79 (accessed 28 March 2003).

Mullin, B., Hardy, S and Sutton, A. (2000). *Sport Marketing*, 2nd edition. Champaign, IL, Human Kinetics.

Piercy, N. (2000). *Market-Led Strategic Change: Transforming the Process of Going to Market*. Oxford, Butterworth-Heinemann, Chapter 6.

Pugmire, L. (2002). Check's in the mail. *The Los Angeles Times*. 17 July. www.sportsethicsinstutute.org/sports_marketing_ethics (accessed 28 March 2003).

Raissman, B. (2002). TV's fight foe, Inc. *New York Daily News*. 14 May. www.sportsethicsinstitute.org/sports_marketing_ethics (accessed 28 March 2003).

Raissman, B. (2003). All bets off with NFL: Vegas ad out while beer flows. *New York Daily Times*. 17 January. www.sportsethicsinstitute.org/sports_marketing_ethics (accessed 28 March 2003).

Shank, M. (1999). *Sports Marketing: A Strategic Perspective*. London, Prentice Hall International (UK), Chapter 12.

Special Olympics (2003). www.2003specialolympics.com/en/?page=spo_pre_01 (accessed 16 April 2003).

Sponsorclick (2003). www.sponsorclick.com/en/mktag (accessed 24 March 2003).

Sponsorshipinfo (2003). www.sponsorshipinfo.co.nz/Site (accessed 24 March 2003).

Varey, R. (2002). *Relationship Marketing: Dialogue and Networks in the E-Commerce Era*. Chichester, John Wiley & Sons, Chapter 6.

Wilcox, J. (2002). *Tech Partners Go for Gold*. 7 February. www.news.co.com/2100-1001-831393 (accessed 19 March 2003).

www.alamobowl.com/sponsorships2.asp (accessed 26 March 2003).
www.thefa.com/home/thefa/fapartners (accessed 26 March 2003).
www.hksevens.com.hk/sponsors (accessed 26 March 2003).

Research and evaluation

After studying this chapter, you should be able to:

- understand the importance of event evaluation and feedback in the sports events industry.

- understand the roles of pre-event, continuous and post-event evaluation.

- identify evaluation methods and their appropriate use.

Introduction

The importance of event evaluation cannot be understated and yet it is a much under used operation. The majority of event planning theory recommends the use of post-event evaluation and yet in practice event managers are all too quick to move on and not commit funds or time to this important undertaking.

There is also in practice a perception that there is only one form of evaluation, that which is conducted post-event. This chapter will consider three phases of evaluation, pre-event research and feasibility, iterative evaluation and the monitoring of an event in progress, and post-event evaluation. It will also identify the various processes, types and methods of evaluation that can be undertaken and the forms of reporting that are necessary. Consideration will also be given to the cost implications involved as they are, more often than not, the reasons for not undertaking the activity.

The evaluation process

This chapter is intrinsically linked to the events planning process. In Chapter 3 it was established that evaluation of success is against the objectives that were first set. Therefore, the extent to which evaluation can be an effective tool is totally dependent upon these objectives. If they are specific, have timeframes and performance indicators (PIs) that can be measured then an evaluation process can be designed that can provide objective and meaningful performance feedback to aid future decision-making.

Hall (1997) maintains that evaluation is no afterthought for event management. It is a strategic necessity in order to achieve the organizational change required for future success. Event management texts agree that evaluation not only assists an event to become more successful it also helps professionalize the industry (Allen et al., 2002; Getz, 1997; Hall, 1997).

The methods of evaluation can be both quantitative and qualitative but the final analysis of all research results will ultimately depend upon one or more managers' interpretation. There is therefore clearly room for bias and in order to achieve as reliable an evaluation as possible, it is essential that several types of research be conducted in order to provide triangulation. This is perhaps more obviously important to the operations for larger events where the same managers may no longer be involved when it comes to consulting past reports. It is just as important however for smaller events and continuous management, because time and memory will erode the detail of evaluation needed to feed into the next event.

The usefulness of evaluation and its reporting is further highlighted by the assistance it provides to the industry at large. The Olympic Games Knowledge Service (OGKS), started in 2001, had vast resources from the Sydney 2000 Olympics and provided

operational guidance to Manchester 2002, the operating organization for the 2002 Commonwealth Games. See Case study 12.1 for
a description of the Transfer of Olympic Knowledge Study (TOK)
programme. The Torch Relay that worked so well in promoting
the 2000 Olympic Games all over Australia prior to the event, was
one concept that Manchester directly adopted. For 3 months the
Commonwealth Torch, as launched by Her Majesty the Queen in
her Jubilee year, not only served as a promotional tool but also
provided community events all over the UK and beyond. The Torch
Relay Director, Di Henry, also directed the Sydney Torch Relay.

Case study 12.1

Event evaluation: Transfer of Olympic Knowledge

The Transfer of Olympic Knowledge (TOK) programme was initiated following recommendation 16 of the International Olympic Committee (IOC) 2000 Commission whereby
the organization recognized the role it had to play in enhancing the transfer of games
management knowledge from one Organizing Committee of Olympic Games (OCOG) to
the next. It began with Sydney 2000, continued with Salt Lake 2002 and is currently being
undertaken at Athens 2004.

TOK documentation and archives work in tandem with the Olympic Charter, host city
contract and IOC guides and specifically provide descriptions of the operations used to
manage the games. The process used in compiling this provision consists of the following:

- *Observers programme*: Up to 40 observers are installed at the games ($-2/+1$ weeks) to
  analyse the strengths and weaknesses of each functional aspect. The observers are
  made up of members of National Olympic Committees, International Federations,
  area expertise and future OCOG's. A series of regular reports are then produced on the
  previously identified 20–25 key areas of the games.

- *Visual TOK*: This consists of photographic imagery of 'behind the scenes' operations. Only
  so many of those concerned with the next games are able to attend the preceding event
  and so this visual knowledge source is used to help show them key aspects in operation.

- *Games debriefing*: This aims to draw main conclusions from the games and give recommendations for future operations. It also allows the IOC to amend and update its
  requirements and guides. It consists of 3–4 days of meetings that cover the key areas of
  the games. In attendance will be current and future OCOG management together with
  hired expertise.

The TOK programme is now provided in addition to the Official Report that is produced
and is a more readily available source of feedback as the latter takes some 2 years to compile.

The IOC also set up a new service in December 2001, the OGKS currently headed by
Craig McLatchey, the former Secretary General for the Sydney Games. Its remit is to use
TOK and other sources of information to deliver tailored education to games and other
sports events management teams. It assisted the 2002 Commonwealth Games.

Source: Felli (2002).

There are costs involved in evaluation and the more sophisticated and extensive are the methods, the more event managers fail to justify this expense. The cost can be in time and effort alone if there are no external agencies involved and for most event managers this can be perceived as too valuable to give. Methods that do incur costs can include the production of materials and/or wages/fees and the important factor regarding planning is that these costs need to be included as part of the assessment of event feasibility. There is therefore an amount of planning that is associated with evaluation because in order to budget for it, the nature of the evaluation, the reporting procedure and the timing involved all have to be considered. It may be that an amount is prescribed for evaluation per se and there are those that recommend a percentage of the event budget be devoted to the task. Those that do make such recommendations would appear to have a vested interest of course, the likes of those organizations that provide impact analysis and sponsorship evaluation services for instance. The key to the costing of evaluation lies, as ever, in the objectives set and who requires it. Is it an internal requirement or are there wider stakeholder needs for such information? The task therefore is to identify those that require evaluation, when they need it, in what form they will accept it and to prioritize what can be produced within budget. This is more comprehensively covered later in this chapter.

Phase one – pre-event research

Having first considered and determined the objectives for the event the next stage in the planning process is to determine the concept that will deliver these requirements. There is therefore a place for research into the opportunities and resources that are available in order that the most appropriate concept is designed. A key part of this process would be to identify customer needs. Further research is then required to determine if the event is in fact feasible. This first phase of evaluation is critical because if it is not thorough and conclusive and a decision is made to go ahead with the event then there will be unknown forces, internally and externally to the organization, which may ultimately prove damaging.

The research that is required can be acquired via situational, competitor and stakeholder analyses. An advanced SWOT analysis for example will not only reveal the existing resources and match them with the best opportunities that are available but also identify any resources required in order to turn weaknesses and threats into opportunities including how to achieve or maintain competitive advantage in response to a competitor analysis. Piercy (2000) maintains that SWOT analysis can be made to work for the realization of strategic insights and is not just another analytical technique that does not produce anything in reality, and this is considered in depth in Chapter 9.

A stakeholder analysis will determine those that are important for the event's success and the nature of the relationship that is required. The identification of event stakeholders is important at this stage so that the event can determine those that are necessary for partnerships, provision of resources or indeed those that might influence whether or not the event can go ahead. This analysis would therefore include the determination of the nature of any bid, license or funding application processes and an identification of the event's target markets and publics for the production of an eventual communications plan. The research process and nature of information required for event marketing are discussed in more detail in Chapters 9 and 10. As with any management tool these tasks are only as good as the ultimate decision-making performed by event managers.

Chapter 3 identified the need for a cost versus benefit analysis for the event and any long-term objectives provided as a result of staging the event. This is accompanied at this stage by the determination of the event budget. From an evaluation point of view it is critical that the budget targets that are linked to the achievement of the event objectives have measurable PIs. These PIs are critical for the monitoring of the event throughout its planning in order to maintain an alignment with the objectives.

It is possible to determine a set of criteria by which an event programme can be produced and in order to determine if the criteria are met there are areas of research that will be required. Sheffield Event Unit has a clear set of criteria that are inextricably linked to its annually monitored programme of objectives. Its remit is to contract events that are able to meet city objectives that include achieving a higher international profile for example. Therefore, a number of events in any one year are required to receive television coverage to a certain level. This emphasizes the importance of monitoring on an on-going basis as well as post-event evaluation and of programme evaluation as well as individual event evaluation. Because the Unit has to look to a provision of some 30–40 events per year (Coyle, 2002), it can balance its requirements out over the whole programme (see Case study 12.2).

Phase two – iterative evaluation

The second phase is the remainder of the planning process itself. Throughout the pre-event period there needs to be continuous evaluation, feedback and alignment with objectives in order to execute the desired event. There is, then, the much needed monitoring of the event throughout its duration. Wood (2004) maintains that the research required to support evaluation needs to be formative as well as summative in order to create a process which rolls from one event into another.

All aspects of the event need to be evaluated on an on-going basis throughout this period and due to their nature there will

Case study 12.2

Event programme criteria: Sheffield Event Unit

The following criteria are used to assess each event Sheffield promotes and/or hosts.

Major sports events selection criteria

- Does the event offer an opportunity for the continued development of links with governing bodies of sport emphasizing Sheffield's potential as a venue for their particular major events?
- What are the financial implications and the nature of the deal with the governing body of sport/event promoter? At this stage involvement and input from sponsors may assist in the decision whether or not to press for a particular event.
- As much intelligence work and information gathering as possible is carried out to assist the decision-making process. Past financial and statistical information is analysed. Potential income sources are assessed against projected expenditure in a cost–benefit analysis.
- Despite the costs of staging major events there are numerous economic benefits notwithstanding those of civic and community pride, national and international profile (city marketing) together with other forms of secondary income. How does the event fulfil these?
- What will the economic impact be for the city?
- What will the level of media exposure be? In terms of developing Sheffield's regional, national and international profile (city marketing) in particular via the medium of television.
- Is there external funding via Sports Council or grant aid sources available?
- Will the event promote opportunities for sports organizations and governing bodies to relocate to the city? What is the city's potential as a major base for associated activities (training, seminars, conferences, etc.).
- How will the event stimulate the local community to collaborate and participate in sport?
- Are there possible links with the development of centres of excellence and the appointment of sports specific development officers?
- Are there opportunities for involving and providing for the sporting disabled?
- What is the status and credibility of the event? How it is perceived in the events market place? Into which category does the event fall, i.e. calendar, participation, entertainment and hybrid/created event?
- Can the city manage the operational implications of the event? In terms of staff, availability of suitably trained volunteers, appropriate resources, etc.
- What will the timing and scheduling be? Where possible bid preparations and deadlines need to be identified and assessed to see if they are realistically achievable.
- Is Sheffield Event Unit able to provide a quality service to the customer and satisfy their demands and expectations?
- What will the event bring in terms of 'added value' and also in quantifiable aspects such as Television coverage, estimated viewing figures, over-night stays, etc.?

Source: Coyle (2002).

need to be the use of both quantitative and qualitative techniques. For financial aspects there is the quantitative use of the ultimate revenue and expenditure targets at the end of the event whereby final accounts will reveal the extent of success. However, the setting of timely deadlines for the achievement of certain levels of revenue, such as for ticket sales for example, will serve as useful PIs that will provide feedback in to the performance of the communications programme, the sales operation and ticket distribution. The use of deadlines as PIs is a straightforward method for the monitoring of a number of qualitative aspects too, for example the quality of the individual or team participants that have qualified through to a competition can also be useful for communications, sales and distribution decisions.

There is a need for flexibility in the event planning process whatever the duration and continuous monitoring will only be an effective tool if there can be feedback into those aspects that need modification in order that they remain aligned with objectives. If there is no flexibility and this feedback is not actively used then the event's success is in jeopardy. How else can the long planning periods that are involved with major sports events be monitored and the planning of an event be always contemporary if it is not flexible enough to allow for modifications? The planning period for the Olympics is 7 years during which the social and legal attitudes and standards may change. Therefore, it is imperative that continuous evaluation be used to ensure an event still meets the objectives it was meant to.

This process also acts as a control for quality. The continuous monitoring against quality guidelines enables the event to control the eventual output through the planning process. This is also important for the delivery of the event itself where the need for a control of the quality of output is most required. Control measures and PIs are therefore required whilst the event is running.

Phase three – post-event evaluation

The third phase follows the event and whilst it is difficult not to bask in the aftermath of the event and/or move on to the next project, it is essential that an overall event evaluation be undertaken. This is, of course, important for the organizers so that there can be feedback into future practice, but it is also of value to stakeholders such as client event rights owners, sponsors, participants, employees and suppliers, partners, investors and local communities, and pressure groups. Evaluation has to be against the objectives originally set for the event and because these can be short or long term, a key consideration is also at what point in time the evaluation is conducted. Post-event evaluation may therefore consist of numerous forms of report. This only emphasizes the fact that the event is not over until evaluation and feedback has been disseminated and that may be long after the proverbial fat lady has indeed sung.

It will be necessary to prioritize which stakeholders are key recipients of evaluation reports. Getz (1997) recognizes the importance of accountability and the identification of those that require such reports. In many cases the responsibility to provide these reports lies with the event organizer. For example financial reporting is required by the state for registered organizations for corporate performance and tax purposes and by investors on their investments performance.

An evaluation of the success of the event may also be a requirement by sponsors. Whether it is contractually required or not it might be of benefit to the event to supply research led data on target market awareness, sales figures and media coverage. A successful evaluation can make a convincing presentation of the success of the relationship and more importantly make for easier negotiations of renewal or enhancement of the agreement. Sponsors may of course produce their own evaluation and their requirements may also be unique. This offers another perspective on the costs of supplying tailored evaluation for each sponsor.

Government at local, regional and national levels may require or be interested in economic and tourism impacts. Funding bodies and government agencies such as those managing the lottery in the UK may also require evaluation as to where the funds have been allocated. National and International Governing Bodies of sport as event rights owners may require evaluation against their criteria. They may also require a host or management company to supply an assessment of impact on the development of their sport. All of these requirements shape the eventual reporting format and each can adopt a number of different methods by which to collect the information required in order to make the report. The following are available as part of the evaluation process.

Data collection

Much of this information and data is obtainable via internal processes and operations. It is available right the way through the planning process and the fact that it is gathered over time means that it is also an obstacle to its effective collection and analysis. Management practices need to ensure that not only is data collected but that it is also collated and therefore more easily analysed at the appropriate time. The very nature of the data in question shows why this is a critical factor. Sources include:

- *Sales data*: Numbers, price levels and dates/times of sales of tickets, corporate hospitality, sponsorship, advertising, programmes, food and beverage, merchandise, car park and space. Applications for purchase may also include important additional data such as postcodes, gender, age, corporate activity, etc.

- *Audience traffic*: A picture of how the audience flowed in, around and out of the event by collecting attendance figures, times of entry and duration of visit available from turnstiles, car park, transportation or policing sources.

- *Participant data*: A picture of the participants can be gained from their entry forms including dietary requirements, sports activity preferences as well as other demographics data.

- *Budgets and cash flows*: Financial reporting that is indicative of performance against prescribed and timely PIs.

- *Meetings records*: Chronological collection of agendas, minutes and compendious reports.

- *Communication programme*: Updated and corrected mailing lists and copies of all documentation, letters and proposals despatched. Copies of all printed materials such as posters, flyers, leaflets and brochures. Communications plans and schedules including promotions, media release copies, media advertising and public relations (PR) schedules. These may need to be obtained from appointed agencies.

Observation

Observation of the event and then the opinion of the observer are of great value to the evaluation process and all stakeholders can provide such feedback. Alongside the reports of event staff the police and emergency service groups, sponsors, venue operators, strategic partners and even pressure groups can provide valuable information that can be incorporated into the evaluation process.

Observation by staff in particular can be of more use if they are trained beforehand. Allen et al. (2002) advocate the use of benchmarks in order to achieve some level of standardization in the process. By using checklists for example a grading can be given on performance of certain aspects of the event so that when it comes to an overall analysis, appropriate comparisons can be made. Getz (1997) goes further and maintains that it is a mistake to rely on casual comment and so there is a necessity for such attempts at standardizing the process.

Observation can also be bought in. In the same way as the retail industry contracts the visits of trained mystery shoppers the event industry can do the same in order to access perhaps a more objective view (Shone, 2001).

- *Photographic record*: There are two sides to every event, front of house and backstage or behind the scenes. Both can be captured on film for important visual evaluation that if achieved in enough detail can provide a snapshot of the whole planning process and the implementation of the event itself. There are two uses for such footage. Edited visuals are important tools for both future management and for new and developed sales.

The results of the analysis of all collected data and observed information can be used to reflect on target market demographics and operations performance for both internal and stakeholder information. It can also be used constructively in future sales operations.

Debriefs

The use of debriefing meetings takes on many forms. At one extreme it is the celebration of the event and even a post-event party. These are important aspects and they have a substantial place in the management of an event but the purpose of debriefing is a separate issue. Having been 'briefed' it is essential that 'debriefing' readdresses the objectives and at a level where all stakeholders have an opportunity to contribute.

The form of debrief will differ from event to event but may involve one meeting, sub-meetings and even a series of meetings. The agenda will address all the aspects of the event but has an important role to play in formalizing the process. For example, there are 20–25 key aspects of evaluation for the Olympics in the TOK programme and Allen et al. (2002) suggest something similar with a generic standard 21 point event checklist. Another starting point worth considering is the area of responsibility as given in the briefing of individual roles and as developed in the implementation of the event.

The question of timing is important too. For some events the scale and size of evaluation will necessitate a long period before meetings can be convened. In the case of the Sydney 2000 Olympics the final report was only concluded 2 years post the event. The general guideline is to stage the meetings as early as possible after the event has closed. It is possible to stage a first meeting within a week of the event whatever the scale and this is an important factor if memory is not going to detract from the process.

There is a question of control. It is important that evaluation does not become either self-congratulatory or highly critical particularly at a personal level. The purpose is constructive evaluation that should feed into the enhancement of performance, not false dawns or recrimination. Therefore each member of a debriefing session needs time to prepare or contribute to a report for that debrief. Essential considerations for those that lead this process therefore, are the content of the agenda, meetings control and timely notification of meetings dates.

Surveys

A number of event aspects can be surveyed. All stakeholders can be given questionnaires to complete pre-, during and post-event and these can be collected immediately or over time. Audiences are key of course, and their perception of the event is of paramount importance in an industry that needs to be driven by customer focus. Therefore, feedback on the event from ticket buyers, sponsors, advertisers and participants is required but it is important to question suppliers, partners, investors, local communities and agencies too.

In addition to questionnaires there are also the more direct methods of interview, either on a one-to-one or in groups. Technology has opened up the opportunities where video links and electronic discussion supplement the normal methods.

The quality of the information given from surveys is always of concern and events may well have to seek the guidance if not the services of trained professional assistance. Generally speaking the greater the scale and depth of information required, the greater the costs but the decision will depend upon who requires what kind of evaluation. Allen et al. (2002) nevertheless maintain that the key considerations when formulating surveys are a clear purpose and targeting, simple designs that have unambiguous lines of questioning, a representative sample size, avoidance of bias via the use of randomness in the selection of participants and the need for supporting data for more accurate analysis.

Impact analysis

This form of evaluation is of common use by event hosts in the determination of an event's economic contribution to its locality, region and/or nation. It can provide much needed information of the wider benefit gained over and above the events operational cost or profit. It is therefore also used to calculate a forecasted impact for a potential event by hosts and as a consequence becomes a much used reference point for media scrutiny.

Economic impact in this context can be described as the net change in an economy as the consequence of staging a sports event (Crompton, 1995). The change is caused by the use of new or existing sports facilities and services by the event and the resultant visitor spending, municipal spending, employment opportunities and tax revenue as a consequence of staging the event. The impact can consist of three different effects. Firstly direct effects that are the wages and profits to local residents and businesses as a result of event visitor expenditure. Secondly indirect effects that represent the rippled effect of this expenditure through to other businesses and workers who supply those who first receive the spending. Thirdly induced effects where the income received is re-spent locally.

The key data for an economic impact study is derived via surveys of the event visitors. The essence of the study is who spent what and where. Data is required on who visited the event, why they came and where they came from in an attempt to determine who necessarily came to the event as opposed to who would have been in the locality anyway. Were they spectators, participants, officials or media? Data is then required on spending patterns in relation to the event and could include that spent on tickets, food and beverage, accommodation, merchandise and travel. An average spend per type of visitor can be determined having next obtained the attendance figures.

UK Sport was set up to support elite sport at the UK level as well as programmes such as anti-doping and major events. It also manages the international relationships and co-ordinates a UK-wide approach to any international issues. The body is funded by, and responsible to, the UK Governmental Department for Culture, Media and Sport and their Blueprint for Success (UK Sport, 1999) is a strategic framework for the securing of major sports events for the UK. It provides a five-phase approach for the analysis of host city economic impact and includes the use of multiplier analysis.

A calculation can be used in order to analyse the extent of the impact. Multiplier analysis is widely used to achieve this and is discussed in more detail in Event management 12.1. There is contention with the use of multipliers as identified in the Event mangement. Coates and Humphries (2003) comment on the use of flawed multiplier techniques and they recommend the use of further empirical study and methods in the evaluation of economic impact rather than using calculations that can be manipulated to the users benefit. The consistent use of such calculations by event organizers to project future economic impact and consequently win over stakeholders should be of concern to the industry.

It has been argued in Chapter 4 that there is more to event impact than just economic benefit and it is important that impact analysis considers the more intangible as well as the tangible such as cultural and social impacts. Conversely, there are also the often neglected negative impacts as a result of staging an event, those of traffic congestion, vandalism, environmental degradation and social disruption that are an important factor in the determination benefits versus costs. It is also important to consider the long-term as well as the short-term impacts as over the longer period the benefit may well be of greater value.

Case study 12.3 describes the brief set by Manchester City Council for a Cost–Benefit Analysis of the 2002 Commonwealth Games. The Case shows that the city was mindful for the immediate as well as the long-term view. Whilst it might be implied, there is however a distinct lack of specific reference to the requirement of a report of any negative impacts. Cambridge Consultants beat six other tenders for the job. See Case study 4.3, in Chapter 4, for a summary of the results of their immediate impacts report.

Case study 12.4 shows two further examples of methodologies used to report on economic impact and the different objectives of

Event management 12.1

Multiplier analysis

In order to calculate the economic impact of an event, multiplier analysis takes the total expenditure whether direct, indirect or induced and converts it into a net amount that accounts for any leakages that have occurred. Leakages include the income that does not remain locally, for example payments to suppliers that are based outside of the area or income that is not re-spent locally.

The aim of multiplier calculations is also to produce estimates of job employment as a result of staging the event. Claims as to the creation of jobs as a result of a one-off event might be somewhat tenuous. Crompton (2001) explains that the use of an employment multiplier assumes that all employees are fully occupied and infer inaccurately that an increase in visitor spending will necessitate local businesses to increase their level of employment just for a one-off event. He maintains that they are more likely to utilize existing levels of employment with short-term transfers. In support of this a number of Manchester City Council employees were seconded, and 25 former Sydney 2000 Olympics management staff drafted in, to Manchester 2002, the organizing body for the Commonwealth Games. A more common calculation is of equivalent job years. This is where the additional income locally is divided by an appropriate average wage to determine a number that is expressed as being in full-time equivalent job years.

There are numerous multipliers that can be used and as a result there is some contention in their use. UK Sport recommends the proportional multiplier be used, (UK Sport, 1999). Others are income, value added and employment multipliers, (Archer, 1982; Getz, 1997; Mathieson and Wall, 1982). There are also the discrepancies that can occur due to the inexact nature of calculation. Crompton (2001) maintains that this is not always as a result of a genuine lacking in economic understanding, moreover it can be deliberate exaggeration that is used to maximize a case for the bidding of an event or the justification for staging one.

There would appear to be a need for consistency in the methods of measurement used across the industry.

Case study 12.3

Impact analysis methodologies: 2002 Commonwealth Games

On 28 August 2001, Manchester City Council dispatched a brief for the commission of a Cost–Benefit Analysis of the 2002 Commonwealth Games. The consultancy brief was to provide a quantitative and qualitative assessment of the impacts associated with the games and in particular the following.

Immediate impacts and pre-games

- The building and preparing of the games facilities
- Associated environmental and infrastructure improvements
- Associated regeneration activity (including land reclamation, inward investment and employment)
- Training games volunteers
- Pre-games operational employment
- Marketing and promotional campaigns
- Enhanced partnership working in order to deliver facilities, infrastructure, etc.

Intermediate impacts – during games

- Operating the games
- The opening and closing ceremonies
- Games related events and cultural activities
- Visitor spend
- Marketing, promotion, media coverage and exposure
- Volunteer activity

Strategic impacts – post-games

The regeneration of East Manchester and wider economic benefits for the City as a whole, including:

- Increased inward and retained investment
- Increased employment opportunities for local people
- Diversification of the economic base
- Increased gross value added
- Enhanced sporting facilities and attendances
- After-use of the stadium by Manchester City Football Club and for other events
- After-use of other games facilities by local residents, visitors and other sporting events
- Improved environment and visual amenity
- Enhanced national and international image
- Increased visitor numbers and spend
- Cultural renewal
- Social benefits such as health benefits brought about through the improved participation in sport, a sense of civic renewal, pride and well-being, personal pride and well-being from securing a job or being a games volunteer.
- Spin-off benefits for the wider region: increased profile, enhanced image, growth in target sectors of the economy, increased education and skill levels, health benefits and stronger regional centre.

Source: Manchester City Council (2001).

Events Halifax in Nova Scotia and the Hong Kong Sports Development Board.

Media coverage

In response to the event communications plan and to supplement the collection of communication materials as above there should be as comprehensive a collection of media coverage records as possible. The sources of information are:

- *Press cuttings*: This can be a bought in service but the more successful the event the more expensive this is. This should be

Case study 12.4

Halifax, Nova Scotia

In 1999 Events Halifax, a Canadian Province agency with a mission to bring more events to the city, undertook an impact study of all its events. The strategy was to conduct a multi-event survey of representative events in every category including winter and summer sports. The methodology consisted of random personal intercept interviews of 809 sports event attendees and 12 promoter surveys.

The sports events included Canadian National Canoe Trials, Nova Scotia Special Olympics, Marblehead Ocean Race, New Minas Soccer Tournament, Equestrian Championships, Kentville Harvest Valley Marathon, Labatt Tankard Curling, Alpine Ski Championships, SEDMHA Easter Hockey Tournament, Provincial Artistic Gymnastics Championships, Masters National Swim Competition and Mastercard Memorial Cup.

The attendees surveys acquired data on expenditure patterns for 11 categories of spending: tickets, restaurants, accommodation, concessions, merchandise, entertainment, retail shopping, local transportation, bars, car rentals, equipment and other.

Survey information collected also included general demographics including sex, age, education, residence, household income, plus travel arrangements, reasons for travel in order to determine the numbers and nature of event visitors.

Average daily expenditure for summer sports events attendees was CAN $72 and for winter events it was CAN $108. The economic impact for 1999/2000 summer events was calculated at CAN $12.7 million and for winter events at CAN $30 million.

Source: Events Halifax (2001).

Hong Kong

Business and Economic Research Ltd (BERL) undertook an economic impact study of sport in Hong Kong on behalf of Hong Kong Sport Development Board (HKSDB).

Broad industry data sources were used such as the Hong Kong Census and Statistics Department's Household Expenditure Survey, trade statistics and public sector data, and tourist information from the Hong Kong Tourist Association. A selection of face-to-face interviews was also conducted with representative companies in specific sports related industries.

The data analysis indicated that the direct economic impact of sport in Hong Kong is a contribution of $21 billion to Gross Domestic Product (GDP) per year. The impact including indirect and induced effects was estimated at $26 billion or 2.1 per cent of GDP. Employment multipliers were also used and estimated that the total contribution of sport to Hong Kong's employment was 81 000 jobs. For comparative purposes the study reflected on impacts of sport in Scotland (1.8 per cent of GDP), in the US (2 per cent of GDP), in the UK (1.7 per cent of GDP) and in Canada and New Zealand (just over 1 per cent of GDP).

Source: HKSDB (2002).

compiled in chronological order and if the coverage has been created via the use of communication tools such as releases or launches then that too should be recorded. It can therefore be effectively conducted in-house if there is the time available to scour a prioritized list of media.

- *Broadcast coverage*: This can be of the event itself or of the acknowledgements made to the event pre, during and post. Accessibility to material will be easier via the broadcast media themselves. For higher profile events the task of collection for any media material may involve national or international review and so outsourcing assistance may be more effective and efficient than in-house.

- *New media*: It is important to keep archives of Internet activity. This should track the content and the timing of any changes, and the traffic both to own and link site activities. Interactive television traffic for event programming can also provide meaningful information.

The difficulty in financing evaluation is clearly an issue in the industry. There are many other financial pressures that take priority. Time too is a resource that is scarce for most event managers. The prospect then of contemplating long-term evaluation, when short-term assessments are rare in the industry, is daunting. There are also further problems associated with the adoption of long-term evaluation. Organizations, staffing, budgets and even objectives change over time and so usefulness can decrease if focus is not maintained during such longitudinal studies. Whilst these issues are important they should not detract from there being an acknowledgement that there is an optimum need for evaluation that can provide the basis for improved future performance.

Reporting

There are a number of reports that can be produced, written or otherwise. The first consideration is who requires the report and this can often depend on the exact individual personality involved. The report must be written for the reader and this clearly dictates the format that will be adopted.

There is also the consideration of when the report is required. In the case of impact analysis and the evaluation of long-term objectives there may be a case for an evaluation process that extends long after the event has concluded, as discussed in Chapter 3. Post-event evaluation can therefore be immediate or up to several years after the event. The argument put forward in Chapter 3 maintains that if there are objectives that involve long-term legacies then they can only be evaluated over that long term, even if that involves handing over the responsibility for evaluation to after-users.

The next consideration is what kind of analysis of the data should be undertaken and this again is reader focused. The internal requirement for future management decision-making is a comprehensive report that covers all aspects of the event. Not all other stakeholders will be interested in so much detail or should indeed be shown the aspects that are confidentially sensitive. Sponsors for example may require or be interested in the media coverage obtained, branding activities and target market reach success and the report for each sponsor may also be confidential of course. Investors would be interested in audited accounts and licensing bodies, such as local municipal authorities, in health and safety and economic impact.

The media coverage presentation should be available as a separate and individual record of the results of the communications programme. It can be presented in addition and in support of other stakeholders' evaluation reports. The presentation can then be used in future corporate sales operations in an attempt to increase existing revenue as well as develop new business.

There is no prescribed form to the report but it is a presentation and so all the normal business guidelines apply. It needs to be concise, comprehensive, accurate and reader friendly. There are some elaborately produced forms of event evaluation and because they are in the public domain and concerned with large-scale events they have also been expensively produced. Not all events have to go so far. If all an event needs to produce is one written evaluation, for internal use, only it need only be at minimal cost.

At least one comprehensive report is required. This will cover all the key aspects of the event and will consider and incorporate the individual reports of as many stakeholders as required. Someone needs to collate it and produce it on time. Other reports, such as those for sponsors, investors and partners can be compiled out of the main report and delivered accordingly. Any debriefing needs to have taken place previously and so the presentation of such reports should not be the first post-event meeting a contributor has had for example. Their input is an integral component.

Summary

The evaluation process may be at the back end of the planning process but without it the event is not complete. It provides a measurement of performance that is necessary on the one hand for an assessment of success against objectives and on the other, an important feedback tool for improved future management.

It is not just a post-event operation however. There are three phases that in fact encompass the whole of the planning process. Research and evaluation is necessary in order to develop the event concept and in order to establish feasibility. Then throughout the event there is a need for a continual monitoring process thus ensuring that planning is flexible enough to accommodate change, particularly for longer planning periods. Finally there is post-event evaluation that together with important feedback aids decision-making, not just for management but also for all the events' stakeholders.

The shape and form of evaluation reporting is determined by the requirements of stakeholders. The final reports that go to the investors, sponsors, strategic partners and management are different and the needs of the process itself is such that it is incomplete without all their contributions.

Questions

1 Analyse the importance of pre-event research prior to the decision to go ahead. Support your analysis with your own examples of what types of research can be undertaken?

2 Evaluate the importance of an iterative event planning process and the role of continuous evaluation for the 2002 Commonwealth Games.

3 Discuss the importance and use of post-event evaluation by Sheffield Event Unit.

References

Allen, J., O'Toole, W., McDonnell, I. and Harris, R. (2002). *Festival and Special Event Management*, 2nd edition. Queensland, Australia, John Wiley & Sons, Chapter 15.

Archer, B. (1982). The value of multipliers and their policy implications. *Tourism Management*, **3** (4), 236–241.

Coates, D. and Humphries, B. (2003). *Professional Sports Facilities, Franchises and Urban Economic Development*. University of Maryland, Baltimore County, working paper 03-103. www.umbc. edu/economics/wpapers/wp_03_103.pdf (accessed 7 January 2004).

Coyle, W. (2002). Interview: Manager, Events Unit, Sheffield City Council at Events Unit, Sheffield City Council, Sheffield. 12 noon, 19 July.

Crompton, J. (1995). Economic impact analysis of sports facilities and events: eleven sources of misapplication. *Journal of Sport Management*, **9**, 14–35.

Crompton, J. (2001). Public subsidies to professional team sport facilities in the USA. In: Gratton, C. and Henry, I. (Eds), *Sport in the City: The Role of Sport in Economic and Social Regeneration*. London, Routledge, Chapter 2.

Events Halifax. (2001). *Economic Impact Analysis: Sporting & Cultural Events 1999–2000*. www.sportnovascotia.com/contents/pubs/ EconImpactAnal.pdf (accessed 16 April 2003).

Felli, G. (2002). Transfer of Knowledge (TOK): a games management tool. A paper delivered at the *IOC-UIA Conference: Architecture and International Sporting Events*, Olympic Museum, Lausanne, June 2002. IOC.

Getz, D. (1997). *Event Management and Tourism*. New York, Cognizant, Chapter 14.

Hall, C.M. (1997). *Hallmark Tourist Events – Impacts, Management and Planning*. London, Bellhaven Press, Chapter 6.

HKSDB. (2002). *Economic Impact of Sport:* Report to Hong Kong Sport Development Board. August 2002. Produced by Business and Economic Research Ltd (BERL), Wellington, New Zealand. www.hksdb.org.hk/hksdb/html.pdf/research/economicimpactofsportinhk (accessed 16 April 2003).

Manchester City Council. (2001). *Commonwealth Games 2002 – A Cost Benefit Analysis: Brief for Consultants*, 21 November 2001. Manchester City Council.

Mathieson, A. and Wall, G. (1982). *Tourism: Economic, Physical and Social Impacts*. Harlow, Longman Scientific & Technical, Chapter 3.

Piercy, N. (2000). *Market-Led Strategic Change: Transforming the Process of Going to Market*, 2nd edition. Oxford, Butterworth-Heinemann, Chapter 7.

Shone, A. and Parry, B. (2001). *Successful Event Management: A Practical Handbook*. London, Continuum, Chapter 12.

UK Sport. (1999). *Major Events: A Blueprint for Success*. London, UK Sport.

Wood, E. (2004). Marketing information for impact analysis and evaluation. In: Yeoman, I., Robertson, M., Ali-Knight, J., Drummond, S. and McMahon-Beattie, U. (Eds), *Festival and Events Management: An International Arts and Cultural Perspective*. Oxford, Butterworth-Heinemann.

Index